Habits of a Successful Orchestra Director

Also by Christopher Selby, Scott Rush, and Rich Moon
Published by GIA Publications, Inc.

Habits of a Successful String Musician
A Comprehensive Curriculum for Use During Fundamentals Time

Conductor's Edition (G-8628)
Violin (G-8624)
Viola (G-8625)
Cello (G-8626)
Bass (G-8627)

Habits of a Successful Orchestra Director

Helpful Tips and Practical Strategies for Improving String Instruction

Christopher R. Selby

Edited by Scott Rush

GIA Publications, Inc.
Chicago

Habits of a Successful Orchestra Director
Christopher R. Selby
Edited by Scott Rush

G-9363
ISBN: 978-1-62277-223-0

7404 South Mason Avenue, Chicago 60638
www.giamusic.com

Contents

Foreword

Peter Boonshaft

The very first time I met Christopher Selby, I felt as though I was being reunited with a long-lost friend. I was drawn to his warmth of spirit, genuine kindness, profound sincerity, and gentle manner. At once, it was obvious that this was a man who was passionate about music education and a truly gifted teacher. As the years have passed, I realized that sentiment was a gross understatement. Christopher is a master teacher who is as remarkable a person as he is talented as an educator.

Now, with this book, *Habits of a Successful Orchestra Director*, every reader can come to know the person I am fortunate enough to call my friend. As one reads each page, it is clear that this tremendous book was written by someone who has a wealth of experience, has mastered his craft, and has clearly detailed virtually every aspect of string education. However, equally important is the spirit, manner, and enthusiasm with which this material is delivered. Put simply, Christopher has dedicated his life to string teaching, and he selflessly shares that vast reservoir of wisdom and lifetime experience with every reader.

The subtitle of this book, "Helpful Tips and Practical Strategies for Improving Instruction," does not do it justice. Yes, it is all of that, but it is also so much more. It is a manual for developing every detail of a successful string music education program. From the broad strokes of philosophy, planning, organization, repertoire, overcoming challenges, assessment and communication, to the detailed teaching and training of techniques such as hand position, bowing, shifting, and vibrato, this compendium offers insights into every facet of string education. Whether one is starting an orchestra program or growing a program, this book will offer helpful answers and superb strategies, but it will also excite you and inspire you.

In short, the powerful information in this book is as important as the way it is expressed. It is practical and pragmatic, as well as accessible and thought-provoking. But at all times, that warmth of spirit, genuine kindness, profound sincerity, and gentle manner I saw the first time I met Christopher shines through.

This exceptional book will energize your passion for teaching string students as much as it will empower you with ideas and techniques. I congratulate my friend Christopher for this wonderful contribution to our professional library with a book that will surely become a valued resource and sincere catalyst for all that is so spectacular about string music education.

—Dr. Peter Loel Boonshaft

Peter Loel Boonshaft is currently on the faculty of Hofstra University in Hempstead, New York, where he is Professor of Music and Director of Bands. He is extremely active as a guest conductor and clinician for festivals, concerts, and workshops nationally and internationally. He is author of many books on teaching and leadership.

Introduction

It is an exciting time to be an orchestra teacher. The number of string programs in America is growing along with the number of string teaching positions. As we see new programs emerging in schools, it is easy for people to think that string education is "the new kid on the block"—but it's not new at all. Though we are seeing a renaissance in string education, it is validating and reassuring to know that we are a part of a long history that extends back before Vivaldi at the Ospedale della Pieta.

The modern job of being an orchestra teacher, while wonderfully rewarding, has many challenges. Even as our numbers grow, we tend to be some of the most isolated teachers in the public school. The vast majority of us go for weeks or months at a time without seeing a fellow string teacher, so our jobs can often feel both overwhelming and lonely. The good news is that there are thousands of us teaching children to make music on stringed instruments, and we share many more similarities than differences. While our programs are unique to our specific schools, we face many common challenges and find ourselves looking for solutions to similar types of problems. Our answers may not all be the same, but we have many of the same questions:

- How do I teach my students to play better in tune?
- When and how do I teach vibrato, spiccato, shifting, and thumb position?
- How do I get my students to work harder in class and practice better at home?
- What do I need to do to earn Superiors at concert festival every year?
- How do I correct technique problems with my upper-level students? I know what I want to rehearse with them, but what am I supposed to teach?
- How do I get my students to count and sight-read better?
- What is the best way to get through all of the string instrument technique so I can spend more time in class teaching students how to make music?
- How do I get my principal to listen to me and support my program?
- What can I do differently to get more students to sign up for orchestra? How do I make my program the place where every student wants to be?

- Is it possible to create a long-range plan that is useful and makes my daily planning easier?
- How do I get my parents to help with fundraisers and field trips? Do I need a booster program, and if so, how do I start one?

Habits of a Successful Orchestra Director was written for you, the busy orchestra teacher. This book is filled with strategies and well-sequenced skills and objectives that will help teachers break down the job of string instruction into its fundamental parts. Let this book help you find your own answers on your way to making your students better musicians. My hope is that it will also help you make this challenging job a little easier—or at least more organized—so you can be the best teacher you can be for your students.

How to Use This Book

Habits of a Successful Orchestra Director can be read from cover to cover, and it can also be used as a resource for extracting information that is helpful at a particular time. When you are ready to create assessments or long-range plans, or if you are looking for strategies to improve your group's technique, tone, or intonation, just jump to the chapter that answers your questions and addresses your needs.

Chapter 1

Learning Comes First

By learning you will teach; by teaching you will learn.

—Latin Proverb

IN THIS CHAPTER:

- I Want to Learn to Teach *That*!
- Giving Ourselves Permission to Learn
- Our String Education Community Has Much to Learn
- Young Teachers Have the Most to Learn in the Shortest Time
- Getting Past the Old Dog's Roadblock
- Good Teaching Makes a Difference—So Learn as Much as You Can

I Want to Learn to Teach *That*!

Have you ever gone to a concert festival to sit in the audience and listen to the different orchestras? When I listen to orchestras at a concert festival, I find myself wishing more teachers were there to see and hear the differences between groups. Nowhere in our field do we have a better opportunity to see the impact that our teaching has on students.

I'll never forget the first time I sat in the audience at a concert festival. It was my first year of teaching in northern Virginia, and I remember the moment I heard a middle school orchestra that changed my life. They were performing an arrangement of a Corelli Concerto, and I learned more from that three-minute performance than I learned in my years of college. The level of precision in their intonation and articulation blew me away; it was truly *beautiful.* The music was not terribly difficult, but the performance was clean, and more: it was *musical.* My eyes had been opened, as if I had eaten the fruit from the Tree of Knowledge. I became immediately aware that it was possible for students under the right instruction to play string instruments with refined accuracy and artistry, and it was up to me to figure out how. It was then that I started to ask myself:

How do I get my students to sound like that?

In this book, I aim to answer that question and many others. Our jobs are difficult, even for older veterans. We are asked to do an extraordinary amount of work. And even though we often don't encounter fellow string teachers for weeks on end, we can find some comfort in knowing that we are not alone.

Many string teachers struggle to find answers to questions like the following:

- When do we find the time to create well-planned, standards-based lessons using technology, differentiated instruction, and the latest cutting-edge techniques to teach large classes of students learning four different instruments with different method books and music?

- Where do we find the energy to prepare lesson plans and long-range plans, record grades, communicate with parents, do duty, attend meetings, plan and conduct concerts, bring in guest artists, and plan and run field trips and fundraisers when we are teaching so many students spread over multiple schools?

- How are we to find time to address all of the standards and teach students how to read and interpret music, how to compose and improvise new music, and how to listen, analyze, and talk about music, musical performance, music history and cultural relevance, and music-related careers, and still have any time to teach students how to play these complicated instruments well enough to get a Superior at concert festival?

- How do we do all that this job requires and still have time and energy for our friends and loved ones?

One of the first things we learn as string teachers is how to survive. Once we get past this stage, we start looking for ways to organize everything we are expected to do so we are not just surviving, but rather managing and enjoying our work. How are we supposed to do our jobs well? The short answer is that we don't need to do more. There are ways to organize or possibly reorganize what we are already doing so the workload is more manageable.

In the following chapters you will find helpful answers and strategies for organizing all that you do. As you read this book, you may come across tasks and planning strategies that you don't already do. Our goal is not to expect you to do more as a string teacher, but instead to help you reorganize what you do and how you plan and teach so you can improve your efficiency and make your job more manageable, effective, and enjoyable. We do a lot, and my hope is that some of the ideas and strategies in this book will help you enjoy your job—and the life outside of your job—even more.

Giving Ourselves Permission to Learn

About three weeks before I heard that first eye-opening performance at concert festival, I had a completely different, more painful kind of professional awakening. Everyone said the first year of teaching would be the hardest. I knew I would encounter challenging students, but I was prepared for them. I spent most of my first year in a cloud of blissful naiveté that carried me right up to the day that I took my middle school orchestra to my first festival. I felt confident that I was a great teacher, and I was ready to show the world how good my orchestra was!

We earned a III rating for our performance, and if you are familiar with festival grading, that was not "good" at all. In fact, it felt more like we had gotten an "F." I was completely stunned. I sat on the bus heading back to school devastated and frustrated, reading and listening to the judges' comments, fighting feelings of anger and bitterness that their criticism stirred up inside me. At first, I refused to believe anything they had to say, discounting their comments and discrediting their authority to judge my orchestra and my teaching. I thought, "Who are these judges, and what do they know? They don't know how hard my kids worked or the obstacles we had to overcome to perform as well as we did." Looking back now from my current vantage point, I realize I was saying the very same things that I've heard so many other teachers say after receiving a poor evaluation. I was not prepared to hear criticism, and I was not prepared to believe that this wonderful career that I had chosen was considerably more difficult than I thought it was going to be.

This lesson learned is common among orchestra teachers, but it is not painful because we have a problem with learning from our mistakes. In fact, learning is not a problem at all for most teachers. The problem is that teachers are under a lot of pressure to *not* make mistakes, which makes learning a little more complicated. We are held to a very high standard, and we are expected to be masters of our content and classroom. We are TEACHERS, and in our tough jobs of confidently delivering our lessons to questioning students, we have to be strong and believe what we are teaching is correct. When students make a mistake, it might affect their grade or it might not; but when teachers make a mistake, it does affect the students. For teachers who care a lot about their students, mistakes can stir up feelings of guilt and doubt. So when students, parents, or administrators ask questions, we feel a lot of pressure to be right. And naturally, as a result of this constant pressure, we harbor a lot of fear about being wrong.

Our job as teachers is hard, and we are working as hard as we can. It makes sense that one of our deepest fears may be that we need to do a better job, but no matter how hard we work, it may not be good enough. We have to be mindful to keep our inner voices in check so our fears do not limit our learning. Some teachers avoid taking their groups to concert festival for fear that they will not receive a satisfactory rating. Others would rather not even sit in the audience for fear that they may hear orchestras better than their own or discover that other teachers have skills that they have yet to learn. It is important for us to remember that we are not perfect, and if we are to learn and improve what we do, then we must give ourselves permission to learn and permission to make mistakes along the way.

Our String Education Community Has Much to Learn

Before I took my current job teaching the high school orchestras at the Charleston County School of the Arts, I spent eleven years as an orchestra coordinator supervising string curriculum and instruction in a different school district. Having listened to performances of school orchestras from across America, I can comfortably say that some of the following systemic challenges were not confined to our school district. They are everywhere, including my own classroom, and possibly yours, too.

1. Learning to play a string instrument requires so much technique and knowledge that teachers of younger students struggle to keep musical expression and the joyful parts of music making a regular part of daily instruction.

2. Teachers of older, more advanced students do not have a comprehensive plan for teaching advanced string skills. Instead, they try to teach string skills as they appear in concert repertoire. Since concert music does not present skills in any pedagogical order, this inefficient practice requires teachers to spend large amounts of rehearsal time addressing technical problems and allows less time for teaching musical expression and artistry.

3. Without a comprehensive teaching plan, most music directors—band, choral, and orchestral alike—fail to tell students at the beginning of class what they are expected to learn. Instead, they give students an agenda of what they are going to do or rehearse that day, without a clear learning goal or focus of instruction. Not only would students learn more efficiently if we explained what they are expected to learn, but we would do a better job of teaching when we have a clear goal for what we want the students to learn.

4. Most orchestra directors, and especially young teachers, habitually select repertoire that is too difficult for their students to successfully polish in the time they have before a performance. This mistake is rooted in a well-intentioned desire to challenge students technically without knowing how to challenge them musically. As a result, teachers select music with challenging notes, rhythms, and bowings, and they fail to take into account the skills or rehearsal time required for end-game skills, such as blending pitch and tone; agreeing on tempo, balance, and phrasing; matching rhythms, articulations, attacks, and releases; and watching, cueing, and breathing together.

5. Orchestra, band, and choir directors claim that the arts foster creativity, but we tend to focus so much on performance that we leave little room for creativity in our classroom. Our most creative students are forced to look outside of our classes to create their own music, and some leave music altogether to take other classes that nurture their creativity.

6. A silent, but significant percentage of string students are musically illiterate when they graduate high school. They struggle with independently deciphering and performing rhythms correctly, understanding how the notes are mapped out on their fingerboard, how the key signature affects finger patterns, and sometimes even naming the notes in first and third positions. Most students also have significant difficulty writing out melodies as simple as "Twinkle, Twinkle Little Star" with or without using their instrument as an aid.

7. Leaders in the music education community have some challenges to resolve when it comes to agreeing on how to plan and teach to music education standards. NAfME has just created new standards for the country's music teachers. ASTA has a curriculum full of standards for string education. Most states also have their own standards for music education; my state is creating a new set this year. When the standards are vague or difficult to understand, it can take years for a veteran teacher to adopt and absorb one set of standards, let alone three.

8. Modern string education has been around for decades, and so far as I can tell, most string teachers are still struggling to write their own curriculum from scratch. Though programs differ from one school to the next, the way we teach a string instrument in the classical tradition is pretty much the same no matter where we teach. So why are we all in our separate schools struggling to reinvent the wheel? Our hope is that this book will bring much relief to all teachers trying to write their own curriculum and long-range plans.

Though the music education community has much to learn, we are on the brink of a renaissance. As an industry and field of study, we are developing greater awareness of systemic mistakes within string education. Each of us has a choice to make as a member within this community of educators. We can continue to do things the way we always have, or we can choose to take a deep look at what we are doing and grow from it.

Young Teachers Have the Most to Learn in the Shortest Time

While veteran teachers know that every year presents challenges, most will agree that the steepest learning curves occur in the first years of teaching. Our job is hardest on young teachers who often find themselves in the toughest teaching situations with little experience. It is not uncommon to see administration ask young teachers to piece together a full-time job between several schools or take on additional non-orchestra classes, like guitar or general music. Some teach upwards of seven different classes that require distinct preparation. Young teachers already need more time to plan to make up for their lack of experience, and yet some barely have time enough to eat in the car between schools.

In my first year, I taught 3 levels of middle school orchestra in the morning—beginning, intermediate, and advanced—and then I had 15 minutes to get to my high school orchestra class 3 miles away. After high school, every Tuesday and Friday I drove to the elementary school to teach 3 more 40-minute classes to fourth, fifth, and sixth graders who were each at different stages of development. As a first-year teacher, I was teaching 7 distinctly different levels of strings/orchestra to students ranging in age from 9–18, and I was eating lunch in the car. I turned down other jobs that had more difficult schedules, including one that required teaching at 15 different elementary schools per week—yikes!

Younger teachers, especially first-year teachers, are more successful when they get help—but they don't get enough help because they tend not to ask for it. Some don't ask because they don't understand the kinds of help available to them, or they don't know how to ask for it. Others are afraid that a supervisor will think they are struggling and cannot do the job.

Young teachers must make an effort to find colleagues and administrators who can answer questions and serve as sounding boards for the many fresh, new ideas young teachers have. Most veteran teachers and administrators are more than happy to drop what they are doing to help teachers when asked. Experienced mentors can help young teachers sort out which ideas have good chances for success and which ones have hidden dangers attached to them. New teachers can learn more quickly if they just ask more experienced professionals to help them learn the tricks of this complicated trade. They will save themselves time and energy, and avoid a lot of stress, headaches, and heartaches. The sad truth is that teachers who do not learn quickly typically do not last very long.

Christine, a first-year teacher, once asked me, "How do I know if I'm doing a good job?" I had already seen her teach, and I knew she was a talented young teacher who worried about being good enough. I told her she was doing great, and then I added what I tell every teacher who asks that question: Most of the good teachers ask themselves if they are good enough, and they push themselves to learn how to be better. The teachers who do not challenge themselves to continually improve fall behind and get stuck in poor teaching habits. We know that great musicians practice and learn their entire lives, or at least as long as they want to remain great musicians. Late in his life, Pablo Casals was asked why he continued to practice four hours a day, and he replied, "Because, I think I'm making progress." It is the same for music teachers. Teaching orchestra may take a lifetime to learn; the good news is that we can inspire students along the way as we learn to do our jobs better.

Getting Past the Old Dog's Roadblock

It's true that younger teachers face many challenges as they learn how to survive and thrive, but veteran teachers face a few challenges of their own. Most veteran teachers do not fit the adage that "you can't teach an old dog new tricks." They have a quick-witted ability to stay way ahead of their students and have an insatiable desire to learn. That said, there must be a grain of truth to the saying about "old dogs," or it wouldn't exist. We have seen so many educational initiatives come and go that some of us roll our eyes every time someone says he or she has a great new idea. So before we go further in this book about teaching methods and strategies, let's call our attention to some of the roadblocks that may keep us from learning all that we can.

While great teachers are always looking for new things to learn, some teachers have found so much comfort in what they already know that they seem less open to new ideas. As a result, they limit their own learning by seeing the world through the lens of their own experience. At in-services or faculty discussions about teaching, you'll hear the veterans start talking about themselves and how *they* do things. "Oh, this is how *I* handle that. What *I* do is...." In fairness to veteran teachers, they have spent many years by themselves in the classroom surviving on their own creativity, patience, and perseverance to solve the challenges that hundreds if not thousands of students have thrown their way. Their solutions are their survival skills, and they are hard earned. Not only are they proud of their well-worn teaching methods, they hold on to them, form an attachment to them, and learn to trust and believe in them. Their world becomes shaped around them.

If we are not careful, however, the comfort we find in our methods can also create unintended barriers to learning. When we spend a large part of our life believing that the world is a certain way, we are going to have to cope with some fears and take a few leaps of faith before we accept another point of view. In a very similar way, when teachers spend a large part of their career hearing their own students play out of tune, they begin to believe that out of tune is normal, and they sometimes face personal roadblocks when confronted with another reality.

So how can we embrace what we have already learned without shutting ourselves off from future learning opportunities? As you read about strategies that are familiar and unfamiliar to you, pay attention to the feelings that arise, whether they are happy or fearful. We can and should celebrate when we read something in a book that we already do; we can say to ourselves, "I do that already," believing it is further evidence that we are doing the right thing. But when we read or see new ideas or strategies, the opposite feelings can creep in. Our voices might say, "I haven't been doing that. *Should* I have been doing that for the past 25 years? Maybe I'm not as good as I should have been." Since we cannot change the past, we must keep that negative voice in check because it gets in the way of our learning new skills. The best we can do is learn as much as we can today and continue to become the most skilled and inspiring teachers we can be.

Good Teaching Makes a Difference—So Learn as Much as You Can

Have you ever noticed that teachers don't like to talk about the differences in skill or ability between teachers? That subject makes teachers uncomfortable. Instead of acknowledging that student performance is largely a reflection of a teacher's skill, some orchestra teachers would rather point to other reasons for differences in student performance: "My students don't take private lessons," or "My students don't practice enough." Or they point to teaching conditions: "My administration isn't supportive," or "I don't have a booster organization," and so on. Maybe we don't discuss teaching ability out of social politeness, in the same way we don't talk about differences in our weight, age, or income—but I think it's more than that. The fears we have about our own teaching ability have created an educational culture in which teachers downplay their own skills and the abilities of others, too. When a group at concert festival plays with great technical accuracy and artistry, some will undercut the role of the teacher and instead talk about huge numbers of students taking private lessons—*which means the school teacher is credited with teaching what?*

It's true that this job does not always have easy solutions, and to help each other maintain our hope, faith, and morale in our stressful career path, we choose to accentuate the teaching conditions and the positive. Let's pay attention when we hear excuses from other teachers or from the voices in our own heads. Acknowledge the fears that give rise to these excuses because we need to keep these fears in check.

We don't like to talk about teaching ability, but it does matter a lot to the students; how much they learn is a direct result of how well we teach. Our skills and abilities do matter, and nowhere do we see this better than in the auditorium at a concert festival. When we hear one group after the next, we start to notice the differences in student performances that are largely the result of differences in teaching. Then we begin to realize that what we do or don't do in the classroom makes a significant difference in student learning and performance.

This realization may be a little frightening, but it is powerful, too, because it provides us with more reason and incentive to continue learning as much as we can about teaching effectively. Good teachers:

- Embrace learning opportunities and ideas that they get from other teachers.
- Attend conferences to see what orchestras like their own are capable of doing.
- Read articles to learn new tips and strategies, and books that inspire fresh ideas and improve their teaching.
- Go to concert festivals to get feedback from experienced clinicians, and to sit in the audience to hear the differences between groups. They just listen, with an empty mind, free of all voices and doubt. They have the courage to temporarily let go of their version of the truth and ask, "How does that teacher teach that? What do I need to do differently to get my groups to sound like *that?*"

FINAL THOUGHTS:

Deep down, all good teachers want to be great teachers, like the people who inspired us to become teachers ourselves. When our challenges make us question our own greatness, we should remember that our inspirational mentors also must have learned lessons from their own challenges and failures. Maybe we underestimate all that they must have endured. We have to give ourselves permission to learn and be okay with discovering new ways of doing things. To do this, we may have to retrain some of our voices because learning new teaching skills is a good thing, and it doesn't mean we have been doing a bad job or making mistakes prior to learning the new skills. Mimi Zweig, a masterful violin teacher, tells her students that mistakes are neither good, nor bad; they are just information from which we can learn a great deal. We should celebrate the fact that we have been given an opportunity to improve. Good teachers choose to embrace this.

Before students or teachers can learn anything, they must be willing to welcome the personal change that comes with learning. When they resist change, the ideas and learning opportunities pass them by.

When I was preparing my high school string orchestra for our first National Orchestra Festival (NOF) in 2009, I got the February *ASTA Journal* that listed some of the other groups my students would encounter in this national competition. After surfing around one of our competitor's websites, I came across a page with links to their recordings of the works they were preparing for the competition. One of the pieces on their page was the "Elegy" movement from Tchaikovsky's *Serenade for Strings*, which coincidentally was one of the pieces our group was preparing for the same competition. I was curious to hear what we were up against, so I clicked on the link—and what I heard set me back on my heels. Their tone and intonation were in a completely different league than my own students. I thought I was a great teacher, but clearly I had much to learn. I found myself swallowing my pride and digging deep, questioning myself and my methods, and over the next several days I began searching for strategies that would take my group to *that* level—a level of refinement I had never heard before. My group was still out of tune compared to them. I could hear it, and I had to figure out how to correct it—how to *teach* it.

Several days later, I was speaking to my friend Gail Barnes, the string education professor at the University of South Carolina, where I had done my graduate work. As we discussed this group's tone and intonation, she could tell that their recording had deeply affected me; so she listened to their NOF recording of the "Elegy" and some other recordings on their website. After hearing them, she said, "I don't think those are kids. I believe those are professional recordings that the students are supposed to use as models to help them learn their music." It took a moment for this to sink in; I went back and listened to the recordings again, and it all started to make sense. At first I found myself relieved to discover these "kids" were actually professionals, but I was also immediately presented with a choice.

For those several days, I had believed I could do better. I searched for ways to improve my group's intonation and I started creating new out-of-the-box strategies for getting them to listen and finely tune their chords. Upon hearing that the recordings were of professionals, I could have said, "Oh, that explains it. Those are professionals; my kids can't sound like that. My students are younger, their instruments aren't as nice, they haven't had as many private lessons, they don't practice as much, etc." But I couldn't get past the fact that for several days I believed I could get them to sound better, and I started to learn to teach intonation at a whole new level.

To this day, I listen to my own groups and ask: "Do they sound like the Orpheus Chamber Orchestra? No? Why not? And what am I going to do about it? I do this because I want my group to sound like that! And I don't want my own limitations and preconceptions to keep my students from reaching their full potential.

Chapter 2

Creating a Culture of Success

Think for a moment about the type of orchestra program you would like to teach. Maybe you are happy with the program you currently have. If not, what would it take to build your orchestra program into the job of your dreams? Let's look at some different ways to communicate with your principal and your school community to build your program, increase enrollment, and create a culture of success for your students.

IN THIS CHAPTER:

- Why Orchestra?
- Recruiting Students and Selling Your Program
- Retention—Making Orchestra THE Place to Be
- Helping Parents Make Good Decisions About Quality String Instruments
- Getting Support from Your Principal
- Starting in a New School

Why Orchestra?

Whether you are recruiting new students, maintaining a strong orchestra program, or trying to keep a program from being cut, orchestra teachers need to be able to articulate why string education is important. When communities question the value of music and the arts in the public school, teachers and parents frequently site scientific research to help bolster support for the arts. Amidst the mountains of evidence that musical study increases math scores, improves emotional health, and contributes to a raft of other benefits, we can easily lose sight of the real reasons we study and teach music.

Ask any students why they signed up for orchestra, and they probably will not mention the research findings regarding enhanced cognitive development and emotional well-being. As music educators, we have experienced firsthand the ways the study of music has enriched our lives. But kids don't have these experiences yet.

Instead, they have their own reasons for signing up for orchestra: maybe they thought it sounded like fun, or their parents made them, or their friends were in orchestra. No matter what reason motivated them to sign up, they trust us to show them the value of music. They want us to share the enjoyment that comes from making music on a string instrument and to teach them the important place music holds in a variety of cultures, including their own.

Why orchestra? Why not band, chorus, piano, or guitar? The answer is that all genres of musical study are important, and different arts media reach different people. Orchestra kids are different than band kids or chorus kids, and there should be an orchestra program wherever there is enough interest and support for one. Children have been studying string performance for centuries; strings have a rich musical history and a value all their own. Can you imagine a Beethoven symphony being performed by an orchestra with no strings?

String instruments are beautiful and versatile tools for musical expression, but they are not easy to learn. Sometimes we wish we could tell our students to press a key like we can on a piano and easily produce a note that has a pleasing tone and is perfectly in tune. It takes time and energy to learn a string instrument, which can be a tough sell for today's children who easily find more immediate enjoyment by picking up a smartphone or video game console. One of the hardest lessons we teach students is the difference between immediate gratification and lasting value. Of all the music classes schools offer, this lesson may be hardest for string students.

Parents want to know: What is the value of being in orchestra? What will their children learn musically and otherwise, and will they have fun? Here's what you can tell parents:

- Their children will learn to use every part of their brain in powerful ways to play an instrument and artistically express musical ideas.

- Their children will learn to simultaneously perform the required cognitive, affective, and psychomotor tasks to create, shape, interpret, and perform music.

- Their children will learn how to express themselves in new ways, to explore the ideas of great composers.

- Their children will love learning because making music with their friends is FUN!

- Through rehearsal and home practice, their children will learn problem-solving skills, how to cope with challenges, and how to face personal fears when performing for tests or concerts.

- Their children will make new friends though orchestra. Unlike most year-long academic classes, orchestras engage students in a wide variety of activities during and after school, year after year, where students can develop meaningful, lifelong memories and friendships.

Our ability to articulate a message about the value of string education to students and their parents will determine the number of students coming into our orchestra programs. Even after they have signed up, we must continue to inspire students and their parents to love music and appreciate the values of being in orchestra, or they will quickly find something else to do. Today's schools offer so many attractive and engaging fine arts classes in addition to athletics options and an explosion of new academic courses. With so many options, students are constantly forced to make difficult choices. Keeping these students in your orchestra simply comes down to making your program more inspiring, attractive, and valuable to students than their other options.

Recruiting Students and Selling Your Program

Are you satisfied with the number of students in your orchestra program? If not, what would it take to build your numbers so your classes were full? If you are an itinerant teacher, do you want to teach full time at one school? If you have been using a recruiting model that is not generating the numbers you want in your program, it might be time to make a few changes to your recruiting machine.

Every school is different, so recruiting plans need to be tailored specifically to each school. The recruiting model below is designed to bring in large numbers of students for big programs. It takes years to build a program primarily because it takes years to build a machine that can feed a large program. The model below may not be appropriate for all programs, but it can serve as a template to help you create a recruiting plan that works for your school and future string students.

1. Write down all of the benefits and great reasons students enjoy being in your string program.

2. Get the word out to students and their parents.

    a. Create recruiting posters and hang them in feeder school music rooms.
    b. Create a "Why Orchestra?" page on your school website that has links to research and videos about the benefits of studying music.
    c. Include a "How to Sign Up Your Child for Orchestra" page on your school website that walks parents through the registration process.

d. Prepare and print information letters and/or brochures about your program; they should look as professional as possible and direct parents to your web pages for more information.

3. Visit each feeder school.

a. Contact your feeder school principal or music teacher to schedule a visit.
b. Go to feeder schools to speak to potential string students, and if possible, perform for them. Get up close and personal, and excite them about being in orchestra. Kids want to hear how much fun it's going to be.
c. Show a video of your program describing classes, concerts, trips, etc.
d. Have your students perform for prospective students; make sure it sounds great.
e. Have your students interact with the audience; distribute information letters or brochures to prospective students.
f. Have your students answer questions from the audience, provide testimonials, and explain what they like about orchestra.

4. Hold an evening information and registration meeting for interested students/parents.

a. Organize parents of your current students to help set up and staff the welcome table, hand out information packets, and answer new parents' questions.
b. Have your top students perform for prospective students and parents.
c. Show an inspiring recruiting video/slideshow about your program to parents explaining how strings will enhance the lives of their children.
d. Have stations set up for students to try different instruments staffed by local private teachers or trained music education college students. These professionals can play for prospective students and help them choose the right size and type of instrument.
e. Explain where and how to get the right size and quality of instruments—or better yet, invite representatives from local music stores to be on hand to answer questions and register students for instruments. Let the music stores know the minimum quality level of instrument that is acceptable in your program.
f. Have a table where students and parents can sign up for orchestra. Make sure they include their contact information and which instrument they intend to play. When they sign up, give them their orchestra shirt (like NCAA teams do when students sign up for an athletic program).
g. Review sign-up sheets and place students into classes based on ability and instrumentation; submit lists to guidance.

5. Compare student interest sign-up sheets with the official class list printed out by guidance. Follow up with parents of students who are missing from the official class list.

6. Prepare and send acceptance and welcome letters.

7. Hold a Beginner Night in the second or third week of school staffed by private teachers or string education students.

    a. Divide students into small groups by instrument. Have private teachers give students small group lessons on the basics of instrument position, determining the correct endpin height and shoulder rest placement for each student.
    b. Have the private teachers ensure that beginners have the correct size and quality of string instrument (good hair, working fine tuners, good strings), and a good shoulder rest or rock stop, rosin, and music stand that they will use at home.
    c. Invite instrument vendors to Beginner Night to help parents and students get set up with the necessary equipment.
    d. Remember to have fun; host an ice cream social.

8. While students attend Beginner Night, give an orientation to new parents.

    a. Explain what students need for orchestra.
    b. Give an overview of the calendar and schedule.
    c. Go over grading and after-school rehearsal and concert policies.
    d. Answer questions; introduce the booster board.
    e. Pair up new parents with veteran parents willing to answer questions about the program.

Each school uses a different process for enrolling students in class. Get to know how the process at your school works, and talk to the guidance department to find out what they need from you or the parents to enroll and schedule students into the correct classes. Do they need parents to physically come in and sign up, or can you hand guidance a list of student names with parent signatures? By helping to make the enrollment process easier, you can be more in control and reduce the number of hurdles in the enrollment process. Inevitably, there will be names that get dropped in the process, so it is extremely important to get a hard copy list of names of interested students, preferably with a parent phone number and signature. This way, the teacher can reconcile the student interest list with the official class list and follow up with parents of students who are not officially signed up.

Retention—Making Orchestra THE Place to Be

Building your recruiting machine is only the first step. Recruiting is about "selling" your product and convincing students and their parents to "buy in" to what your programs offer. To retain the students who have signed up, you must stand behind your product and follow through with students and parents. Fortunately, we are not selling used cars; our product is much more valuable and should last a lifetime. Don't be shy about selling what you teach; be proud about your program and enthusiastic about the prospect of sharing your love of string music with as many children as possible.

Are you fun? Pay attention to not only what you say, but how you say it to convey the enjoyment that music has brought to your life and to show all of the ways students have fun making music together in your program. Whether you are teaching beginning or advanced students, it is important to stay fresh and remember to share the love, enthusiasm, and joy you get from making music with your students. When the joys of making music do not outweigh the challenges of learning the string instrument, students will eventually lose interest and quit.

Are you successful? Students want to feel proud to belong to a successful program that earns Superiors at concert festival. They want to wear a cool T-shirt that says they are a member of the club. They want to have concerts and field trips that their friends hear about through posters and daily announcements. Parents want their children to be successful, too, and they value and support programs where excellence is standard practice. Explain what students are learning from you, and regularly announce the successes students experience in your program. Do not underestimate the power of a professionally designed logo to put on your letterhead, posters, and at the entrance to your orchestra room. Build a brand that means quality, artistry, and fun, and make your orchestra the reason people come to your school.

The teacher's message and tone are extremely important, but nothing is more powerful than having successful students communicate the value of your music program to prospective students and parents. You are not the best recruiter in your program—your best recruiters are your students and their parents. Kids listen to other kids. When they love your class, they tell their friends, and their parents tell the parents of younger students. Have a couple of your veteran parents speak to prospective parents. Your message is much stronger and more convincing when you have others providing testimony and giving proof that what you are selling is the real deal.

Finally, when selling the values of orchestra, be careful not to downplay the challenges of learning a string instrument. While you don't want strings class to sound miserably laborious, it is important for students and parents to know that learning a string instrument can be hard work, which can be valuable and rewarding. If you tell students it's easy, then they will be disappointed when they find out it isn't. If you tell parents it's easy, then they will perceive the value of the process to be worth less. In marketing, this is called *perceived* value. When something is free, it's perceived value is worth relatively little.

Learning to play a string instrument is a challenging and valuable endeavor. We must convince parents that their children's music education is worth renting a quality instrument and setting up a good place at home to practice. We do these things for all children because string education helps them learn to become more skilled, successful, and healthy human beings.

Helping Parents Make Good Decisions about Quality String Instruments

Inviting students to join orchestra involves a little more than signing up for class; parents will need your help getting the right instruments and accessories. Parents are strongly motivated to find a good deal, but they do not understand the detriment they cause to their child's education when they get a poor-quality instrument. Veteran teachers and instrument dealers will tell you that fighting the wave of cheap instruments flooding the market is an ever-increasing battle—a battle we cannot afford to lose. One of the most challenging and important parts of our job is to set students up for success by educating parents about the importance of putting a quality instrument into their hands.

What is your process for ensuring that parents do not get the cheapest instrument they can find on the Internet? Some parents will need a lot of convincing before they understand why the more expensive instrument at the store is a better choice for their child than the $99 special they discovered on the Internet. When speaking to parents, appeal to their interest in seeing their children succeed by explaining, "If I, a professional string teacher, have difficulty tuning and making a good sound on your child's instrument, then your child has no chance, and children who cannot tune or make a good sound on their instruments are usually the first to quit. String instruments are difficult enough to learn, so the least we can do is find an affordable quality string instrument that is easy to tune and makes a good tone when played correctly. We both want your child to be successful, so please, let me help you find an instrument that will give him/her a good chance for success."

Explain to parents that renting a quality instrument is better than purchasing a bad one. Also, let them know that cheap instruments break easily and tend to be more difficult and expensive to repair. Many music stores refuse to even try to repair cheap instruments because when they break again, parents mistakenly blame the music store. Parents appreciate knowing what questions to ask music stores, so I arm them with questions, such as:

- What does basic rental include?
- What are the cost differences between the various levels of instrument?
- When upgrading to a bigger size or higher quality, what percentage of my investment transfers to the new instrument?
- What is the store's repair policy?
- How long does it take to make minor repairs or re-hair a bow?

Write a letter that you can send home and give out at recruitment and information nights (see Appendix A). This letter explains to parents how a better instrument will help their child succeed.

Orchestra teachers can save themselves, their students, and parents much grief by talking to the store manager directly about the quality of instrument you want to see coming into your classroom. Arrange a time to meet with the manager of each store, get to know them on a first-name basis, play their instruments, and work together with them to make a list of approved instruments from each store. Also talk to the managers about their trade-in process when it's time for students to get a step-up instrument. Create a list of high-quality beginner and step-up instruments, and then send this list home and post it on your website so parents of beginners know what instruments to get.

Invite all of the instrument vendors who agree to stock quality instruments for your students to your parent information night. Go out of your way to include every store, and be careful not to endorse one store over another. This allows parents an opportunity to compare prices of competing vendors, and more importantly, it reminds everyone that we are all on the same team. Vendors value the opportunity to set up shop and talk to future customers, and you have the microphone telling everyone in the room about the importance of quality instruments. Remember, the quality of your concerts depends on this. If you have an orchestra full of bad-sounding instruments that cannot stay in tune, it will reflect poorly at your concerts and result in high dropout rates, which is a reflection of you and your work.

Store managers know their business, and competing against the cheap Internet instruments is not easy, so don't be surprised if you get a little pushback. Store managers want your business and the business of the many students you could send to them year after year. Everyone wins when you work with the music stores.

Getting Support from Your Principal

We cannot build successful programs without the support of the principals. Some administrators value and support the arts, even when tight budgets pressure them to cut funding. Others are less understanding, sometimes because they grew up in a place with no orchestra or because they had a bad experience in a music class when they were young. The best way to get their support is to help them understand what we do, why it's valuable to students, and how they can help. We want them to understand what we understand, but to communicate well with administrators, it's important for us to try and understand their perspectives, too.

Put yourself in the shoes of your principal, a person who is in charge of an entire faculty of teachers who are focused on their own programs, classes, and students. It is the principal's job to see the big picture and, with the limited resources at their disposal, support all of the teachers fairly in a way that is best for all students in the school. Our principals want to give us the support we need to teach the students as much as we can, but they have to make difficult choices about how to distribute their limited time and resources.

Principals can support our programs by:

- Resolving conflicts with parents and supporting policies, procedures, and discipline;
- Providing funding for instruments, repairs, and other educational supplies;
- Approving trips and festivals, and understanding that string students may miss class;
- Determining what classes we teach and where we teach them; and
- Scheduling students and resolving schedule conflicts.

Principals also have the authority to hire teachers and give us evaluations, and they can lobby for our jobs when money is tight. When they understand what we teach and why it's valuable, they are more likely to support our program. The good news is that our choices and behaviors can and do shape principals' views of us and our program.

Principals look for many things in their teachers, but we will look at three factors that shape how much principals trust and support us. Remember, they are busy, so don't make your principal do a research project to find out the answers to the following questions:

1. Can your principal trust you?
2. Are you an invaluable part of your principal's faculty?
3. How do you communicate what your students are learning, and what support can your principal provide for them to learn better?

Earn Your Principal's Trust

Principals need to be able to trust the adults in their building to take care of other people's children. They want to know that their teachers will show up to work on time, supervise their students, keep students safe from harm, and teach students the skills and knowledge they were hired to teach. We must earn their trust by consistently demonstrating that they can count on us to do our job; any teacher they cannot trust is a big liability. Principals are also in charge of making sure the faculty and staff work well together, and they cannot make everyone happy all of the time. Principals want teachers to be able to speak their mind, and even have the courage to disagree at times, but at the end of the day, they need their teachers to come together as a team. You must be willing to work with your principal and other teachers for the good of the students.

A word to younger teachers:

Work hard to learn and speak the language of your administrators because you probably communicate differently than they do. It is everyone's responsibility to reach across generation gaps, but younger teachers must learn how to communicate with the older generations if they want to get the best support from their students' parents and administrators. Young teachers must also take extra precautions to make sure they are not misunderstood or accidentally perceived as being disrespectful or unreasonable. This happens too often, and it is easy for young teachers to end up on the losing side of that misunderstanding.

Make Yourself Invaluable

There is an extraordinary amount of work that must be done effectively to keep hundreds or thousands of students safe and to teach them all they need to learn. While principals appreciate teachers who are good at what they do, they also want to know that those teachers are willing to help them when they need help. In so many schools, the string teacher position seems to be the first one on the list to be cut. We cannot afford to be perceived as isolated or unwilling to be a part of the school community. Make yourself valuable on the faculty; make yourself indispensible.

If you need your principal's help, provide several solutions and ask for your principal's advice and support on the best one. Don't complain; speak in terms of solutions only. Principals face more problems each day than any one person can handle; make yourself valuable to your principal by bringing solutions to the table. Once you show that you are a valuable member of the team who is willing to help others, your principal will be much more likely to help you and give you and your program the support you need.

Communicate What Your Students Are Learning and What They Need

Your principal probably doesn't completely understand all that your program requires or the direction you want to go. Conversely, we probably don't understand all of needs the principal is trying to meet to satisfy parents, the district office, the students, and various factions of teachers. Your principal needs to hear from you to better understand what you do and to learn about what your students need. Here are a few things you can do:

- Invite your principal to speak at your concert. Put your principal up on stage with a microphone and a list of all of your group's accomplishments, so he/she can tell the audience of extremely powerful parents how well you and your students are doing.

- Tell your administrators what your students are learning each week, and invite them to visit and observe classes that you know will be good. Even if they only come a fraction of the time, they always know what you are teaching, that you are excited about teaching it, and that you appreciate their presence. Principals LOVE this, and it helps them understand what we do.

Starting in a New School

Whether you are starting a new program or taking over a developed orchestra, there a many details to consider and pitfalls to avoid when taking a new job. Middle and high school directors who also teach elementary strings frequently find themselves teaching in different elementary schools.

If your initial challenges include finding a good time and place to teach orchestra, the solution usually involves convincing the principal that your program is legitimate and the students deserve a proper place to learn. Develop a good relationship with the principal and the other teachers. Get to know them, their challenges, the layout of the school, and the school's schedule. Dress well, show up early, and show them a level of professionalism that says you mean business. You will have to put forth some effort to convince them that you are a real teacher, an expert in your field, especially if you are teaching an elementary string class in their school only once or twice a week. After you have earned their respect, they will be more likely to listen and consider your solutions regarding the problems of teaching space and schedule. Be firm, but also be understanding and patient. Depending on the school's schedule and available space, a resolution to this problem might take a year or two.

If you are starting a new program from scratch, you will need to make two lists for everything your students need to be successful in your class:

- **List #1** – Items the teacher or school provides, like a place for students to store their instruments at school, good chairs and stands, large instruments, and music.

- **List #2** – Items that students' families provide, like a home instrument, method books, a music binder, and a music stand for home, along with a quiet time and place to practice.

After making your lists, create a plan that clearly identifies how students will get each item. Only when your plan is clear for you can you make it clear to the students and their parents.

When taking over a well-developed orchestra, you must be acutely aware that students, parents, and administrators will have preconceived notions of how they think the program should be run, and you might face decades of tradition. You might also face a situation where the person you are replacing burned some bridges and created negativity towards the orchestra program. Regardless of the circumstances you inherit, there are two basic rules that need to be at the forefront of your mind when you take over a program:

1. *Never* say anything bad about the previous director or past performances.

2. During the first year, change as little as possible, and only cut or adjust things that you simply cannot live with. There is plenty of time to make it your own.

Successful programs have a culture of excellence that draws students to the organization. Transitions are tough enough for everyone, and the last thing you should do is go into a new job upsetting the apple cart and changing everything at once. Instead, make an appointment with the outgoing director and find out as much about the program as possible. Meet with the school's band and/or choral directors to get their perspectives. You will want to know about the class schedule, after-school rehearsals, number of concerts typically given each year, and what types of trips the students are accustomed to taking. Ask for a copy of the previous director's handbook and several years of past programs to find out what was expected and performed in the past. Also ask to meet with the parents to hear what they liked about their previous director's methods or program so you know which changes might meet more resistance.

Students and parents don't care how much you know until they know how much you care.

After you spend the first year proving that you care about them, you can then slowly begin infusing new ideas into the program. Let your students and parents know that you intend to have an incredible orchestra program and to build on the traditions of the past. If there really were no past traditions, you can have a discussion with your new students about developing a tradition of excellence and establishing a culture of success. After three or four years, the program will reflect your philosophy and ideals.

Chapter 3

The First Days of School

We become string educators so that we can teach and share with younger generations the joys of creating and performing music that we have experienced in our own lives. Shortly after taking our first jobs, though, we quickly learn that making music is a relatively small part of all that we do. Have you ever tried to list all of the things you do? Consider "The Life of an Orchestra Director" (see Appendix B), which is a sample list of responsibilities.

It's exhausting to read, and more exhausting when you think about all of the work that will be required to accomplish every task. Most of the tasks are non-pedagogical in nature, which presents us with a dilemma. We want to spend our time making music with our students; however, the reality is that we must create and communicate all of our policies and procedures to the parents, fill out field trip forms, handle string repairs, prepare a events calendar for the year, and the list goes on and on.... If we are not well organized, we can become overwhelmed by all of the non-pedagogical tasks, but it doesn't have to be this way.

This chapter is chock full of strategies to help teachers get their year started off right. Our job becomes considerably more manageable and enjoyable when we organize what we need to do, create and communicate clear policies, and complete all of the other non-musical tasks an orchestra program requires.

IN THIS CHAPTER:

- Organization—What, When, and How
- The Orchestra Handbook and Policies
- Rules, Consequences, and Expectations
- Preparing for the Expected and the Unexpected
- First Week Plans and Opening Checklist

Organization—What, When, and How

Good organization is critical for orchestra teachers to be successful. When we are not organized enough, we find ourselves in crisis mode, racing from one problem to the next, trying to put out all of the fires that occurred from being disorganized. It is up to us to figure out what, when, and how we will do everything we need to do. Once we organize the various aspects of the program, our job becomes more manageable and enjoyable.

The first thing you need to figure out is what you need to do. Your job doesn't come with an owner's manual, so you must create one yourself. Before the students arrive on the first day, prepare the following:

- Events calendar
- Grading policy, including concert attendance
- Rules and procedures for class and rehearsal
- Quality instruments—both school- and student-owned
- Music and method books

This is a partial list of required materials for all string teachers. See Appendix B for a more thorough list for established orchestra programs.

Knowing *when* to initiate and implement all of these tasks is also critical. For example, if you wait too late in the year to recruit for your program, many prospective students may choose other activities. One of the most important organizational frameworks you can establish is a yearly timeline for implementing all of your tasks. In the Timeline for the Academic Year (see Appendix C), we map out a sample timeline for accomplishing the following tasks:

- Develop a handbook and determine long-range plans
- Prepare the event calendar for the year
- Order method books and music
- Send instruments to the shop for repair
- Schedule string recruitment
- Prepare for concert festival
- Schedule trips
- Organize booster meetings and elections

Using Appendix C as a guide, take some time to write your own timeline for the entire year. It will be the compass that keeps you on course and keeps your program running with the precision of a well-oiled machine.

Finally, it is also important to figure out *how* you will complete many of these tasks. Ask yourself these questions:

- How am I going to communicate with parents?
- How am I going to make sure students get quality instruments?
- How am I going to distribute and collect forms and fees efficiently so we get to music making as fast as possible?

Being organized includes figuring out a process for:

- Scheduling students into the correct classes;
- Assessing students and assigning grades;
- Paying bills and filing paperwork;
- Organizing field trip forms and fundraising;
- Structuring boosters with clearly defined responsibilities;
- Prioritizing daily and weekly tasks;
- Organizing the music library and instrument inventory;
- Maintaining and repairing instruments;
- Setting up the classroom; and
- Creating thoughtful long-range and daily lesson plans.

There are programs on the market to help music teachers organize their music library, instrument inventory, communications with students and parents, and fees and fundraising. Put some time and effort into getting organized. With the myriad tasks a successful program requires, good organization will help you keep your sanity.

The Orchestra Handbook and Policies

The orchestra handbook may be the most important piece of communication you create for two reasons:

1. It is a document that helps you organize your own thoughts regarding how you want your program to function and what you expect from your students.

2. It communicates the organizational framework and expectations to your students, parents, and administration, giving everyone an opportunity to learn the expectations and minimizes surprises. Parents and administrators dislike surprises more than anything else.

Every orchestra handbook must have the following components:

- Event Calendar for the Year
- Course Descriptions (with a list of required materials)
- Grading Policy

- Expectations, Procedures, and Student Responsibilities
- Rules and Consequences
- Uniform Information
- Financial Obligations
- Audition Information
- Policy for Attending Field Trips
- Prior Commitment Form (communicating a conflict with a concert)
- Parent/Student Contract and Signature Page

In addition, your handbook might also include:

- Table of Contents
- Letters from the Director and/or Principal
- How Parents Can Help
- Instrument Recommendations
- List of Private Teachers
- Directory of Students
- And much more

You can include a lot of information in your handbook, but at the very least, your handbook must answer the following three questions:

1. What are the required costs, materials, and equipment for this class?
2. What after-school events are required, and what is the grading policy if my child misses one of these events?
3. How do auditions work, and how do they affect my child's seating or placement into a higher-level orchestra?

First, parents need to know up front about the costs associated with your program. Be very clear about your instructional fees, the costs of materials and method books, and whether uniforms and/or instruments need to be rented or purchased for students to participate in class. It is also helpful for parents to have a ballpark idea about how much field trips typically cost so they can prepare for them. Costs can quickly add up, especially when students are taking lessons and qualifying for district, regional, and all-state orchestras. If you are planning a big trip with a large price tag, announce it in the spring of the previous year so students and parents can start saving up over the summer. Also, be sure to include clear policies for students on free or reduced lunch.

Second, your handbook must include the Orchestra Event Calendar and your policy for grading after-school rehearsals and performances. Parents need to know when these rehearsals and performances will take place so they can prepare for them. Young teachers may not know how busy a parent's life can be; parents appreciate clear communication about when and where their children need to be months in advance.

On the Events Calendar, indicate which events are required and graded. Refer parents to the page of the handbook that describes what happens to a student's grade if a required event is missed. If you are a new teacher, copy the "Grading Policy for After-School Rehearsal and Concert Attendance" (shown below). Show it to your principal and find out if there is anything in it your principal cannot support or would like to change. It is important for your principal to see, understand, and support this policy because it will be tested *every single year.*

Sample Grading Policy for After-School Rehearsal and Concert Attendance

Grading Policy for After-School Rehearsal and Concert Attendance

Concerts and after-school rehearsals are considered part of the class requirement for orchestra. Good communication between teachers, students, and parents can prevent misunderstandings. So please communicate immediately with the director when there are problems and schedule conflicts.

The orchestra's performance calendar is on the front page of our website and on the back of the front cover of the Orchestra Handbook. Students are expected to arrive 15 minutes early to rehearsals and 45 minutes early to concerts to unpack, warm up, and get ready. They are also expected to stay for the entire rehearsal or performance. Students will receive grades for every after-school and evening rehearsal and performance. Students who are absent, tardy, or leave early for any unexcused reason may receive a low grade or a zero. Students who come to a concert performance in unacceptable attire will have their concert grade reduced, and in extreme cases will not be allowed to perform. Students who have after-school jobs are expected to communicate with their employer and request that their work schedules be arranged to accommodate all rehearsals and performances. Employers should be informed that orchestra is a class, not an extra-curricular activity. After-school rehearsals and concerts are a required part of the class, and school policy states that student employment is not an excused reason for missing class.

Absences and tardies for a rehearsal or performance are only excused when they meet the following criteria and parents immediately send a written note informing the director. Verbal or written statements from students are not excused.

1. **The student is too ill to attend school.** The parent should send a written note to the director as soon as possible. In most cases, a signed doctor's medical excuse will exempt the student from making up the grade. Students who were present at school on both the day of the after-school event and also the day after the event will not be excused without a note from the doctor.
2. **There is a death in the family or comparable family emergency**. The parent should send a written note to the director as soon as soon as possible. If the student's family crisis is a death in the family or comparable, the student will be exempt from making up the grade. All other cases are excused at the discretion of the director; unexcused absences will earn a zero, and excused absences must submit a recording as described below.
3. **The student has a prior commitment.** If the student has a prior commitment that was planned before the orchestra rehearsal or concert was announced, the parent must communicate this conflict using the Prior Commitment Form (see Appendix D). Established religious holidays are excused but should be communicated by the parent using the Prior Commitment Form. *Prior Commitment Forms for communicating conflicts with events that are announced in August with the calendar in this handbook are due September 1.* If the orchestra has a schedule change during the year, parents will have 10 days to inform the director of conflicts. Students with excused prior commitments are allowed to make up their event grade by submitting a recording *before the date missed.*

Making up the grade for excused absences – Students with excused prior commitments, illnesses without a doctor's excuse, and family emergencies that are not comparable to a death in the family must make up the grade of the event missed. To make up a grade, students must record themselves performing all of the music from the event they will miss. This recording will be graded and will replace the zero for the grade of the event missed. Students will lose 10% of their grade for every day the recording is late. For prior commitments, students are to submit their recordings to the director before the date of the missed event. For illness and family emergency, students must submit the recording within 3 days of the end of the absence.

> Students who miss a significant number of in-school or after-school rehearsals for excused or unexcused reasons may lose their leadership seating and, if necessary, may not be allowed to perform at the concert. This affects students who miss:
>
> - More than 20% of the classes in the 6 weeks leading up to a concert
> - More than 40% of the classes in the last 2 weeks before a concert
> - Unexcused absences from any required after-school rehearsals or dress rehearsals before the concert
>
> Students who miss too much class to perform will be required to make a recording, as described above, and submit it before the day of the concert in lieu of their concert grade.

There are rare cases in which a conflicting event was not organized by the student or parent, and the event forces the student to make a terrible choice. Examples include a student who was asked mid-year to be in the bridal party of her sister's wedding, or a star athlete whose team made it to the state championship game that was not on the regular calendar. In cases like this, the parents must communicate as soon as they foresee the likelihood of a conflict, and the concert make-up grade requirement would be the same as any other prior commitment.

If the sample policy doesn't work for your teaching situation, then change it or create one that meets the needs of your program. Children are busy these days, and some have a different activity every night of the week. Students will come to you requesting to be excused or asking for special exceptions, and you need a policy to protect you and your program. When students ask for an exemption, do *not* make any quick decisions. Instead, *refer to your policy and follow your policy*. Sit down with the student and the policy, and let the student decide between the consequences of his/her actions in light of your policy. If you cannot follow your own policy, do *not* make an exception. Instead, *amend the policy*.

A good policy removes directors from the treacherous and exhausting position of having to make decisions every time a conflict comes up. Directors who do not follow their own policy create all kinds of problems for the principal and, consequently, themselves. They also weaken the other orchestra policies that give the program much-needed strength and structure.

After money and grades, include any information about how you will determine a student's course placement or chair. Some parents are extremely sensitive about seeing their children upset about the chair they earned or the level of orchestra they will take the following year. If you have auditions for chairs or for course placement, your handbook should include clear information about the requirements and also how final decisions are made.

Every handbook should have a contract that parents sign and return to verify that they read and understand your policies and expectations. When a parent issue arises, the principal is going to ask, "Do you have this policy in writing?" Your answer should be, "Not only do I have this in my handbook, but the parent signed the contract stating that he or she read it and understood all of the policies and procedures within the program. Here is a copy of the signed page." At that point, your principal will smile and thank you for making his or her life easier. An example of contract wording is shown below:

Sample Contract Wording

By signing below, I affirm that:

- I have read and understand the policies stated in the Orchestra Handbook.
- By enrolling in orchestra, I agree to comply with these policies, procedures, and expectations.
- I have this year's orchestra calendar and am responsible for attendance at all required events.

Student's Name: ______________________________

Parent's Signature: ______________________________

Date: ______________________________

To be clear, a parent's signature does not mean the parent agrees with your policies; it is simply a way of communicating to you that the parent has read and understands your rules and expectations. The parents already agreed to follow your policies when they signed their child up for the class, and students are given ten days in most states to change their minds and drop a class without penalty if they don't want to agree with your policies.

Rules, Consequences, and Expectations

How do you want your students to behave in rehearsals, concerts, and on field trips? What is your plan for teaching those behaviors? Rules, consequences, expectations, and procedures give structure and order to classroom behavior.

Rules and Consequences

Well-run classrooms have rules and clear consequences when the rules are broken. Rules work best when students understand what the rules are and what happens when they are tardy, disruptively talk, eat in class, or engage in any other behavior that you deem inappropriate.

Remember:
A consequence is something the student chooses.

"If you choose to break this rule, then you have also chosen this consequence." It's best to keep your list of rules short and clear, as shown in the list below:

1. Be on time to class and early to every rehearsal and performance.

2. Bring the materials you need—your instrument, music, and a pencil—and not the ones you don't: cell phones, work for another class, food/drink, or other distractions.

3. Follow instructions the first time they are given, and mark your music without being asked.

4. Speak or play your instrument only when you've been instructed to do so.

5. Put your name on your instrument case and store it in your locker.

Post your rules and consequences in your handbook and somewhere in your classroom. All consequences should follow the discipline plan of your school. Here's an example:

Students who choose to break the rules are also choosing
to receive the following consequences:

- First offense – verbal or visual warning
- Second offense – lunch detention
- Third offense – removal from rehearsal and parent contact
- Fourth offense – administrative referral
- Extreme offenses – referred to administration immediately

There is a rule for teachers, too:
Be consistent and follow through with your consequences!

Teachers who choose to break this rule are choosing their consequence as well: Students will misbehave and then blame the teacher for unfairly applying consequences to some students and not others.

What you do when a student doesn't follow your rules may be more important than the rules themselves. When a student breaks the rules, implement consequences in your office or away from other students. It's the teacher's job to be the adult and make every effort to *de-escalate* the situation. For habitually unruly students, additional consequences may be appropriate, including the loss of leadership, suspension from performance, or loss of field trip privileges.

Young teachers have the most difficulty enforcing rules; classroom discipline is the biggest problem for many first-year teachers. They want their students to like them and they tend to avoid confrontation with students. The reality is that students may whine when disciplined, but they want a disciplined classroom anyway. They are tougher than we think, and they respect teachers who are clear and consistent with their rules. Teachers can hurt students' feelings more when they give out consequences inconsistently. Students will take advantage of "nice teachers" all day long, and those teachers naturally become frustrated at the students. Don't get frustrated; just enforce your rules.

Expectations

Expectations help define the culture of your program by simply saying to students, "In this orchestra, we expect certain behavior." Expectations might include listening skills, appropriate language, saying thank you, or keeping the orchestra room clean. Students need to know that although there is no consequence for not thanking the chaperones, it is what you expect of students in your program. This is your opportunity to teach "life lessons" that are so important in the people business. You may even want to have your students make a list of behaviors that are important to them so they take ownership in the expectations of the class. A statement about expectations in your handbook does not have to be long or preachy. Consider the example below:

Sample Statement of Expectations

We make every effort to teach students more than just the vocational skills they will need to work. In orchestra, students are expected to learn and demonstrate a strong work ethic, professional and respectful conduct, and good communication skills that are required in every workplace. In class and especially in the community, students are expected to:

- Show up early to events
- Prepared with the materials and attitude they need to perform their best
- With a respectful, responsible, and positive demeanor toward themselves, each other, and their teachers, parents, and community members

Preparing for the Expected and the Unexpected

Procedures help students understand "how we do what we do." Most teachers learn the hard way that nothing happens the way they want unless they figure out a way to make it happen that way. Experienced teachers have a procedure for everything, including how students should enter the room, turn in fundraising money, or execute fire drills. Whether or not you put procedures in your handbook, at least write them down because your students will learn and follow your procedures when you are able to thoughtfully articulate them.

In the first weeks of school, students should learn how to enter the room, unpack, tune and cross-tune, without reminders from the teacher. This will ensure that the start of class is not delayed while you take attendance, address slipped pegs, or even when you have a substitute.

What are your procedures for:

- Unpacking and setting up class?
- Tuning and taking attendance?
- Distributing new music or forms?
- Collecting old music and returned forms?
- Collecting money (including how to handle cash and what goes on a check)?
- Setting up and breaking down the room or concert stage?
- Having students record their assignments?

Practice procedures by walking students through the process.

Remember:
Procedures have no consequences;
you just practice the procedure until it is right (like practicing music).

Create a "What Would I Do If..." list. Young teachers frequently encounter situations for which they are unprepared. Creating a list helps you stay in control of your class even when surprises arise. Consider how you would handle the following situations. Also consider if there are any others not included that you think you might have to address.

What would I do if a student:

- Talked constantly and then cussed at me when I asked him/her to be quiet?
- Forgot his/her instrument for the third time?
- Told me his/her instrument broke and they can't afford to get it fixed right now?
- Lost his/her music?
- Said "no" when I asked a student to sit in his/her seat?
- Purchased a new violin that was so poorly made that it does not keep its pitch?
- Asked to go to the bathroom every day in your class?
- Said someone else had been playing his/her personal instrument?
- Told you he/she didn't want to play 2nd violin?
- Fell in your class and started to bleed?
- Was making out with another student in your practice room?
- Came to your room crying?

This is an especially valuable exercise for young teachers who are not accustomed to having to deal with the variety and volume of problems that arise in a classroom. In addition to a response for students, you might also create one for parents.

What would I do if a parent:

- Showed up in my classroom unannounced and angrily told me they needed to talk to me immediately?
- Said his/her son should be playing near the front of the 1st violins?
- Said his/her daughter doesn't like the music you picked?
- Asked you not to grade his/her student too hard because he/she has a learning disability?
- Informed you that his/her daughter is thinking about quitting because she thinks you don't like her?
- Said his/her son's orchestra grade is hurting his GPA and it's not like he's going to play an instrument after high school?
- On the other end of the phone started yelling angry insults, and nothing you said seemed to help?

Remember:
If you don't know the answer to a question, the best response is, "Let me think about it and get back to you on that."

Then you give yourself time to think and ask a mentor or your administrator for advice so you can respond with a thoughtful, prepared answer. Being prepared for surprises can greatly reduce teacher mistakes, parent anger, and administrative repercussions. Educating parents is not much different than educating students in this regard. No matter who we are in the process of educating, we do a better job of it when we are prepared to teach the lesson at hand.

First Week Plans and Opening Checklist

On the first day of school, new kids are nervous and returning students are excited to see their friends. By the end of the day, however, the students have heard four to six lectures about rules, consequences, expectations, and procedures, and it will likely take them and their parents weeks to sort out all of the new information. Orchestra classes can feel especially challenging in this regard because, in addition to the normal classroom rules and expectations, you must also assign instruments and lockers, and explain rentals and fees, performance calendars, concert attire, and concert grading policies before you can do what you were hired to do—make music!

Don't try to teach students about your rules, consequences, expectations, and procedures all at once. Create a first-week plan that spreads the information and start-up details out over several days. First impressions are important, and you don't want all of this initial information to smother the excitement students feel about orchestra. If you haven't read *The First Days of School* by Harry Wong, we highly recommend that you order it. While it won't tell you anything about teaching orchestra, there is no better book for helping school teachers set up classroom rules and procedures.

According to the Chinese philosopher Sun Tzu, "Battles are won or lost before they begin." Your success depends largely on how well you have prepared for the year. The checklist below might help you organize your program and your year, and put yourself one step closer to great music making. Do as much as possible during the summer, before your first official work day.

- ❑ Create your "To Do" list using "The Life of an Orchestra Director" (Appendix B).
- ❑ Plan your year using "Timeline for the Academic Year" (Appendix C).
- ❑ Complete the Orchestra Handbook.
- ❑ Plan procedures for how you want everything done in your classroom.
- ❑ Update your instrument inventory and assign instruments/lockers to students.
- ❑ Have handouts, concert music, and method books ready for distribution.
- ❑ Create and review your first-week plan.
- ❑ Set up your class lists and grade book.
- ❑ Compile a list of student/parent phone numbers and e-mail addresses.

Chapter 4

Structuring Class Time

Children appreciate structure and routine, especially when they are young. Even older, free-spirited teens understand how time frames and deadlines are helpful for synchronizing group efforts and making teamwork more efficient. And while we want to be careful that our routines don't become a mindless treadmill, we know orchestras work and learn most efficiently when everyone understands not only what they are supposed to be doing, but also when they are supposed to do it.

In this chapter we will look at how we organize class time. The bell schedule tells us when a class begins and ends, but how we structure the time in between bells will determine whether our classes are chaotic and directionless or organized, focused, and efficiently moving forward. Moreover, when students independently and punctually do what they are supposed to do, our jobs become significantly easier. Efficient classes save us time that we can devote toward optimizing planning and instruction, and they also save us energy for that life that waits for us after work.

IN THIS CHAPTER:

- Classroom Set-Up: Rows vs. Rehearsal
- Stretching
- Teaching Young Students to Tune Themselves
- Fundamentals Time
- Rehearsing, Performing, and Making Music

Classroom Set-Up: Rows vs. Rehearsal

How you choose to set up your room depends on the dimensions of your teaching space, but more importantly upon the type of instruction you plan to deliver. Beginning string classes are often taught in rows, whereas older orchestra classes typically rehearse in semicircles. Each has benefits and drawbacks that influence instruction in different ways.

Teaching in Rows

Teachers of younger students in elementary or early middle school frequently line up students in rows instead of the traditional orchestra semicircle format. The focus of the classroom instruction is on developing the musical performance skills of individual students. The primary resource is usually a sequential method book, and separate concert music is often added to the folder as concert time approaches.

There are several benefits to teaching classes in straight rows:

1. Rows require every student to be responsible for bringing their own instrument, accessories, and music.

2. Rows give the teacher better access to every student to help them tune and assist with instrument position and left- or right-hand technique.

When determining where students will sit, put the students who need the most help up front. Then teach from the front of the class to the back of the room, verbally pushing the most advanced students in the last rows while silently assisting the front-row students who need the most help. Don't put the bass players in the back just because they are play bass; young bass students need as much attention as any other students—and sometimes more. Also, have students keep their cases and book bags under their chair or against the wall, but not in the aisle. You will want to be able to move quickly and easily up and down the aisle to help students with their technique without tripping or leaning over all of their stuff—and kids have a lot of stuff.

In middle school, teachers often start the year in rows and then transition to a semicircle set-up mid-year, toward concert time. If you use different set-ups for classes throughout the day, students can learn how to set up and break down the room. This will save you time and energy, especially around concert time.

Traditional Orchestra Format

In the traditional orchestra format, students sit two per stand and in sections (e.g., violin 1, violin 2, viola, cello, and bass). To keep bass players from being forgotten, some teachers prefer to put them directly behind the seconds and violas. Orchestra seating is preferable when the students are playing concert music because they can better hear and blend with the other members of their section.

The traditional orchestra format has one significant drawback: it limits the teacher's direct access to individual students and inhibits one-on-one technical instruction. This is an important problem to recognize because we tend to program challenging music for upper-level orchestras and then forget to teach students the performance skills these advanced pieces require. The following strategies reduce the impact of this problem:

- If the room is big enough, leave space between the podium and the first stands, and also between each section. Use this space to move around the room and give students individualized instruction.

- Pair weaker students on a stand with stronger students. If you seat students in order by ability, put the 2nd chair student behind the 1st chair on the outside of the 2nd stand; put the 3rd chair player on the outside of the 3rd stand. After the outside seats are filled, then seat the remaining students on the inside. Use this seating for concerts as well. Don't put all of the less-skilled students in the back where it is most difficult to hear and away from the instruction they desperately need.

- Change up the seating for variety, but also to improve instruction. For example, on days when you plan to focus on technique, put weaker players in the front. Mondays and Wednesdays might be technique days, Tuesdays and Thursdays might be traditional concert set-up, and Fridays might be a different seating altogether.

Stretching

The older students get, the more they sit. Studies have shown that students sit too much. Stretching is especially important for high school students, who have more technically demanding music and spend longer hours at the computer. Stretching only takes a minute, and you will find that when students stretch, they are not only more physically prepared to learn, but they are also more prepared mentally.

At first, students may feel socially uncomfortable and resist standing up and stretching. As they grow more comfortable, they will even ask to stand up and stretch. When time is short, do a few stretches that focus especially on the back, shoulder, arm, and hand muscles. After a couple weeks of leading the stretches yourself, have a student take over and lead the class. Include any additional stretching you deem important for playing.

Use the stretches below, or create your own:

- Roll the head from one shoulder to the other, slowly stretching out the neck. Place the chin on the right shoulder and move it slowly to the left shoulder.

- Roll the shoulders in large, slow circles, forward and backward.

- Perform wrist circles with your hands moving in opposite directions.

- Move the right elbow across the body to the left shoulder, with the left hand on the back of the right elbow. Repeat with the left elbow.

- Move the right arm over the head to the left shoulder, with the left hand on the back of the right elbow. Repeat with the left arm.

Teaching Young Students to Tune Themselves

Consider this:
The most one-on-one instruction many beginning students receive is during the time the teacher spends with them to tune their instrument.

If teachers took only a few extra seconds with each child to improve their technique, their playing positions and tone quality would improve greatly over the course of a year. The extra time and energy teachers spend employing the tuning strategies below will pay off handsomely in the long run. If done correctly, instructional time will be gained, not lost, and students will get 5 to 10 more minutes of uninterrupted practice every day.

If the strategies listed below don't work for you, do some research and figure out what works best for your situation.

The goal is always the same:
Students' strings must be in tune before rehearsal begins.

Beginning Students Who Are Not Yet Using Their Bow Well (first 6 months):

1. Before students enter the classroom, write a tuning time assignment on the board.

   This is my favorite: Have the method book accompaniment CD playing over the sound system as the students come in and quietly unpack. They can review, sing, and pluck the book exercises along with the CD or MP3 while you tune individuals. Most of these exercises are in tuning-friendly keys, so you can listen to the tuner in the background (or just tune to the CD) while the students play.

2. Have the violins and violas stand while they play with the CD. As you approach each student, check the student's instrument and hand position, and correct students as necessary. This is a good time to check shoulder placement and cello/bass endpin height, too.

3. Take the student's instrument and tune it with a bow. Using the bow is not only more accurate, but it allows the student to see good bow technique up close and hear a good tone on their own instrument. To save time, take your bow around the room to tune students' instruments.

4. After the instrument is tuned, hand it back and ask the student to place it correctly back into playing position. Assist or correct the student as necessary.

5. Take attendance while students are actively practicing and reviewing.

Beginning Students Who Can Use Their Bow (6–18 months):

1. Write a tuning time assignment on the board. Turn on the tuner, and have violins and violas stand. Check each student's instrument placement, endpin height, as well as their left-hand position. Assist or correct them as necessary.

2. Have students use their bow to play the A string. Check each student's bow hand, bow angle, and tone, and make any corrections necessary. Tune the A as the student plays. Then, have the student play the A-D string together while you tune the D; move on to the G and other strings. This process will take a little time at first, but it allows the students to receive daily one-on-one bow and tone instruction during these critical months. Students will also hear and learn the sound of tuning by fifths as their instrument sits right under their ear—a valuable aural memory that students will need later when tuning by fifths themselves.

Teaching Intermediate Students to Tune One String at a Time:

1. Students should stop playing and talking. Have a student leader operate the tuner so the tuning process continues if/when you need to help students who are struggling with slipped pegs.

2. The student leader plays the A on the tuner. The students listen quietly for 5 seconds, hum and match the A, and then tune their A strings at the tip of the bow using a good, transparent tuning tone. Students who cannot tell if the note is sharp or flat should tune the note unmistakably flat, and then raise the pitch until it is in tune.

3. When students are finished tuning the A, the student leader turns the tuning pitch to D, and everyone tunes their D string. This process repeats for the G, C, and E strings. String bass students should begin using octave harmonics to tune their strings.

Teaching Intermediate Students to Tune in Fifths:

1. Select a student leader to operate the tuner; this allows the tuning process to continue if/when you need to help students who are struggling with slipped pegs.

2. The student leader stands in front of the class and plays an A on the classroom tuner. The students listen quietly for 5 seconds, hum and match the A, and then tune their A string at the tip of the bow using a good, transparent tuning tone. Students who cannot tell if the note is sharp or flat should tune the note unmistakably flat, and then raise the pitch until it is in tune.

3. The leader turns the tuning pitch to D, and the students play both the D and A strings together. Teach students to listen to both strings as they tune the D string and to listen especially to the "beats" that occur when the strings are out of tune. Demonstrate the sound of two strings coming into tune as many times as necessary for the class.

4. When the D strings are tuned, the leader turns the tuning pitch to G, and the students play their G and D strings together to tune the G, and so on.

5. To tune the C string, violins and basses continue playing the G string. To tune the E string, the violas and cellos continue playing the A.

6. Double basses should use third position harmonics to tune one string to another. In third position, the first finger harmonic on the A string produces an A two octaves above the fundamental; the fourth finger harmonic on the D string in third position produces the same pitch. The students should play each pitch separately, adjusting the D peg until the harmonic on the D and A strings match. Then tune the other strings the same way.

Eventually, students reach a point when they are ready to tune their instruments on their own. The leader plays the A; the students listen for 5 seconds and then tune their A string at the tip of the bow. Once the A is in tune, the leader turns off the A and instructs the students to tune the rest of their strings. The students tune their instruments quietly using the tip of the bow, and they stop playing when they are finished. At this point, even older, advanced student orchestras will still be slightly out of tune. There are additional cross-tuning strategies for finely tuning older orchestras (see Chapter 9: Intonation).

There are a few other methods to help younger orchestras get in tune:

- **Electric tuners** – Some teachers have found electric tuners to be very helpful for tuning large classes of young students. You would have to figure out logistics for distributing and sharing tuners, but when used correctly, they can help beginning students develop independence—and even give them the confidence to tune their instrument at home.

- **Planetary cello pegs** – What would it be worth to you and your students to never, ever have to tune a cello's slipped peg again? Planetary cello pegs cost a little money up front, but they are worth it! Talk to your local instrument shop, have a fundraiser, and get planetary pegs. Not only will they make your life significantly easier, your students will do a better job of tuning.

Cheap instruments are quickly becoming the biggest tuning problem teachers face. If an instrument is difficult to tune, the student should consider taking the instrument back to the store. Parents need to hear from teachers that students must have instruments of a certain minimum quality to be able to learn to tune their own instruments. They need to know that the cheapest instruments, especially those purchased online, are so difficult to tune that their children will be much more likely to give up out of frustration.

Fundamentals Time

In a city or countywide youth orchestra, the music rehearsal begins immediately after the orchestra tunes. Youth orchestras can do this because the job of teaching students how to play their instruments is left almost entirely up to the private teacher. In school orchestra, however, the director's job includes more than conducting students through inspiring rehearsals and performances of great music; it also involves teaching students the technical and musical skills that the great concert pieces require. The majority of this instruction occurs during fundamentals time after the students tune, but before the rehearsal of concert music begins.

In younger orchestras where students are lined up in straight rows, fundamentals time is a very natural part of the class. Teachers use sequential method books to teach technique, and they have to be careful not to let fundamentals time take over the entire class. For directors of older orchestras, the challenge is to figure out ways to teach and review the skills that advanced music requires. Teachers tend to model and run their classes and rehearsals like the orchestra experiences of their youth—those same experiences that inspired many of them to pursue music education. "We teach the way we were taught—not the way we are taught to teach."

We want our students to play great orchestra music, but the performance skills many of these pieces require can be well over the heads of what our students are able to do well. Like the directors of our youth, many public school orchestra directors rely on private instructors to teach older students advanced technique. Instead of figuring out ways to teach technique in class, we tell students to get private lessons. We know private instruction is a powerful and good component of the technical development of any serious string student, and we reason logically that if it worked well for us, then it should work well for every student.

When we were younger, however, it was difficult for us to see and realize that every student was not like us. We were the students getting lessons and thriving in the youth orchestra model; we were the leaders who would eventually become music teachers.

Of course, students who are serious about their musical development should seek out the best private instruction they can find, and orchestras with high numbers of serious string students will also naturally have many students taking private lessons. But there is a significant difference between encouraging private instruction and telling students to get a private teacher because they are going to dive right into the music right after tuning and won't be taught the string technique that the music requires.

Even if every student could afford it, at what point are string teachers no longer responsible for teaching string technique?

School orchestra is different than youth orchestra.
***All students*—not just the ones taking lessons—deserve sequential, comprehensive instruction that enables them to learn the knowledge and skills that orchestral works require so every child can make great music.**

Fundamentals time is what makes school orchestra different from youth orchestra. It is an important part of every orchestra class, regardless of age or ability level of the students, and it is up to you to figure out what skills your students need to learn and then continue teaching the technique that the advanced repertoire requires.

Just think about it: There is so much for you to teach. During fundamentals time, you can review and improve skills and knowledge, and teach technique, creativity, tone, articulation, intonation, rhythmic literacy, musicianship, and much more. By devoting time toward continued technical development, you can review the skills students already "know," and you can also continue developing upper-level skills and knowledge to better equip your students to perform more advanced repertoire.

There is plenty of rehearsal time after fundamentals time for concert music, and when you devote the first part of the class to teaching skills and knowledge, your students learn more and perform their concert music with better skill and musical understanding.

Teaching technique during fundamentals time with exercises designed for developing technical skill is more efficient than teaching technique through the concert music.

When done correctly, fundamentals time saves time, and students will develop better technique and musicianship resulting in concert performances with improved accuracy and artistry.

Structuring Fundamentals Time

Fundamentals time can and should be organized into the groups of skills you want your students to learn:

- Right-hand skills – technique, bowing, tone production, and articulation
- Left-hand skills – technique, shifting, vibrato, etc.
- Musicianship – theory, creativity, expression, interpretation, and sight-reading skills

The length of your class will determine how you structure fundamentals time. In a 45-minute class, address the skills from one or two categories before moving on to the concert music rehearsal. In a 90-minute block, you not only have time to address something from each category, but the instruction of the different skill groups will help break up the long block into smaller chunks of learning time. Especially as students get older and more advanced, the amount of skills to address during fundamentals time increases. Be selective about which skills need to be taught each day. You may want to designate different days of the week for emphasizing certain skills. For example, emphasize right-hand skills on Monday and Wednesday, left-hand skills on Tuesday and Thursday, and theory and creativity on Friday.

There is so much to teach that it can be a little overwhelming to try and create a long-range plan that organizes everything you should teach. Busy orchestra directors are easily tempted to skip the extra work of planning and teaching skill development during fundamentals time, and they just hand out another piece of music. This is one of those times when the easiest thing for us is not what is best for our students. The good news is that this book has been written to help teachers organize what they need to teach.

The next eight chapters address the process of planning and teaching skills during fundamentals time and rehearsal time. These chapters contain learning objectives, teaching strategies, and pitfalls and solutions that will benefit all students, regardless of their age and ability level. We will look at strategies for introducing and reviewing skills during fundamentals time, and also ways to address these skills in the concert music rehearsal.

Students cannot realize the full potential and artistry of their concert music if they lack the skills to perform the music. String instruments require a great deal of skill to perform well, and it is up to us to structure our class time and strike the right balance in the time we devote to teaching technique and making music.

Rehearsing, Performing, and Making Music

Music does not have to be complex or challenging for it to be enjoyable or rewarding. Even when students have just begun learning their instruments, you should devote a significant part of class to making music. For beginners, plucking an open D string along with a musically pleasing method book sound track is musically gratifying. Students experience the joys of making music when they can play the correct notes (in tune) and rhythms (together with their friends) with an aesthetically pleasing tone. As students become more musically mature, give them opportunities to improvise slow, pretty melodies with some teacher-directed parameters. Anytime students can make music from within, something beautiful happens. Always have a couple of fun pieces in the folders that your students love to play, and end every class making beautiful music so your students leave class wanting more. Chapter 12 is devoted entirely to concert music, including rehearsal objectives, strategies, and how to select music that is right for your students.

What is the right amount of time to devote to fundamentals vs. concert music? Every day is different, and each class is different. The risk of writing about daily structure in a book like this is that it creates the illusion that daily structure is fixed, when in reality, the structure varies constantly. It depends on the age of your students and the type of instruction you plan to deliver. In September, you will find that you tend to spend more time on technique; as the concert approaches, you find yourself allocating more time for polishing concert music. Always try to keep a good balance, and make time for fundamentals and concert music in every class. The closer you get to the concert, the more concert music should occur in the last half of class. Dividing the class time into equal parts—fundamentals and concert music—will help remind you to balance technical development and music.

Though your plans will and should vary from one day to the next, the sample framework below is a common one because it works well:

Sample Daily Structure

Daily Structure

Bell Work:
- Students enter, set up, and unpack without reminders.
- Students lead tuning, stretching, warm-up routine.

Announcements:
- Upcoming assessments, concerts, trips
- What will you learn today?

Fundamentals Time:
- Right-hand skills – technique, bowing, tone production, articulation
- Left-hand skills – technique, shifting, vibrato, etc.
- Musicianship – theory, creativity, expression, interpretation, sight-reading skills

Concert Music:
- New concert music
- Review concert music

Closure:
- Review assignments and upcoming assessments.
- End with a fun piece.
- Pack up and reset room.

Chapter 5

Instrument Position

A complete book of strategies for teaching all string class instruments—violin, viola, cello, and double bass—would require thousands of pages if it exhaustively addressed the myriad body types, learning styles, and schools of string teaching. These next chapters include strategies for introducing instrument and hand positions to students, but the greater focus is on how to review and improve student technique year after year. There are many different schools of string education, and veteran teachers will certainly encounter strategies in these chapters that are different than their own. In the end, you must find the method that works best for your students, remembering that every student is a little different.

This resource aims to provide thoughtful and proven strategies that you can read and replicate in a classroom setting. We will also troubleshoot some of the more common and persistent problems all students face and provide suggestions for helping resolve these issues. You can find many good online video demonstrations that show the technical skills described in these chapters, and videos illustrate the movement of string performance much better than we can with pictures. You can supplement videos with the pictures in their beginning methods books. If you are looking to hone your own string skills, you are encouraged to enroll in a university summer string education course or boot camp. These camps are a fun way to make new friends and develop new teaching skills, especially on secondary instruments.

IN THIS CHAPTER:

- When Do We Stop Reviewing Fundamentals?
- The Goal Is Balance
- Balancing the Violin and Viola
- Balancing the Cello
- Balancing the Double Bass

When Do We Stop Reviewing Fundamentals?

Before we dive into the next three chapters on position and technique, we need to address the way that skill review is minimized in our current public school culture. School academic classes focus heavily on teaching large amounts of new material to students as fast and as efficiently as possible. In these classes, teachers introduce new facts and practice new skills quickly to prepare students for an upcoming unit test or end-of-course exam. "Review" refers to that last thing a teacher does right before the unit test.

Musicians, on the other hand, spend a relatively small amount of time learning new skills compared to the vast majority of time spent practicing and refining skills. In the school climate, we frequently find ourselves having to explain the importance of practice, and defending the rehearsal and review that is so important to success for all musicians. We only introduce a skill once, and the introduction is important, but how we review skills every day after that introduction is even more important. So don't shy away from reviewing fundamentals, especially with advanced students who have the most to review.

The reality is that our bodies are constantly changing, especially during the teenage years, and it is important for all musicians, even professionals, to review instrument and hand position and technique. Position problems restrict movement and create tension, which can lead to injury as well as problems with vibrato, shifting, fine-tuning, velocity, articulation, and tone production.

All students need to be reminded about the value of review, especially when they say, "Oh, I already *know* that." Each time you teach a new skill, you have an opportunity to begin by assessing and reviewing basic technique, to make sure there are no problems that might inhibit the learning of more advanced skills. Fundamental skills are not "kids' stuff"—they are important for string musicians of all ages.

The Goal Is Balance

Playing a string instrument requires extraordinary freedom. The body works best when it is free of tension. When we "hold on" to the instrument to manipulate it and make music, our arms and hands must maintain the freedom to *move around* the instrument so the instrument itself does not get in the way of our concert music. The mere idea of "holding on" suggests gripping and tension, so it's better to think of our relationship with the instrument as one of *balance*.

This chapter contains strategies for helping students set up their instrument position in a way that promotes good balance instead of good "holding on." Let's begin with an overarching goal for teaching instrument position:

Instrument Position Goal and Objectives

The goal is to balance the instrument with the body in a way that allows the left hand to move freely around all parts of the fingerboard and the entire bow to easily play all four strings. This goal guides all of our instrument position instruction, regardless of what students play. It can be broken down into several objectives that can be reviewed with a homogeneous or heterogeneous class of students. The students will:

1. Sit or stand with a balanced head, relaxed shoulders, and lengthened spine.
2. Bring the instrument to the body and balance it in a way that allows:
   a. The left hand to move freely around all parts of the fingerboard; and
   b. The bow to easily access all four strings.

The following sections address specific performance objectives and strategies for teaching individual instrument position. Each instrument requires a distinct set of skills, and learning all of the performance objectives takes time. To help students learn the objectives that they are expected to demonstrate, create a rubric with the objectives and have students use it to assess their own performance, evaluate the performance of their peers, and identify one or more goals for learning at home.

To help you organize how you think about instrument position and set-up, first begin by learning the general goal and objectives listed above, as well as this "Golden Rule" for instrument position:

Golden Rule for Instrument Position:
First, stand or sit tall with a floating head, lengthened spine, and shoulders back. Then bring the instrument to the body; don't bring the body to the instrument.

Humans instinctively adapt to their environment, and our brains have learned to do this without even thinking about it. When balancing an instrument, our bodies naturally want to meet the instrument halfway, unconsciously causing our heads and shoulders to lean forward to play the instrument. The Golden Rule reminds us to first sit or stand with a relaxed and well-balanced head, spine, and shoulders. Then, while maintaining excellent balanced position, bring the instrument to the body in a way that does not disrupt this balance.

When standing, the feet should be shoulder-width apart, and the body's weight should be evenly balanced over both feet. Gently swaying back and forth promotes good balance and keeps joints from locking. The head should float, pulling the spine up tall, and shoulders should rotate back, not forward. The head, spine, and shoulders remain tall and balanced, whether standing or sitting.

When seated, the body's weight is spread across a tripod of support, balanced between the two feet and the sitz bones that support the body on the edge of the chair. The chair should be tall enough to keep the hips even with, or slightly higher than, the knees.

Balancing the Violin and Viola

The violin and viola are balanced between three points of the body: 1) the left clavicle/shoulder muscle, 2) the left jawbone, and 3) the left hand. Most of the support comes from the relaxed shoulder and jawbone. The left hand provides enough support to counter-balance the action of the fingertips and the weight of the bow; the primary job of the left hand is to play the instrument, *not* hold it up.

Violin/Viola Instrument Position Objectives:

Teach and assess student position using the following objectives.

Violin/Viola students will:

1. Stand/sit with a lengthened spine and well-balanced head and shoulders.

2. Keep both shoulders back and relaxed when supporting and playing the instrument:
   a. The left shoulder does not raise up to support the instrument.
   b. The right shoulder does not break dramatically forward to chase the instrument.

3. Rest the instrument back over the left shoulder far enough for the edge of the left lower bout to be close to the plane of the player's back.

4. Face the chin to the left so the jawbone rests lightly in the chinrest.
   a. The back of the player's head remains balanced over the spine, not craned forward to meet the instrument.
   b. The chin stays tucked and does not raise or lower to meet the chin rest.

5. Support the scroll over the left foot at a height that keeps the strings parallel to the floor—not sloping downward.

6. Rotate the bridge slightly to 1:00, keeping the instrument almost flat.

Setting Up Good Instrument Position:

Use the following strategies to set students up with correct, healthy instrument positions. Have students stand when they are learning to balance their instrument; it's easier to hold the instrument correctly and also easier for you to see and correct problems that arise.

1. Stand with a lengthened spine and well-balanced head and shoulders. Sit on the front of the chair with tripod support and a lengthened spine and well-balanced head and shoulders.

2. Keeping the head still, feel the clavicle (collar bone), shoulder and back with the right hand.

3. Remember the Golden Rule: Stand or sit in a tall, healthy way, and then bring the instrument to the body; keep the head still and do not bring the body or the head/chin to the instrument.

4. With the left hand on the right shoulder of the instrument, raise the instrument up high over the left foot, then turn the instrument, lower and rest it onto the clavicle so the scroll is over the left foot and the strings are parallel to the floor. The lower left bout should be close to the back of the neck.

5. Without raising or lowering the chin, gently turn the head to look left, and rest the jawbone lightly in the chin rest; the nose, bridge and scroll should align.
   a. The jawbone should move horizontally; it should neither reach up to get over the chinrest nor clamp down.
   b. The shoulder should remain relaxed and back; it should not come forward or hike up to balance the instrument at the correct angle (see below, "Troubleshooting 2: Shoulder Rest and Chinrest Height").

6. Remind students to "grow an inch" and continue standing with a lengthened spine.

Troubleshooting – Violin and Viola

1. Most problems, such as holding the instrument too far in front, with the scroll pointing down or up, with their head craned forward, with their neck crooked, etc., can be corrected with the same solution. Take the instrument from the student and have him/her stand or sit correctly. Then place the instrument onto the student's shoulder and help the student turn his/her head to support the instrument. Remind the student to place the instrument far enough back on the shoulder so the left lower bout is almost touching the plane of the player's back. Many position and technical problems stem from

not having the instrument back far enough on the shoulder. Older students with ingrained bad habits will need their teachers to repeat this process a number of times until they understand how the new, correct placement is, and how it looks and feels.

2. **Shoulder Rest and Chinrest Height** – Many players require a shoulder rest or a taller chinrest—and sometimes both—to comfortably balance the instrument without hiking the shoulder up or clamping down with the neck and jaw. While shoulder rests have been popular for decades, we have recently seen more chinrest solutions from companies creating taller, even custom-fit chinrests. Many believe taller chinrests are superior to shoulder rests because they allow violinists to balance the instrument lower and closer to the arms than a tall shoulder rest.

3. **Viola Problems** – Bigger is not always better, and this adage holds true for the viola as well. Many viola problems and injuries are the result of having an instrument that is simply too big for the player's body. If the viola is so big that the player cannot hold it correctly, then it is too big. Students are happier and play better when they have an instrument that is properly sized.

Balancing the Cello

Cellists should sit tall, with a lengthened spine, and with their sitz bones on the edge of the chair. Heels should be firmly planted on the floor and far enough apart to create a 45-degree angle between the two legs. This "tripod of support," including both heels and the sitz bones, is the supportive framework that balances the cello and the rest of the body. The chair must be the correct height, allowing the hips to be slightly above the knees. It is best for a cellist's legs to slope slightly downward from the hips to the knees, allowing the cellist to balance the instrument with the sternum.

Cello Position Objectives:

Cello students will:

1. Use a chair that is tall enough to keep the hips slightly above the knees.

2. Sit on the front of the chair on the sitz bones with a lengthened spine and well-balanced head and shoulders. Keep both feet planted with heels and toes on the floor, and the knees apart so the legs meet at a right angle.

3. Pull out the endpin to a height that allows the student to cradle the cello comfortably between the knees and sternum.

4. Rest the upper bout of the cello against or near the sternum over the heart.

5. Keep the lower points of the C-bout above the knees.

6. Angle the cello so the C-peg is behind the left ear and the neck is next to, but not touching, the cellist's neck; the cello should not lean left so the cellist can see the left hand.

Determining Endpin Height and Placement:

First, cellists need to determine how far to pull out the endpin and where to place it on the floor. Before the endpin was invented, cellists balanced their instrument between the knees and sternum for 300 years. It wasn't until the mid-nineteenth century that cellists started using an endpin as a supplementary means of balancing the cello. The following endpin strategy is a good starting point for helping students find the length and position that is correct for their body:

1. With the endpin all the way in, hold the cello for the student while the student sits up tall on the edge of their chair with a good tripod of support.

2. Carefully place the cello between the student's legs and sternum so it balances comfortably in the body without the endpin. The lower points of the C-bout are above the knees, and the upper part of the cello rests "over the heart."

3. Once the student is comfortable and the cello is in the correct position, let the endpin out to the floor and secure the tightening screw. Remind the student to keep his/her body tall and forward, and not to collapse under the cello.

4. Readjust the legs and firmly replant the feet so the tripod of support is re-established. Minor adjustments may be needed, but this is generally the correct length and floor placement for the endpin. The student should take a moment to look and visually measure it, and get adjusted to what it feels like to have the endpin support a cello that is balanced in the student's body.

Setting Up Good Cello Position:

After the correct endpin height and placement is established, use the following process to balance the cello between three points of contact: the areas around the left and right knee, and the sternum. When it is supported correctly between the legs, the cello will lean back against the sternum so the cello neck rests next to (but not quite touching) the neck of the cellist.

1. Pull out the endpin to the correct length (see above).

2. Sit with the "tripod of support" and set the tip of the endpin in front of the feet to the center or just right of center; use a rock stop, if necessary.

3. Keep the body forward and balanced, and bring the scroll back, past the left ear. Rest the cello lightly on the sternum and position the C-peg behind the ear.
   a. Do not let the cello push the body back; the body supports the cello.
   b. The cello neck rests near the student's neck.

4. The inner knees support the cello on the sides below the "points" of the lower bouts. To make sure the knees don't "squeeze," take the cello away and bring it back frequently to promote light contact.

5. The cello angle should be approximately 45 degrees, depending on the student's body size and type.

6. Drop both hands to the side to check for good balance.

Troubleshooting – Cello

As with the upper instruments, most problems with cello position have the same basic solution: the teacher takes the cello from the student and has the student sit correctly; then the teacher replaces the instrument and balances it between the player's legs and sternum.

1. Young cellists frequently lean their cello left so they can see what their left hand is doing. Take the cello way, have the student sit correctly, and replace the cello so the cello neck is close to the student's neck. The students should use senses other than their eyes to listen and feel if the left hand is correct. If they need to look, cellists should use "sly fox" eyes (moving their eyes, but not their head). It may be helpful for them to close their eyes, or even blindfold them to help them realize they don't need their eyes. The "bear hug" (crossing arms around the cello to either bout), promotes centering and securing the cello in the body.

2. The collapsed cellist has rolled the hips back off of the sitz bones, and it looks like the cello is pushing the cellist back into the seat, causing the back and shoulders to slouch. First, make sure the chair is tall enough to keep the student's hips higher than the knees. Then take the cello from the student and remind the student to roll the hips forward, sit on the sitz bones, and sit

tall. Then return the cello and instruct the student to lean into the cello to balance it with the sternum. Have the student "rock and roll" (while in the "bear hug," rock on the sitz bones to promote balance and mobility).

Balancing the Double Bass

Whether they prefer to sit or stand, bass players will all agree that the instrument needs to be balanced in such a way that the player has the freedom to move the left hand around the fingerboard and the bow can play all four strings.

Double Bass Position Objectives:

The double bass student will:

1. Stand or sit tall with a lengthened spine:
    a. Stand with the feet shoulder-width apart with the left leg forward.
    b. Sit with the left leg on the lowest rung of a stool and the right foot flat on the floor.
2. Extend the endpin height to keep the left hand first finger in first position at eye level or higher, and the right hand knuckles at bridge level or higher when the arm is relaxed.
3. Rotate the bass slightly so the bridge faces 1:00.
4. Support the right rear corner of the upper bout against the body.
5. Balance the bass with the body so the left hand can move up and down the fingerboard freely.

Setting Up Bass Position:

Balance and freedom continue to be the guiding principles when trying to figure out how each student will best balance and perform double bass.

1. Stand with a lengthened spine and balanced head and shoulders, and with the feet shoulder width apart.
2. With the double bass in front of the body, balance the bass perfectly upright on its endpin with the left hand at the base of the neck.
3. Rotate the bass clockwise slightly so the bridge points to 1:00; too much rotation will limit E-string access. Do not allow students to face the bass to 3:00 and lean the ribs of the bass on their belly.

4. Step forward with the left foot and bring the right rear corner of the bass to the body, and balance it lightly with the body. The lower right rear bout balances lightly on the inside of the knee.

5. Balance the bass mostly upright, not excessively slanted. The bass should balance lightly with the body—between 80 and 85 degrees with the floor—and should not require the left hand to hold it steady. Drop both hands to the side to check for balance.

6. When sitting, use a bass stool set to a height that allows the player to sit comfortably on the edge of the stool with the right foot planted firmly on floor, and the left foot resting on the rung lowest to the floor.

7. Sitting or standing, check and adjust the endpin height:
   a. If LH first position first finger is below eye level, pull out the endpin to raise the bass.
   b. If the RH knuckles on a relaxed right arm are below the bridge, lower the bass.

Chapter 6

Left Hand Position, Vibrato and Shifting

Our brains have a funny habit of focusing attention on smaller things in ways that cause us to miss the bigger picture: sometimes we focus so hard on the trees that we fail to see the forest. When we teach left-hand position, it is easy to forget to address the motion of the shoulder, arm, and elbow that got the left hand to that position in the first place.

In this chapter, we will look at how the left arm and hand work together to give our hand and fingers easy access to all parts of the fingerboard. This chapter contains strategies for setting up the left hand, as well as common pitfalls, solutions, and callisthenic exercises that develop good left hand position and technique. We will also look at the other left-hand skills that include arm and elbow motion, including vibrato and shifting from first position up and around the upper bout into the highest registers of the string instrument.

IN THIS CHAPTER:

- The Left Arm and Hand
- Violin and Viola Left Hand
- Cello and Bass Left Hand
- Vibrato
- Shifting

The Left Arm and Hand

Our hands have opposable thumbs that give humans superior ability to grab and hold on to things. Over time we have evolved to hold on instinctively; a baby's hands, for example, will close reflexively around an object that we place in it. Our grip is one of the more important traits that make us human, but it can get in the way of learning a string instrument. We must retrain our left hand to let go of the instrument so our left arm has the freedom to move the hand to the correct place, and also to shift, vibrate, and do all of the gymnastics good performance requires. The left hand Golden Rule sounds simple enough, but undoing millions of years of evolution requires constant attention and practice.

Left Hand Golden Rule:
Let go of the instrument and rest the thumb lightly on the neck to give the left arm the freedom to move the hand to the correct position.

The best way to teach the left hand to let go is to keep it moving so it does not have the opportunity to stop and hold on. This is especially important for younger students who tend to lock into first position because they have not yet learned to vibrate or shift. We often model or show students pictures of what a good position looks like, but it is considerably more important for them to learn how the hands *move*, and how it *feels* when the motion is correct and relaxed.

Young players who stay in first position in their first years must learn to move their thumbs, move their hands, tap their fingers on the strings, and do other calisthenics that keep the left thumbs from squeezing. They should also learn how to use their arm and elbow to slide their fingers up and down the string, moving their relaxed hand, wrist, and arm around the instrument as one unit.

The String Polishing Exercise:

This exercise works well for all instruments, and it is especially valuable for teaching beginners the feeling of movement, freedom, and letting go. Using an instrument to demonstrate, teach students to slide the third finger lightly up and down the full length of the D string, leading with the elbow to bring the hand around the instrument and then back to its proper first position resting place. This precursor to shifting reduces the tendency to grab the neck and releases the tension that inhibits vibrato and finger accuracy and velocity. Make sure the students' instruments are well balanced and supported by the body, and their left hands are free to move around the instrument without any tension. Then repeat this string polishing exercise every day using different fingers and strings.

Create and demonstrate callisthenic routines that review good technique at the beginning of each class. Once students learn the routines, have students lead the class while you walk around the room and help individuals perform each drill/skill correctly. Be creative; invent drills as students demonstrate a need.

Develop a classroom environment with zero-tolerance for poor technique.

Left-Hand Goal and General Objectives:

The strategies in this chapter address the following goal and objectives:

Goal:

Students move the left arm and hand around the instrument *freely*, keeping the thumb and fingers curved and relaxed.

Objectives:

1. Position the left elbow at a height and angle that allows the wrist to remain comfortably straight and gives the hand and fingers unrestrained access to all parts of the fingerboard.

2. Angle the hand and curve the fingers so the correct parts of the finger tips or pads touch or hover over the string.

3. Gently rest the thumb on the neck opposite the second finger without squeezing.

4. Shift from the elbow with a relaxed, fluid motion, and keep the thumb with the second finger.

5. Vibrate with a consistent, relaxed motion.

The goal and objectives listed above can be applied generally to all instruments in the class. To help students learn the objectives, create a rubric using the objectives and have students assess their own performance, evaluate the performances of their peers, and identify one or more goals for learning at home.

These general objectives are helpful for reviewing good position with heterogeneous classes. More specific objectives are outlined in the following sections; these can be used to set up good left-hand technique with beginners or students who need more focused attention on their specific instrument. There are subtle, but distinct left-hand differences between violin and viola, just as there are between cello and bass. Their similarities, however, far outweigh their differences. So for the purpose of teaching beginners in heterogeneous classes, we have grouped the instruments in pairs to simplify instruction.

Violin and Viola Left Hand

When setting up the left hands of beginning upper string players, keep in mind the cause of most violin/viola left-hand problems. The left hand cannot be free to do all it is required to do when students have a poor instrument position that requires significant support from the left hand. The first step to good left-hand position is to make sure the instrument is balanced properly on the shoulder with a good shoulder rest and chinrest, and then use the following list of objectives to teach and evaluate left-hand position. When the instrument is balanced correctly, the left hand has no reason to hold on.

Violin and Viola Left-Hand Objectives:

While balancing the instrument correctly in playing position, violin and viola students will:

1. Angle the elbow slightly toward the belly, keeping the wrist comfortably straight—neither flat, nor crooked.

2. Rest the first finger "joint line" lightly against the neck near the nut.

3. Gently rest the left thumb on the neck opposite the first finger, leaving space between the palm and the neck.

4. Rotate the hand toward the neck, bringing the pinky closer to the fingerboard.

5. Keep the fingers curved over the strings in a "boxy" shape, and use the thumb-side corner of the fingertips to stop the string.

Setting Up the Left Hand for Violin and Viola:

Use the following teaching sequence to help beginning students learn proper left-hand set-up. Students should stand as they learn left-hand position. They will be less likely to develop bad habits, and you will have an easier time seeing and correcting the problems.

1. Bring the instrument up to the shoulder and balance it between the relaxed shoulder and jawbone. Then lower the left hand back down to the side, and check to make sure the instrument is well-balanced before continuing.

2. Gently shake out the left hand (as if shaking water off the fingertips) and bring the left arm up, with a relaxed, neutral wrist.

3. The visible "joint line" where the first finger meets the palm of the hand should rest lightly against the neck near the nut at the end of the fingerboard.

4. Lift the scroll upwards a few inches with the left hand, and then gently bring it down pointing the elbow toward the belly button.

5. The thumb, wrist, and forearm should be aligned as the student rests the thumb on the neck. The thumb tip should be almost even with the fingerboard and resting against the neck close to where the first finger tip touches

the string. Make sure there is ample space (about the size of a mouse hole) under the neck between the thumb and first finger. Polish the side of the neck with the thumb to maintain a soft hand and straight wrist.

6. Turn the left hand, gently bringing the pinky closer to the neck. Place the thumb-side corner tips of the fingers on to the string; fingers should be shaped like a square or a box and should curve and hover over the string—not stick up in the air.

7. Check finger placement. The half-step fingers should touch, and the third finger should be in tune with the lower string.

Troubleshooting – Violin and Viola

Most left hand problems (like squeezing thumbs and bent wrists) are caused by poor instrument position and support. Check and make sure the instrument is properly balanced far enough back on the shoulder with an effective shoulder rest and chin rest set-up. Then correct any learned tension by reviewing the Golden Rule and resetting the left hand.

1. With the instrument in shoulder position, take the left hand away and rest it at the side of the body.

2. Check the shoulder rest and chin rest combination to make sure the instrument is well balanced between the relaxed shoulder and left jawbone. The left hand should not need to hold up the instrument.

3. Gently "shake the water off of the fingertips" of the left hand, and then bring it back up to the instrument, placing it in the correct position without squeezing.

4. Do the string polishing exercise (described in the beginning of this chapter) to teach the left hand that it is not there to hold the instrument.

Additional Strategies for Retraining a Squeezing Thumb:

- **Polishing the neck with the thumb** – With the fingers resting on the string, polish the neck of the instrument with the pad of the thumb. The wrist should relax and straighten into a neutral position. After polishing, rest the thumb next to the first finger so it leaves a "mouse hole" underneath the neck between the thumb and first finger.

- **Sinking fingers** – Gently sink the thumb-side corner of the fingertips into the string until the string touches the fingerboard. Lift and repeat to teach the hands to use the minimal energy required to stop the string, keeping the knuckles curved and the thumb soft and relaxed.

Correcting Flat Wrists:

- Use the neck polishing strategy (above) to help correct this problem.
- **Skittles** – With the fingers on the string, put a "Skittles" (imaginary or otherwise) on the middle segment of the first finger. If the instrument, arm, wrist, hand, and finger position are all correct, the middle segment should be parallel to the floor and the Skittles will sit atop the finger segment like it is on top of a little table.

Correcting Crooked Wrists:

Crooked wrists make the wrong side of the fingertips touch the string. In addition to doing the "Skittles" exercise, and polishing the string and neck, try the following:

- **Strumming the strings** – Lightly strum the four strings, from lowest to highest, with the left pinky by moving the elbow, not the wrist. The wrist should stay relatively still and straight through the entire motion.
- **Finger taps** – Tap the thumb-side corners of the fingertips on the string without squeezing; the fingers should be shaped like a square or a box and should hover curved over the string—not sticking up in the air.

Cello and Bass Left Hand

The endpin length and instrument position must be correct before setting up the left hand. After ensuring the instrument position is correct, pay close attention to the position of the elbow, which determines the angle that the wrist and hand approach the string. If there are problems with the wrist and hand position, check the elbow position first.

Cello and Bass Left Hand Objectives:

While balancing the instrument correctly in playing position, cello and bass students will:

1. Hold the left elbow at a height that keeps the wrist comfortably straight.
2. Gently rest the thumb on the neck behind the D-string and opposite the second finger; keep the tip of the thumb from crossing the mid-point of the back of the neck.

3. Keep the middle two fingers curved and perpendicular to the string, and gently angle the **pinky** down the fingerboard toward the bridge.

4. Gently point the first finger toward the pegs. On the bass, the first finger should stop the string in first position around eye level. To create a proper half step, separate the first finger from the other fingers.

5. Keep the fingers curved over the string, and use finger pads and arm weight to stop the string; never squeeze or collapse the knuckles.

Setting Up the Cello and Bass Left Hand:

When setting up the left hands of cello and bass students, remind students to keep their wrist in a relaxed and neutral position. If the elbow is too low—and it frequently is with young players—the wrist bends, inhibiting the facility of the left hand. When the elbow is at the correct height, the wrist has an easier time staying straight, and the fingers will have their best angle of approach to the string. The elbow height varies depending upon the string being played; lower strings require a higher elbow position. The arm should never rest on the upper bout of the instrument.

Use the following teaching sequence to help beginning students learn proper left-hand set-up:

1. Start balancing the instrument in correct playing position. Do not lean the instrument to the left to watch the left hand.

2. Dangle the left hand at the side; then "shake the water off the fingers" and let the hand rest again.

3. Place the left hand on top of the head so the thumb is on the left side of the head and the fingers are on the right. Pick an imaginary soft grapefruit from the top of the head to create a relaxed C-shape formed by the thumb and index finger; use soft hands to hold but not squish the grapefruit.

4. Rest the finger pads on the string so the two middle fingers are perpendicular to the string. In a beginning classroom setting, visual aids like dots or tapes may be helpful with initial finger placement.
   a. **Cello** – The first finger points slightly toward the nose and the pinky points slightly down the fingerboard.
   b. **Bass** – The first finger rests around eye level and the other fingers stay loosely together for support. If the first finger note is not at eye level, adjust the endpin.

5. Relax the shoulder and allow the weight of the arm to sink the fingers into the string. The shoulder should be at rest, not raised; the elbow should float comfortably as if suspended by a string at the correct height to keep the wrist in a relaxed, neutral position.

6. Gently place the corner tip of the thumb on the back of the neck behind the D string and opposite the second finger (this is the same corner tip that many people use to text on their phones). The thumb should maintain its C-shape and not point toward the scroll. To promote light contact, polish the neck with the thumb corner, and then return it to its correct resting place. Cello and bass students tend to bring their thumb too far around the back of the neck, which sets up bad squeezing habits. If you can see the tip of the thumb when facing the student, the thumb is too far around.

7. Finger spacing:
   a. **Cello** – The fingers are evenly spaced between the first and fourth finger; the fourth finger and lower string make an octave.
   b. **Bass** – The fingers are spaced so that a half step exists between the first and second fingers, and also between the second and fourth.

Troubleshooting – Cello and Bass

Most left-hand problems are caused by improper elbow height and thumb placement. Pay special attention to both of these elements as students do left-hand calisthenics.

1. **Elbow placement** – The elbow placement is too low, creating wrist and finger problems, and causing the left hand to run into the bout when shifting or doing the string polishing exercise.

   a. **"Knuckle Knocks"** – Students knock the top of the fingerboard with the left hand from the nut to the bridge while raising the position of the elbow to clear the shoulder of the instrument. Knock on different strings to change the elbow action.
   b. **"Ski Jumps"** – With the tips of the fingers between the D and G strings, move the hand from the scroll to the end of the fingerboard, and finish with a left-hand pizzicato. The arm should continue moving with a circular motion.

2. **Thumb placement** – The thumb is too far around the back of the neck. Drop the left hand to the side and reset the hand position. Shake the water off the left hand, pick the soft grapefruit off the top of the head, and reset

the tip of the thumb pad on the neck in the correct place behind the D string. A non-medicated corn pad is an effective remedy for this type of thumb placement problem.

3. **Knuckles** – The left-hand knuckles are leaning toward the scroll; this is common among lower string players who converted from violin or viola. With the student's permission, place your hand on the student's left hand and gently roll the knuckles toward the floor, letting the student feel the weight of the hand and arm in their third and fourth fingers. Help the student set their first finger on the fingerboard so the fingertip is gently pointing back toward the scroll and not down toward the bridge. After the student feels the weight in the lower fingers, and understands the angle of the first finger, have the student repeat these steps to reset the left hand.

4. **Fourth finger** – The fourth finger is collapsed, causing the left-hand knuckles to pronate toward the bridge. The second, third, and fourth fingers must support the weight of the hand with enough strength to balance the hand and arm weight. Have the student reset the left hand using the sequence above. Then do "Sinks" and "Taps" while making sure the knuckles do not collapse toward the pinky.

    a. **"Sinks"** – Keeping the knuckles soft and curved, use the weight of the arm to sink the fingertips into the string, bringing the string to the fingerboard; lift and repeat. Do this exercise with and without the thumb on the neck. Polish and replace the thumb regularly to promote a "soft hand."
    b. **"Taps"** – Tap all four fingers on the string, with the thumb resting gently on the back of the neck to teach students the minimum effort required to stop the string without thumb tension.

Vibrato

Most string teachers recognize when vibrato is done well. It looks easy and sounds relaxed, rhythmic, warm, and pleasing, and it matches the intensity of the music. Poor vibrato is also easy to recognize, as it usually looks and sounds tense, or maybe it is too slow, too fast, too wide, or simply unpleasant.

The following section is a starting point for teaching elementary vibrato. Modify and adjust the process as needed to accommodate different students and playing styles. Keep in mind that vibrato can vary from note to note, from phrase to phrase, and from one string player to the next. When teaching vibrato, encourage students to begin with a slow and smooth vibrato rhythm. Frequently, students start with a good, slow vibrato that disintegrates into a fast, tense, and jerky vibrato. Encourage students to be patient and stay focused on the slow vibrato. It takes time and practice before vibrato feels, looks, and sounds natural.

Violin and Viola Vibrato

There are two widely accepted types of violin/viola vibrato: 1) arm vibrato and 2) wrist vibrato. Some musicians use arm vibrato, and others use wrist or a hybrid of both. It is possible to do one type without doing the other; however, most players use a little of each, even if they gravitate more toward one.

There are two problems students must overcome before learning vibrato. First, the instrument must be well supported. If the shoulder rest/chinrest combination is not right for the student, the left hand will not have the freedom to vibrate correctly. Secondly, the student must learn to release the first finger knuckle from the neck to eliminate any squeezing and to give the hand the freedom to vibrate back and forth without shaking the entire instrument.

Violin and Viola Vibrato Objectives:

Violin and viola students will demonstrate the following objectives when vibrating correctly:

1. The instrument is well supported and balanced comfortably between the jawbone and shoulder without the left hand. Students with poorly supported instruments have significant problems learning and performing vibrato.

2. The first finger knuckle moves freely and is not anchored to the neck.

3. The thumb and vibrato finger lightly touch the neck and string without gripping.

4. The arm/wrist motion is smooth, relaxed, and parallel to the string.

5. The palm continuously faces the player's eyes and does not rotate like a doorknob.

6. The knuckles of the vibrating finger flex and extend to absorb the motion.

Teaching Strategy:

Use the following strategies to introduce vibrato to violin and viola students:

1. Hold the instrument in guitar position under the right arm.

2. "Salute" with the left hand, then lower the left hand and rest the pad of the left thumb on the side of the neck between the scroll and upper bout.

3. Relax the thumb so the hand can sway comfortably under the neck; the first finger should not touch the neck.

4. Place the second finger on the A string, and "polish" the A string by sliding the thumb and second finger up and down the neck. No part of the first finger should touch the neck and the palm should not rotate like it is turning a doorknob.

5. While continuing to polish, slowly decrease the distance that the left hand travels, until the arm is moving but the thumb gently rests on the neck and the second finger lightly stops the string. The thumb should stay relaxed and the second finger knuckles should flex and extend, absorbing the motion of the arm and wrist. Vibrate with a quarter-note rhythm, and then with eighth notes and sixteenth notes; finally, vibrate freely, without a meter.

6. Repeat Steps 4–5 with the third finger, then the fourth, and finally the first finger, which can be the hardest of all.

7. Put the instrument on the shoulder, hold the instrument stable with the right hand, and repeat Steps 2–6 in shoulder position.

8. Finally, add the bow. Do a slow scale using long bows and no rhythm until the left and right arms adjust to simultaneously doing two completely different motions. Vibrate with a quarter-note rhythm, and then with eighth notes and sixteenth notes; finally, vibrate freely, without a meter.

Troubleshooting Vibrato on Violin and Viola

1. **The vibrato is stiff and shakes the whole instrument** – Make sure there is space between the first finger knuckle and neck when vibrating. Releasing the first finger knuckle is very difficult if the instrument is not well supported with a good shoulder rest/chin rest combination. If the instrument is balanced well and it still shakes a lot, anchor the scroll by holding it against the wall to keep it from moving while practicing vibrato.

2. **The palm rotates like a doorknob** – Place the tip of the second finger on the purfling so the side of the finger touches the side of the fingerboard. With the thumb in the crook of the neck, start the vibrato motion, allowing the side of the finger to touch and follow the side of the fingerboard.

Cello and Double Bass Vibrato

Cello and bass students tend to pick up vibrato a little quicker than upper string students because the instrument is anchored to the ground and is less likely to move around when the hand is vibrated. They also tend to shift more, so they learn to move more and lock up less. Lower string vibrato does require a little more strength to create enough motion to vibrate the larger string. To accommodate for this difference, lower string players sometimes move their thumb and other fingers closer to the vibrato finger to support it.

Cello and Bass Vibrato Objectives:

Cello and bass students will demonstrate the following objectives when vibrating correctly:

1. The instrument position is correct; the student is not turned and looking at the left hand when vibrating.
2. The left elbow is suspended and remains relatively still during vibrato motion.
3. The wrist is relatively straight and relaxed.
4. The thumb rests on the neck behind the vibrato finger.
5. The fingers are curved; when vibrating the fourth finger, the third finger may rest on the string next to the fourth for better support.
6. The arm moves in a smooth, arcing motion; the wrist does not rotate like turning a doorknob.

Teaching Strategy:

When introducing vibrato to cello and bass students, have them place the bow on the stand, set up a good playing position, and follow these steps.

1. Rocking motion with a still elbow:
    a. Look forward (not at the left hand), and shape the left hand as if preparing for a handshake. Bring the left hand into the chest so the fingertips touch the chest below the collarbone.
    b. Keeping the elbow relatively still, use an arcing motion to pivot the arm/hand on the tip of the second finger. This motion should be large, slow, and smooth.

2. Transfer the motion to the string:

    a. Shape the left hand like a "C," placing the second finger lightly on the D string and the thumb lightly on the neck.
    b. Slide the finger and thumb up and down the neck about three half steps in a slow, relaxed motion; the elbow should remain relatively still.
    c. With the arm still moving, decrease the sliding motion to two half steps, one half step, until the thumb and second finger are no longer sliding. Check to make sure the thumb is still relaxed and the hand is shaped like a "C." The finger pad should be rolling (but not slipping) up and down the string.

3. Repeat Step 2 with different fingers. When vibrating the fourth finger, bring the third finger and thumb closer to the fourth to provide additional support.

4. Finally, add the bow, just long bows and no rhythm until the left and right arms adjust to doing two completely different motions.

Troubleshooting Vibrato on Cello and Bass

1. **The wrist is rotating as if turning a doorknob** – Review Step 1 (above) to isolate the motion that comes from the elbow and not the wrist. Then review Step 2 (above) to make sure the elbow is at a height that allows the arm and wrist to be straight. The arm, wrist, and back of the hand should be straight and move as one unit.

2. **Student takes the thumb off the neck to vibrate** – The good news is that the student is not squeezing the neck, but the thumb should rest on the neck even when vibrating. Move the thumb and place it on the neck behind the vibrato finger.

3. **Vibrato is too narrow or too fast** – Review both steps above using large, slow motions. Vibrate with a steady rhythm, starting with quarter notes and then moving in eighth notes.

Shifting

There are many method books on the market to help students learn to shift. Most methods introduce shifting in the third book of the series; however, it's important to begin the string polishing exercise early in the first year of string study—and certainly long before the third book. Bass players often learn to shift within the first several months of study. Cellists begin moving their thumb when they learn forward extensions, and they should also learn to shift into second position around the same time. String teachers must be aware that double bass and cello players shift and move between neighboring positions much sooner and more frequently than the upper string players.

Begin lessons on shifting by reviewing good instrument and left-hand position. Use the string polishing exercise discussed earlier in this chapter to teach students to freely move their hand up and down the entire fingerboard. The string polishing exercise is the basic shifting motion, and all smaller shifts are simply a short segment of the larger shifting motion. Many students mistakenly think that the hand or finger shifts from one position to the next, but it is the shoulder and elbow that initiates the basic shifting motion and moves the left hand.

The simplest shift is a same-finger shift, in which the student moves from one position to another on the same finger. When done correctly, you don't hear the finger slide from one position to the next. The sound of shift is hidden between a bow change or by briefly releasing the weight on the bow to hide the sound of the sliding left hand.

When moving into a higher position for the first time, young players can have difficulty finding the new position. Encourage students to find the notes in the upper positions that match open strings, and use these "anchor pitches" to check their location and orient themselves in the higher position. The exercise shown below (Example 1) is from the method book *Habits of a Successful String Musician*. Violins can check third position G and A with their open G and A strings to verify the accuracy of their shift.

Example 1:

After learning same-finger shifts, students learn to shift from one finger to another. When two fingers are involved in a shift, the finger used before the shift is referred to as the "origin" finger, and the finger arrived on after the shift is the "destination" finger. Begin by teaching the "classical" shift in which the player shifts on the origin finger and places the destination finger on the string only after the shift is complete. The exercise shown below (Example 2) teaches the rhythm of the classical shift as the student moves from the first finger to the second.

Example 2:

In measures 5–6, the origin finger shifts to the note represented by the diamond on the staff. In a classical shift, this shift and the destination of the shifting finger are both hidden by releasing the weight of the bow.

There are many finger combinations and styles of shifts. In jazz, folk fiddle, and romantic era literature, players may choose to make the shift audible to add expressive color to the shift. To do this, the performer places the destination finger down before arriving to the new position, which allows the listener to hear the destination finger slide into the new note.

To access the upper registers on all instruments, the elbow brings the hand around the shoulder of the instrument. On violin and viola, the elbow begins to bring the hand around the bout in fourth position and the thumb begins to come around and under the neck. Neither the heel nor the palm of the hand should ever touch the bout as the elbow moves the hand into the upper positions. The thumb reaches its upper position resting place in the crook of the neck around seventh position. From there, as the fingers continue to travel up the fingerboard, the thumb remains in the crook of the neck. Only in the case of students with small hands (or big violas) will players allow the thumb to continue around the neck and anchor against the side of the fingerboard. Students will need one-on-one attention to help them determine what is appropriate for their hand size. When descending from the upper positions, the thumb travels back the same way it came up.

In the middle register on cello and bass, students place their thumbs in the crook of the neck around fourth position. As they move further down the fingerboard, the elbow continues to lift and carry the hand around the instrument. Beyond seventh position on the cello and fifth position on the bass, students must transition into thumb position to reach the highest notes on the instrument.

Getting to the new position is only half of the challenge; students must also know the finger pattern of the new position. Use the exercises in Chapter 9: Intonation (such as tetrachord study, scales, and simple melodies) to teach students how to play in upper positions, including thumb position.

FINAL THOUGHTS:

In string education, we have been making a few mistakes that encourage rigidity in the left hand. We speak a lot about left-hand "position" as if it is a fixed picture, and we show students what the perfect left hand looks like with its curved fingers and relaxed thumb. As a result, young violin, viola, and cello students stay relatively locked in first position for as long as it takes to get through their first two method books. When we compound these tendencies with poor shoulder rest/chin rest set-ups that require students to hold on to their instruments, it is no wonder we see enormous stiffness in the left hands of our young school orchestra students.

This chapter combines left-hand technique with vibrato and shifting because they are all part of the same set of skills that require fluidity. The arm and elbow move the hand around the fingerboard; this motion is the antidote to the squeezing left hand. When students first put their instruments in playing position, use the string polishing exercise to teach them to move around the instrument before teaching them where to plant their fingers. Make sure their instrument set-up allows them to move, and then keep polishing the string, especially during the early years when students are stuck in first position.

Vibrato is too often treated as an advanced skill that some students cannot do because their left hands are too stiff. When left hands have learned to be fluid, vibrato can be taught earlier than most teachers think. Vibrato can also help force students to address their poor instrument set-up and help them release some of the tension in the left hand. Keep the left hand moving constantly, and use the arm to teach the left hand to be free of the bonds of first position.

Chapter 7

The Right Hand

For hundreds of years, string teachers have taught the bow hand from their own perspective, the way it looks from the teacher's point of view. In private studios, teachers have helped students by holding the bow for them, lavishing students with the one-on-one attention required to keep the fingers curved and relaxed properly. In the modern school orchestra classroom, beginning string students are less likely to have this luxury. In this chapter, we will look at ways to teach the bow hand from the student's perspective, with the bow hair facing up. Not only is it easier for students to see where the stick lies in their properly curved fingers, but when the bow is upside down, the weight of the bow in the fingers more closely resembles the true feel of the bow against the string.

IN THIS CHAPTER:

- Right-Hand Overview
- Setting Up the Bow Hand
- Bow Hand Games and Troubleshooting
- The German Bow

Right-Hand Overview

Before we get to the strategies for setting up a good, relaxed bow hand, let's take a look at the two primary problems that challenge young string players.

First, we need to understand that when we reach for an object, our brain sends signals to our hands to take the shape of the thing we are about to hold. If you reach for a can of soda, for example, your hand will take the shape of a soda can. When beginning string players reach for a bow, their hand forms the same shape they typically use to pick up a pencil; their fingers and thumb straighten and prepare to pick up the stick with their fingertips. The correct hand shape for holding the bow more closely resembles the way we hold a soda can. Un-learning this instinctively natural habit requires attention and kinesthetic bow hand games that re-teach the hand how it feels to correctly hold the bow.

Second, we are back to that word "hold" again. From the very beginning, students need to learn to "balance" the bow *on the string* (either balancing the bow in rest position on our knee or balancing it vertically in the air). If we are going to "hold" the bow horizontally, the only way we hold it is down on the string. We do *not* hold the bow up horizontally in the air—ever. Holding the bow up horizontally creates enormous tension in the pinky, which tries to counterbalance the weight of the stick on the other side of the thumb. Beginners are anxious to get to the bow and learn how it works. Too easily, they quickly learn and ingrain tension in the pinky, which can take months (sometimes years) to un-learn. This brings us to the golden rule for the bow hand:

Bow Hand Golden Rule:
The bow is held up by the string and held down by the bow hand.

Right-Hand Goal and Objectives:

The strategies in this chapter address the following goal and general bow hand objectives.

Goal:
Students will use a healthy shoulder, elbow, wrist, and finger position to provide the best balance of control, flexibility, and power for their bow and instrument.

Objectives:

- Hold the bow down with the bow hand, and allow the string to support the bow up.
- Curve the thumb and set the thumb tip on the stick next to the frog.
- Gently rest the pinkly on the stick, and curve the other fingers over the stick keeping the knuckles soft and fluid as the bow moves.
- In the middle of the bow, hold the right elbow at an angle that keeps the wrist comfortably straight; as the bow moves, bend the wrist to keep the bow angle perpendicular to the string at all times.

To help students learn the objectives, create a rubric with the objectives and have students use it to assess their own performance, evaluate the performance of their peers, and identify one or more goals for learning at home.

Setting Up the Bow Hand

Introduce the bow hand in two stages. First, students must learn to hold the bow correctly in rest position with the bow balanced vertically on the knee or upper thigh. Then, you can teach them how to get the bow to the string without creating tension in their pinky. After the bow hand is initially introduced, follow up with bow games and exercises that teach students how the bow feels and moves horizontally. Together, these set-up strategies and subsequent exercises will reduce the number of stiff knuckles, tense pinkies, and locked thumbs that we often see in the classroom.

Stage 1 – Bow Hand in Rest Position:

Start by teaching beginners how to hold the bow in rest position. Not only is it easier to focus on the right hand without an instrument in the left, but students who can hold the bow properly in rest position are much more likely to transfer this good position to the string.

1. Gently shake out the right hand (like shaking water off the fingertips) and then hold the right hand in front of you in the shape of holding a soda can. Tap the tips of the two middle fingers to the tip of the thumb, making perfect circles with round knuckles in the fingers and thumb.

2. Slide the tip of the thumb from the fingertips down to the first crease behind the knuckles of the two middle fingers, always keeping round knuckles in the fingers and thumb. Gently tap the tip of the thumb on the creases several times.

3. In the *left* hand, hold the bow gently at the balance point so the tip points toward the ceiling and the bow hair faces you; then lean the tip away from you about half way between vertical and horizontal. This angle gives students the best perspective when placing the bow into the fingers of the right hand.

4. Place the bow into these top creases of the two middle fingers so the space on the bow between the frog and the grip go directly in front of the second finger. Depending upon the instrument, the bow will rest in different parts of the top creases of the right fingers.

    a. Violin bows should touch the left side of the crease closest to the fingertip; viola bows should lay directly on the crease. Wrap the tips of the middle two fingers around the stick; the finger*prints*—not *tips*—will gently "hold" the stick opposite the thumb.
    b. Cello bows should touch the crease on the right side of the crease, the side closest to the hand.

c. French bass bows should touch in between the two creases. Wrap the tips of the middle two fingers around the stick so the fingertips will extend down to the metal ferrule.
d. German bows are addressed at the end of this chapter.

5. Tap the tip of the thumb on the bow between the frog and the grip with a curved thumb knuckle, and then let it rest there. The placement of the thumb varies somewhat between upper and lower strings.

    a. **Violin/Viola** – Set the tip of the thumb near the bottom of the stick and curve the thumb more.
    b. **Cello/Bass** – Set the tip of the thumb closer to the side of the stick and curve the thumb less.

6. Release the bow with the left hand, allowing the stick to rest between the top two knuckles of the right hand first finger. The first finger should feel the full weight of the stick. Tell the students to "go fishing" and joggle the bow gently in the right hand so the stick bobs up and down in the first finger.

7. Tap the pinky several times on the stick.

    a. **Violin/Viola** – Tap the tip of the curved pinky on the top of the bow over the circle or center of the frog
    b. **Cello/Bass** – Pinkies wrap around slightly and tap the side of the bow with the fingerprint of the pinky.

The bow is now resting upside-down in the right hand; the hair is facing up, the thumb knuckles are curved outward, the weight of the bow is resting in the first finger crease, and the pinky is curved and relaxed. After the bow feels comfortable and balanced, raise the tip up and bring the bow to vertical; then, place the turning screw on the right leg and balance the bow vertically. With the bow on the knee/upper thigh, tap all of the fingers on the stick to promote loose contact (no gripping). From this "rest position," students can do the vertical bow games described below.

Stage 2 – Getting the Bow to the String:

When students can hold their bows with beautifully curved and relaxed fingers and thumbs, they can learn to bring the bow to the string. Students should *never* hold the bow horizontally when carrying the bow to the string. This causes tension in the right hand—tension that stays in the hand even after the bow is resting on the string.

1. Pick up the bow from the stand or the lap: first rest the bow hair up with the stick in their fingers ("go fishing"), then bring the bow to vertical with relaxed, curved fingers, and then finally "pour" the bow onto the string.

a. **Violin/Viola** – Balance the instrument on the left knee and balance the bow vertically on the right. Then, raise the instrument up and balance it on the shoulder (as explained in the previous chapters) so the strings are horizontal. At first, it may be best to hold the upper bout of the instrument with the left hand for added security. Finally, keeping the bow vertical, lift the bow with the right hand and bring the bow's balance point close to the string. Then, without any pinky tension, "pour" the bow onto the string by raising the elbow so the wrist remains relatively straight. If the pinkies are in danger of becoming stiff, lift the pinky off of the bow while pouring the bow on the string, and then replace the pinky once it is balanced on the string.

b. **Cello/Bass** – Use two hands on the bow to keep it relaxed while the bow gets to the string.

2. Rest the bow on the string in the middle of the bow; then tap fingers and pinky on the bow and readjust the fingers until they are beautifully curved and flawlessly free of tension. Knuckles should be curved, soft and flexible; when the bow moves, the knuckles should be visibly fluid, not stiff.

3. Position the right elbow so the wrist is comfortably straight; as the bow moves, bend the wrist to keep the bow angle perpendicular to the string at all times.

   a. **Violin/Viola** – Pronate the top of the right wrist toward the tip so the first finger digs in to the stick—as if gently pouring the soda out of your soda can hand shape.

   b. **Cello/Bass** – Keep the wrist flat, the fingers perpendicular to the stick, and the knuckles pointing up.

4. Keep the bow hair flat on the string between the bridge and the fingerboard, and rotate the bow so the stick rolls over the hair slightly toward the bridge.

To help students learn all the steps of forming a good bow hand, create a "Bow Hand Mantra" that the students repeat each time they put the bow on the string. It might include short reminders, such as:

"Curve all fingers, pour the bow;
tap the pinky, ready, go!"

Bow Hand Games and Troubleshooting

Good teachers use an arsenal of games to help students keep the hand soft and fluid while holding, moving, and applying weight to the bow. All bowing games must be practiced with excellent bow hand technique. Pair up students with their stand partners and have them teach each other these bow games. Students can also help each other learn how to hold the bow and test each other using assessments you create for them.

Vertical Bow Games:

The vertical bow games below are done with the tip of the bow pointing straight up.

- **"Windshield Wipers"** – With the bow perfectly vertical, move the right arm back and forth so the bow moves like the windshield wipers on a school bus. Then rotate the arm/wrist so the tip of the bow waves back and forth like a windshield wiper of a car. This game helps students keep their thumb, pinky, and fingers relaxed, even as they feel the torque of the oscillating bow.

- **"Rocket Ship"** – Rest the vertical bow on the right knee, and then lift the bow straight up like a rocket. The wrist should rotate outward when the bow ascends and then back inward when the bow comes back down to the launch pad.

- **"Stirring the Soup"** – With the tip pointing straight up, make large, medium, and small circles (as if stirring a big pot of soup or a small cup of hot chocolate). The circular motion promotes balance and fluid wrist/finger motion.

- The Suzuki Method uses a song that works well for young students:

  Up like a rocket, down like the rain;
  Back and forth like a choo-choo train.
  Round and round like a great big drum
  On your _____(nose, head, ear) bent pinky and thumb.

Horizontal Bow Games:

Most bow hand tension, especially the stiff or locked pinky, comes from students trying to hold their unsupported bow horizontally with the hair down. When doing any horizontal bow games with the right hand, help students pay attention to always supporting the bow with the left hand. Before practicing horizontal bow games, pick up the bow at the balance point with the left hand, and then demonstrate a good, relaxed right hand position at the frog. Then slide the left hand out to the tip so the bow weight is supported properly with the left hand while practicing the following right-hand games. Continually have students check for a curved pinky and thumb, and do finger taps to keep the fingers relaxed.

- **"Tug-of-war"** – Gently pull the bow with the left hand so the right hand can feel the bow pull under the fingertips; then pull the bow with the right hand, feeling the resistance coming from the left hand. Young cello and bass students will sometimes let the right wrist "give out" to the right, causing the pinky to collapse. Make sure cello/bass students balance the pull of the left hand by keeping the wrist firm and relatively straight so the fingers are perpendicular to the stick, working together as a "block."

- **"Sandy Towel"** – Holding both ends of the bow, use both wrists to gently flop the bow up and down (like you would to shake sand off of a towel).

Bow Games on the String:

The following games are played with the instrument in playing position. Before beginning, start off in rest position with an excellent bow hold. Then, pour the bow on the string, curve the thumb, and tap the fingers to make sure all fingers are relaxed.

- **"Digging In"** – Use a gentle rotating action in the right hand to apply weight to the first finger while keeping a curved pinky and thumb. Use this strategy to teach students how bow weight is applied, and explain the term **"bow weight."**

- **"Silent Wiggles"** – Using the technique described above, dig in and grab the string near the fingerboard with the bow hair; then wiggle the string back and forth without making any noise. Grab the string at the frog, balance point, middle and tip of the bow; talk about how the parts of the bow feel and behave differently.

- **"Mini Bounces"** – With curved, relaxed fingers, silently bounce the bow at the balance point on the string with mini-bounces (not higher than half an inch off the string). Bounce near the bridge, at the fingerboard, and everywhere in between. Rest the bow back on the string between the bridge and fingerboard; do a few finger taps, and explain contact point.

- **"XXT"** – With the bow on the string between the bridge and fingerboard, move the frog toward the scroll until it is very crooked; then bring the frog too far toward the bridge until it is crooked again. Next, bring the frog back perpendicular to the string and explain bow angle. Finally, do the XXT game at the tip and frog to learn how the correct bow angle feels in different parts of the bow.

- **"Bow Rolls"** – Roll the bow toward the scroll so the stick is on the string; then roll it all the way toward the bridge. Finally, roll the bow so the stick is directly over the hair. Now roll it just slightly toward the scroll (but only a little) so all of the bow hair still touches the string. Explain that the bow rotates some during playing, but the correct bow rotation keeps the stick mostly over the hair and slightly leaning toward the scroll.

Do calisthenics to fun exercise music to make them a lot more entertaining. Cue up the theme to *Rocky* or another favorite exercise tune, and model finger taps, bow motion games, and right- or left-hand calisthenics with the music cranked up. Have a student lead the calisthenics while you move around the room adjusting bow holds. Between each game, remind students to balance the bow vertically on their knee, or hold it upside-down in rest position.

Troubleshooting:

Most bow hold problems are corrected by reviewing the learning sequence and strategies outlined above. Beyond that, the following strategies may also help.

- If the student's pinky is pressing against the stick, even when the bow is being held up by the string – Instruct the student to play in the middle of the bow without the pinky for a few days. Also review bow hold rest position and pouring the bow on the string.

- If the student's thumb is curved the wrong way or poking too far through between the stick and the hair – Review the soda can hand shape and instruct the student to touch the bow with the thumb using the exact point where the thumb touches the phone when text messaging.

- If the student's fingers are straight and stiff – Have the student do finger taps with a curved thumb and fingers. Do four taps with each finger, followed by three taps per finger, then two taps, and one.

- If the student's knuckles are very stiff or locked – Have the student put the bow down and make a circle touching the fingers to the thumb. Then, while keeping the tip of the thumb and fingers touching, collapse the knuckles by bringing the fingertips in toward the palm of the hand (as if there is a sponge in the circle and you are squeezing the water out of the sponge). The knuckles on the back of the hand should flatten. Return the fingers/thumb to their circle and repeat a few times.

The German Bow

The German bow allows double bass players to transfer more weight and power to the string than the French bass bow. What German bow players gain in power and volume, they give up a little in flexibility and dexterity. Neither bow is "better" than the other, so double bass players should ultimately select the bow that feels best for them.

The sequence below is a starting point for introducing the German bow. It may be best to treat bass students to a special lesson on the German bow before or after school. Apple strudel and German chocolate cake are not required, but they are a great way to lavish attention on those frequently forgotten bass students.

1. Place the screw on "upper webbing" of the right hand, between the thumb and pointer finger.

2. Rest the weight of the stick on top of the curved middle finger and ring finger. The bow can be balanced with just these two fingers.

3. Place the thumb and pointer finger in a circular shape on top of the stick.

4. Rest the ring finger in frog indention.

5. Place the curved pinkie on the bottom of the frog.

6. All fingers are curved and tips line up (approximately).

7. The palm is curved, fingers are relaxed and flexible.

The German bow takes at least an inch off of the length of the right arm, so check the endpin height and bass rotation to make sure the contact point of the bow on the string is below the end of the fingerboard during normal playing. German bow players tend to let the tip point down, so remind students to keep the bow parallel to the bridge. Slower bow speeds tend to sound better in most cases. Also, watch out for straight, tense fingers, or students squeezing the frog.

Private teachers are extremely important for bass students for several reasons: 1) bass students are often the most neglected students in the string classroom because of their proximity to the teacher, 2) classroom teachers tend to be least familiar with double bass technique because it is so different from the other instruments, and 3) the instrument is so big and performance solutions (French, German, sitting, standing) are often so personalized that it almost requires a private teacher to guide beginners through all of the decisions that need to be made.

FINAL THOUGHTS:

Students tend to pay more attention to the left hand because it is responsible for playing the correct notes on the big instrument. The misperception is that the right hand "only moves the bow." We must remind students—and even ourselves—that while the ability to play in tune with robotic precision is a wonderful skill to have, most of the other components of music are governed by the right hand. These components include more than just tone, rhythm, and articulation—also the dynamics, phrasing, and timbre control that make music more expressive.

As an orchestra supervisor years ago, I had the very fortunate opportunity to observe many classrooms, lessons, and teaching styles. One of our teachers, Mr. Wilson, made good technique a priority, but he had a particular talent for teaching bow hand technique. He spent months doing bow hand games and would correct poor positions whenever he saw a problem. Visiting one class of beginners in November, I remember walking across the room, looking down each row of students, and seeing entire ranks and files of perfect little bow hands.

Mr. Wilson's success was largely the result of his understanding about the importance of review. You might introduce the bow hand as a new skill in the fall, but you must never stop assessing, reviewing, and improving your students' bow hands.

***Every* day is bow hand day.**

Chapter 8

Tone and Articulation

Tone is the soul *of music.*

—Shinichi Suzuki

Music has many components: tone, rhythm, pitch, volume, form, to name a few. Most of them are related to each other, but possibly none is more connected to all of the others than tone.

When we fall in love with our instruments, the element we tend to love most is tone. Though it may be one of the most important of all the components of music, tone is often overlooked in classrooms simply because we rely heavily upon our eyes to tell us what we need to teach and learn. In all written music, we see symbols and markings that tell us what notes to play, as well as the rhythms and tempos, volume and dynamics, articulations, and even the mood of the piece. The only element that is not visibly depicted through musical symbols is tone.

This chapter contains strategies for teaching tone, the uniquely aural musical component that can only be taught through modeling. We will explore the complex relationships between bow speed, weight, and contact point. We will also look at strategies for teaching articulations, such as spiccato. At the end of the chapter, there is a sequenced list of tone, articulation, and bowing skills to help teachers organize their instruction and long-range plans.

IN THIS CHAPTER:

- The Instrument
- Teaching Tone through Modeling
- Short, Basic Bow Strokes
- Long Bows and Advanced Tone Production
- Teaching Articulation
- Tone and Articulation Goals and Sequenced Objectives

The Instrument

Beginning a chapter about tone without talking about the instrument is like talking about improving intonation without mentioning the tuning of the strings. Instrument quality involves money, so it can be a difficult and sensitive topic to address with students and parents, but we must still address it. There is no escaping the fact that good tone begins with a good instrument—not necessarily an expensive instrument, but at the very least an instrument that is easy to tune, stays in tune, and produces a good tone.

If your school district is preparing to purchase instruments for your program, pay close attention because you may be the only person who understands that picking the lowest bidder and filling a classroom with the cheapest instruments on the market is not good for students. If you have a fleet of student instruments, check them at least once a year to make sure they are in good working condition. At the very least, check for open seams, missing sound posts, warped bridges, and working fine tuners.

Strings are important, too. They don't have to be expensive, but the cheapest steel strings don't sound very good. For beginner instruments, use higher quality steel strings that have a good tone/durability-to-cost ratio. As students get older, they can look around for strings with a better tone and higher price. Even the best strings get old, so make sure you have money in your school budget or through instrument use fees to keep healthy strings on your school instruments. Cellos should have new strings every 12 to 18 months; smaller instruments need them more frequently; and double basses, less frequently.

Last, but not least, is the bow. For beginners, there are good non-wood options on the market that have satisfactory function for the price. Stay away from the cheapest bows, including the cheapest wooden bows, which are as bad or worse than fiberglass. Make sure the bows have real hair of a decent quality. Students will play on a bow with less than half of its hair if you let them, and parents simply don't know enough about instrument upkeep to know when their child's instrument needs to go to the shop. It is up to you to tell parents that hair needs to be changed at least once a year, or sooner if it becomes thin, dirty, or loses its natural "teeth" that grab the string. Teachers who make sure their students have good instruments, strings, and bows can be confident that they have given their students the equipment and opportunity they need to make music with a beautiful tone. Why would we do any less?

Teaching Tone through Modeling

Of all the musical components, tone may be the hardest to explain with words. Indeed, we don't even have symbols that depict tone in the same way notation indicates pitch, rhythm, tempo, volume, or articulation. Tone is uniquely aural, and to produce a good tone, string players must control many moving parts, including bow angle, weight, speed, contact point, and keeping the tone even from frog to tip. String players must also learn the extraordinary number of articulations a bow can produce, and string teachers need to consider how different instruments perform these articulations.

Authors must rely on words to describe good tone production, but good teachers know that modeling tone provides an aural picture that is worth a thousand words. All of the mechanics and variables involved with producing a good tone can be overwhelming to new students. Instead of talking about tone, it is best to pick up an instrument and show students how a good tone looks and sounds.

Good string teachers have spent years watching and listening to conductors, private teachers, peers, and accomplished performers. These experiences help teachers develop a visual and aural picture of a good string sound, and the physical motions and skills required to achieve that sound. Young string students have none of this imagery guiding them. They must rely almost entirely upon the sounds and images they learn from their first teachers.

The most important information you can give to students is a vast and memorable collection of aural and visual examples of good string playing and the joy that music making brings to our lives.

Music is an aural discipline, and there is no better way to teach a musical concept than through modeling. Modeling reaches both visual and auditory learners simultaneously. Also play recordings of outstanding soloists, school orchestras, or professional orchestras. Students will strive to imitate every aspect of the fine playing they see and hear. The fear of rote teaching is no excuse for not demonstrating as much as possible to young students.

Modeling helps teachers, too, because it reminds us of technical issues that need to be taught. It helps us break down a complex process into smaller pieces, and it gives students a chance to see us break it down so they can do the same for themselves. Modeling also reminds students that the teachers are musicians, too. We are not just telling them what to do, but telling them what we do—and there is a very big and important difference between the two. Being a string teacher is consuming, and it can easily reduce our own practice time; playing for the students is a great way for teachers to stay in shape.

Short, Basic Bow Strokes

Tone production warm-ups and exercises are a great way to lead into concert music rehearsal because they get students moving and sounding good from the start.

They also provide mental and aural "pictures" of good tone to remember as you add harder notes and rhythms throughout the rehearsal.

When introducing tone production to beginners, begin with notes of shorter duration because short bows are much easier to control than long, sustained bows. The following call-and-response strategy is a powerfully efficient way to teach students to play with a strong, versatile, and mature tone. Pick up an instrument and model the tone or articulation concept you want them to learn; then without anyone else talking, have them show you right back. With less talking, students will rely more on their eyes and ears to watch and listen to you, themselves, and the ensemble. If you can't model a skill, then have your best student leader model the skill for you.

The Call-and-Response Strategy:

1. On an open string, play the concept, demonstrating exactly how you want the students to look and sound. Then, without speaking, have the students play it back to you while you look, listen, and assess for the following indicators of student mastery.

    - A flawless bow hold, curved pinky and thumb, and relaxed knuckles
    - The correct part of the bow, with the correct bow angle and contact point
    - Bow speed and weight to produce a good tone that projects well
    - Correct rhythms and a consistent pulse

2. If necessary, model it again, and explain what the students need to improve.

3. When the students can perform the skill on an open string, model it again on an easy tetrachord, scale, or arpeggio. Look, listen, and assess again. If it's not perfect, keep practicing or come back to it later.

4. Using a metronome, start with a tempo that is very comfortable and then gradually increase the speed until it is slightly faster than what you intend students to perform in their concert music.

The "Bowing Variations" from our method book, *Habits of a Successful String Musician*, use the call-and-response strategy to teach bowings, rhythms, and articulations in unison and in canon. Model the bowing/articulation on a five-note scale, and then have the students demonstrate mastery on a nine-note scale (Example 3).

Example 3:

Start with simple symmetrical quarter- and eighth-note patterns (Example 4). Use enough bow speed and weight to produce a good tone that projects well. Stay in the middle of the bow, and remind students to bow at an angle that is 90 degrees to the string. Next, introduce triplets and sixteenth- note patterns. Perform sixteenth-note patterns in the middle to upper half of the bow, keeping the upper arm still and opening the elbow like a hinge.

Example 4:

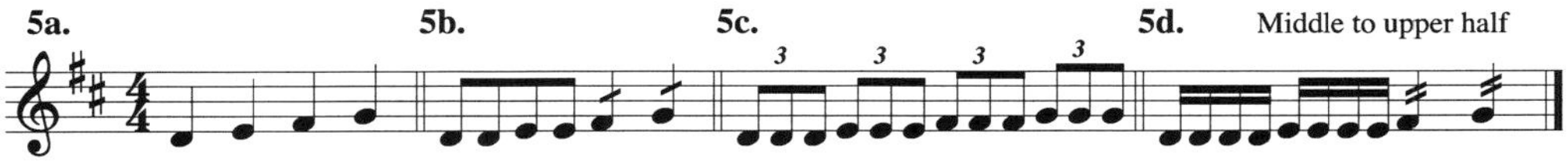

After symmetrical bowings, teach asymmetrical bowings that use the same bow speed. Students will try to play rhythms like those seen below (Example 5) in the same part of the bow. Demonstrate how the bow travels farther on longer notes, and as a result, the shorter sixteenth notes will be played in different parts of the bow.

Example 5:

Next, teach rhythms that require asymmetrical bow speed. In the rhythm seen below (Example 6), if we do not use a faster speed on the shorter notes to get back to where we started the pattern, we eventually get stuck at one end of the bow or the other. This occurs most often with dotted rhythms and in triple meters. The challenge is to produce the same volume and tone on all notes, even as we use different bow speeds.

Example 6:

The most common bowing solution to these uneven rhythms is the slurred staccato, or hooked bow (Example 7).

Example 7:

When learning this bowing, students must grab and release the string with clean articulation and tone. When teaching dotted rhythms, hooked bow patterns, and syncopated patterns, use a metronome to help students hear the beats and divisions contained within dotted rhythms.

The final skill to address with beginners is string crossing (Example 8). Use open strings to develop student awareness of the shoulder and elbow angles. Remind students that the shoulder moves the elbow to the position that gives the hand the best access to the string being played. The wrist should not be crooked, but in a comfortably neutral position. If the wrist looks wrong, it is probably the position of the elbow that needs to be corrected. In faster string crossings, keep the bow close to both strings and use the elbow, wrist, and fingers to change strings. Use different tempos, strings, parts of the bow, and add crescendos and decrescendos.

Example 8:

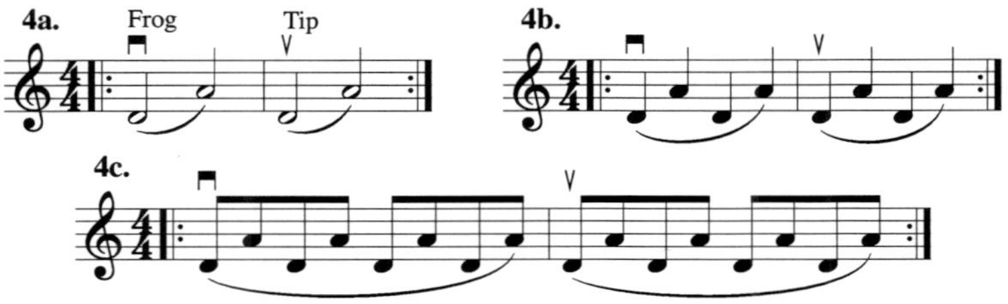

Long Bows and Advanced Tone Production

Once students are comfortable controlling shorter bow strokes, they will need to learn how to use the whole bow to produce a good, even tone from the frog to the tip. Introduce full bow strokes on an open string without regard for pulse or time (Example 9).

Example 9:

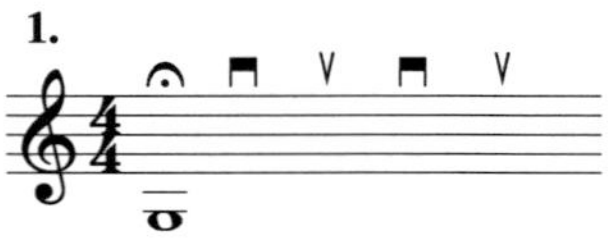

Then add a pulse, counting to four at a tempo of 60 beats per minute. Students will need to focus first on keeping the bow angle perpendicular to the string. Then they will need to learn the **Tone Production Triangle**—how to coordinate bow speed, weight, and contact point to create an even tone from frog to tip. After whole notes, students can continue to learn bow management by adding rhythms (Example 10).

Example 10:

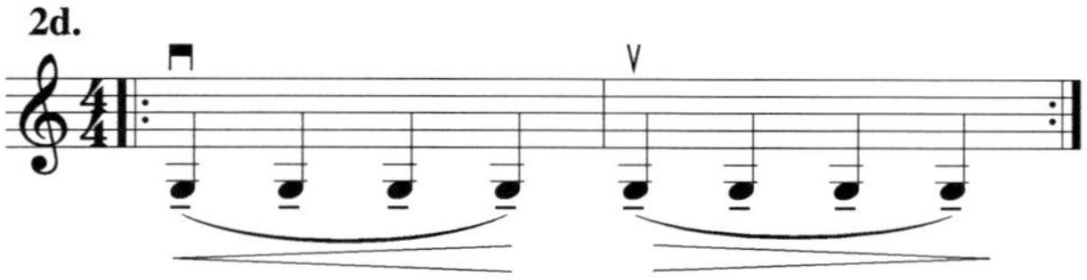

Bow Angle

Tone production involves many variables. The triangle of bowing elements—**weight, speed, and contact point**—are constantly changing and adjusting to each other to produce the desired volume, timbre and tone quality. Among all of the variables, however, there is one element that is relatively constant: The string vibrates only one way, back and forth at a 90-degree angle to the length of the string. For this reason, the 90-degree bow angle is a great place to start a discussion about tone production.

To work optimally with the natural motion of the string, the bow should meet and move against the string at a right angle. This is easier said than done because the strings create a strange optical illusion from the player's perspective. When the bow is at a right angle to the string, it doesn't look exactly perpendicular to the player. Making matters worse, the straight bow feels a little different on each string, so after a student learns what straight feels like on the A string, it can be frustrating to hear that the same feeling on the G string makes the bow crooked. We see most bow angle problems on the outer strings because they are the most extreme angles and the last angles students usually learn.

Bow Angle Strategies:

The mirror is the best answer for most bow angle problems. When students play in front of a mirror on all four strings, they can see when their bow is crooked, and they learn how straight truly looks and feels from the player's perspective. In the classroom, pair up students with their stand partner to watch each other's bow angle. There are several other strategies for correcting bow angle:

1. Hold the student's bow so the tip of the bow is on the string at the correct 90-degree angle. Instruct the student to move the bow hand along the stick to learn the trajectory of the bow hand for that string. After a couple passes with you holding the bow, the student can take control of the bow and practice moving the bow along the same trajectory. Do this with each string.

2. Instruct the student to make a karate chop with the left hand, holding the hand out, fingers straight, thumb on top, and pinky on the bottom. Set the bow upside down on the left hand so the stick rests on the first finger right next to the largest knuckle. With the right hand on the inverted frog, move the stick in a down-bow and up-bow motion, keeping the bow's contact point in one place. This exercise helps students feel the correct elbow motion in the upper half of the bow and also helps them identify tactilely with contact point on the string.

3. The grand martelé stroke (Example 11) is good for developing bow speed and freedom. It is also an excellent way to correct lingering bow angle problems. If the bow is not perfectly straight when the bow is pulled sharply from the frog to the tip, even small deviations from the 90-degree angle will send the bow flying off the string.

Example 11:

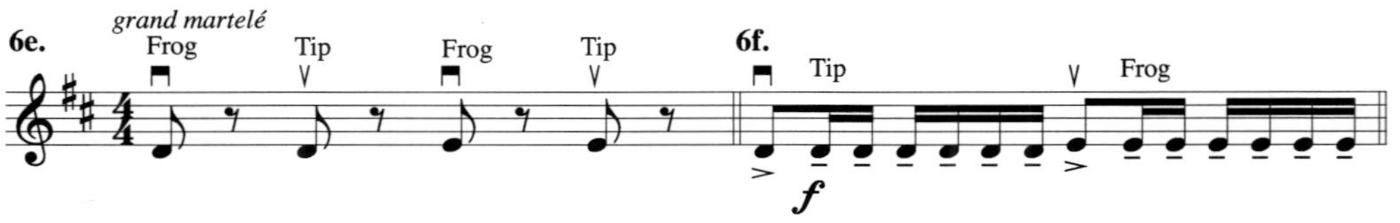

The Triangle of Bowing Elements: Weight, Speed, and Contact Point

The **contact point** is the place *on the string* where the bow hair touches the string. You can change the timbre of the tone by moving the contact point closer to the bridge or the fingerboard. The best place for beginners to start is right in between the bridge and fingerboard, where the string is most forgiving. As students progress, they will play closer to the bridge to project a more focused tone, or closer to the fingerboard to create a softer, more transparent tone. In extreme cases, you can play directly over the fingerboard (*sul tasto*) to create a light, airy, flute-like effect called *flautando*. You can also play at or on the bridge (*sul ponticello*) to create a metallic sound effect. Advanced students also learn that the contact point moves toward the bridge the higher they play on the fingerboard.

Bow weight actually refers to the combined weight of the bow, hand, and arm that you allow to transfer to the string. Increased bow weight generally produces a louder tone, but adjustments must be made with bow speed or contact point to avoid crushing the tone. Bow weight is applied primarily by the first two fingers on the violin, but on the larger instruments, it is spread increasingly throughout the four fingers of the bow hand.

Adjust the **bow speed** to create the best tone quality for the chosen bow weight and contact point. Younger students tend to be more comfortable with slower speeds that are easier to control, and they frequently need encouragement to use a faster speed and more bow length. At later stages, students will learn that it is possible to move the bow too fast, which creates a thin tone. The violin responds better to faster bow speeds than the larger instruments do. Sometimes, teachers mistakenly ask an entire orchestra to use more bow when it's not needed or appropriate for the lower strings.

To help string players understand the relationship between bow weight, speed, and contact point, divide the area between the fingerboard and bridge into different bowing "lanes," sometimes called the "Kreisler Highway." The slow lanes are closest to the bridge; like highway lanes, where the heavy trucks drive more slowly, the lanes next to the bridge sound best with a slower bow speed and heavier bow weight. Conversely, the faster lanes near the fingerboard sound best with a faster and lighter bow, like the smaller sports cars in the fast lanes of the highway.

String players must pay attention to how the bow responds when weight is applied at the frog, middle, or tip. At the frog, bow weight is not applied by pressing down, but by relaxing the arm and allowing the weight of the arm to transfer to the string. Tone and volume naturally wane as the bow moves toward the tip. To counteract this tendency and maintain an even tone, students must consciously add leverage and bow weight as the bow moves toward the tip. Conversely, they must lighten up at the frog to avoid overpowering the string. Cello and bass strings require more weight than the smaller instruments, so lower string players stay closer to the frog than their smaller relatives, and their bows are shorter and stouter to withstand the heavier weight.

If string players must respond to the natural waxing and waning tone in the different parts of the bow just to maintain an even tone, then they must do even more to achieve a crescendo or decrescendo. What's most remarkable about all of this is that after a few years of playing, string players hardly have to think about any of these mechanics when focusing on creating a musically rewarding crescendo. To be good teachers, however, we need to be able to keep these mechanics clear in our own minds so we can explain the technique clearly to our students.

Strategy for Coordinating Bow Weight, Speed, and Contact Point:

- Instruct students to play an open string *forte* near the bridge using the entire bow while counting from one to eight. After the eight-beat note, have them play up-bow, counting to seven and using the entire bow; the student's bow will need to move a fraction faster, and move the contact point just slightly away from the bridge. Then, follow the seven-beat note with a six-beat note on the next bow, moving the bow slightly faster so the entire bow is used, and moving the contact point a little closer toward the fingerboard. Continue with five-, four-, three-, two-, and one-beat notes, moving the bow gradually faster, always using the entire bow and moving the contact point to produce a beautiful tone on each note. Then, go in reverse order, counting up while slowing the bow down, and moving the contact point back toward the bridge.

Troubleshooting Contact Point

Most problems with the contact point are actually symptoms of bow angle problems. When a student's bow chronically drifts over the fingerboard—evidenced by traces of rosin at the end of the fingerboard—the cause is not the student's contact point; that's the symptom. The problem is usually the angle of the bow, and the student will continue to pull the bow back and over the fingerboard until the bow angle is corrected. Earlier in this chapter, we looked at several strategies for correcting bow angle issues. If the contact point problems persist even with a straight bow, then the following strategies might help:

1. Bow may be too long – For smaller students, especially young violinists, the bow can be too long for their little arms. The result of this problem is that students will try to use the whole bow, bowing all the way to the tip, and since they run out of arm before getting to the end of the bow, they start pulling the bow toward their back in an effort to get to the tip. Either use a smaller bow, or identify the point on the bow where the student's arm reaches full extension and mark it with a sticker. Then tell the student not to bow past that point.

2. Incorrect endpin height – Incorrect endpin height will create contact point problems on the double bass, and sometimes on the cello. If the right hand rests too low or high on the string, the endpin or instrument angle may need to be adjusted up or down until the player has easy access to the contact point.

Teaching Articulation

The palette of articulations available to string players is extraordinarily diverse thanks to the extremely versatile bow that provides many ways to attack, release, and end notes. The stylistic differences between Baroque, Classical, and Romantic music are largely defined by the articulations used. Begin teaching articulations like slurs and staccato to students in their first year of study, and as they become more advanced, use the bowing variations strategy described above to model a variety of articulations in combination with almost any rhythm.

Young students tend to sneak into notes with a "swish" instead of a clean attack. The following exercises teach students to grab and release the string to create a crisp attack.

1. **"Silent Wiggles"** – Dig in and grab the string near the fingerboard with the bow hair and wiggle the string back and forth without making any noise. Practice wiggling the string using different parts of the bow.

2. **"Grab and Release"** – On an open string, perform four down-bow eighth notes followed by four up-bow eighth notes (Example 12). Grab and release the string with the bow hair to start each note with a crisp attack followed by a good tone that is not scratchy after the initial attack.

Example 12:

More advanced students can learn up-bow staccato patterns that also develop articulation skills (Example 13).

Example 13:

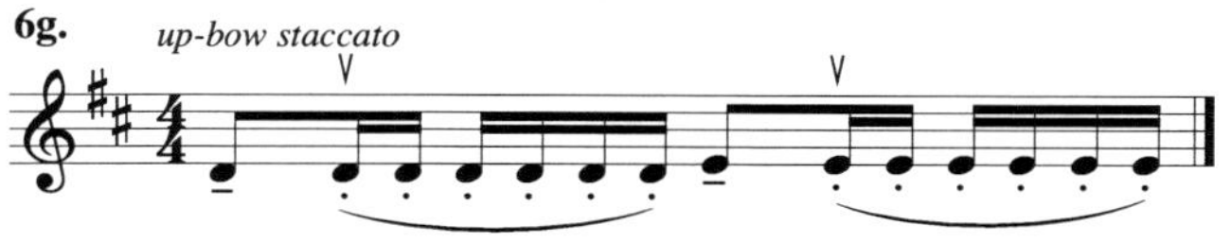

Teaching Spiccato

Of the many articulations taught, few generate as much pedagogical discussion as spiccato. There are different types of spiccato, and similarly different approaches for teaching students to play "off the string." No matter what method you teach, spiccato lessons offer an excellent opportunity to review basic bow hand technique with the advancing student. Spiccato can make a bad bow hand worse, so make sure students have a curved thumb and pinky, and soft and fluid knuckles before beginning. The following pre-spiccato strategies will help prepare students for spiccato by reducing tension and other bad habits.

1. **"Knuckle Pull-Ups"** – Rest the right arm on a table or music stand so the wrist comes to the edge. Hold a pencil in the right hand using good bow hand technique. Raise the wrist to the neutral position so the back of the hand is flat with the arm. Without moving the back of the hand, extend the thumb and fingers to lower the pencil as far as it will go. Then, without moving the back of the hand, curve the thumb and fingers to raise the pencil as far as it

will go. Repeat this motion while gently holding the left hand on the back of the right hand to make sure it remains still.

2. **"Silent Bounce"** – Rest the bow at the balance point on the D string. Lightly sink the bow into the string and then release the weight (not the bow), allowing the bow to spring back up; the bow hair may not leave the string at first. Repeat this step over and over in a rhythm until the bow begins to leave the string. Do not pick the bow, but merely guide the rebound (like bouncing a basketball). Check the pinky and thumb to make sure they are still curved and relaxed. Experiment with bouncing on other strings and in other parts of the bow—closer to the frog or middle of the bow.

Use the following sequence to teach spiccato. Students should learn the spiccato bow stroke at the balance point. In this resource, we teach students to start the stroke from the string.

1. Start by setting the bow on the D string at the balance point. Use the first finger and some hand weight to "grab" the string with the bow hair.
2. **Single Note** – Using a down-bow, pull the bow off the string, and in one motion make a tiny circle and come back to rest on the string at the balance point (Example 14). Check for curved and relaxed pinky, fingers, and thumb. Repeat the down-bow circular motion four times, resting on the string between each time. Repeat this step using an up-bow stroke at the balance point, retaking the bow in a circular motion. After doing four down and up-bows, do three, two, and one.

Example 14:

3. **Two Notes** – Perform two down-bows in quick succession before resting the bow again on the string (Example 15). The goal is to perform two *controlled* off-the-string down-bows without whacking the string. Continue to use tiny circles, always returning to the string to rest. Do four circular double down-bows resting on the string between each one, followed by four double up-bows; then, do three, two and one.

Example 15:

4. Perform pairs of eighth notes as described above, but this time use a down-up bow motion and rest the bow in between each pair—down, up, rest; down, up, rest (Example 16). Do four pairs with the down-up pattern, and then four pairs with an up-down pattern, resting in between the pairs.

Example 16:

5. **Three Notes and More** – Perform three notes: down, up down, rest; up, down, up rest. Continue increasing the number of consecutive notes, setting the bow each time and checking to make sure the fingers and thumbs are curved, and the knuckles are soft and fluid.

6. Perform a series of continuous, controlled eighth notes, pulling the bow off of the string without whacking the string. Stop frequently, resting the bow on the string to check for curved fingers and thumbs, and fluid knuckles.

The bowing variation patterns below (Example 17) can be applied to the strategies described above. Use different tempos, and as students demonstrate increased skill, have them experiment with performing a dry spiccato vs. a brush stroke.

Example 17:

Avoid rushing into teaching spiccato. It is more important to perform spiccato correctly than it is to learn the skill fast. Students need frequent reminders to start spiccato from the string and at the balance point. Also check bow hands to make sure they stay relaxed. The bow does not have to come off of the string very far; if students are lifting the bow too much, the fingers (especially pinky) will become tense and the tone will sound "whacked."

Tone and Articulation Goals and Sequenced Objectives

The strategies in this chapter address the following goals:

- **Tone** – Use a 90-degree bow angle, and the correct balance of bow speed, weight, and contact point to produce a characteristic string tone of the desired volume and timbre.

- **Articulation** – Use the correct part of the bow to perform the bowings and articulations required in the music.

The following sequence is a list of bow strokes organized into difficulty levels. Use the objectives in the order below, or create your own logical and teachable pedagogical sequence.

When creating your unit plan, use the list below to help you:
- Select the objectives introduced in previous years that need *review*;
- Identify the new objectives that you plan to *introduce* for the first time; and
- Sequence the objectives you plan to teach in each course level into an order that promotes good technique and minimizes bad habits.

To help students learn the objectives, use the checklist below or create your own rubric for evaluating the elements of good tone production. Have students use it to assess their own performance, evaluate the performance of their peers, and identify one or more goals for learning at home.

Tone Production Checklist:

- ❏ The **bow hand** is flawless; finger placement is correct; thumb and pinky are curved; knuckles are fluid.
- ❏ The **bow angle** is perpendicular to the string and rotated correctly.
- ❏ The **contact point** is the correct distance between the bridge and fingerboard.
- ❏ The **bow weight** and **speed** are balanced and produce an excellent tone that projects well.
- ❏ The **part of the bow** used is correct for the desired articulation.
- ❏ **Articulations** are well defined and stylistically correct.

First, introduce a new bow stroke or articulation by isolating and repeating it. After students master the isolated bowing, integrate it with other bow strokes. Use a metronome to keep the tempo steady while switching from one bow stroke to the next.

Novice Level:

- Pizzicato with a warm tone and a clearly ringing pitch over the fingerboard about one inch from the end of the fingerboard
- Quarter-bow strokes in the middle of the bow with an even tone and perpendicular bow angle
- Groups of two, three, and four notes on a single pitch at a moderate tempo
- One bow per pitch with good left-right coordination at a slow tempo
- Half-bow strokes in the middle of the bow with an even tone and perpendicular bow angle
- Quarter- and half-bow strokes using detaché and staccato articulations, and two-note slurs at a moderate tempo
- Bow retakes (circle bows) at the frog with a curved and relaxed thumb and pinky
- Two consecutive up-bows at a slow tempo

Intermediate Level:

- Full-bow strokes at a moderate tempo with an even tone and perpendicular bow angle
- One bow per pitch with good left-right coordination at a moderate tempo
- Groups of two, three, and four notes on a single pitch at a moderately fast tempo
- Quarter- and half-bow strokes with staccato articulations at a moderately fast tempo
- Three-note slurs
- Two consecutive up-bows at a moderate tempo

Proficient Level:

- Full-bow strokes at a fast tempo (grand martelé) and at a moderately slow tempo with an even tone and perpendicular bow angle
- Four-note slurs
- One bow per pitch with good left-right coordination at a moderately fast tempo
- Groups of two, three, and four notes on a single pitch at a fast tempo
- Three consecutive up-bows at a moderate tempo
- Hooked up and down-bows at a moderate tempo
- Brush-stroke spiccato at a moderate tempo

Accomplished Level:

- Full-bow strokes at a slow tempo with an even tone and perpendicular bow angle
- Five- to eight-note slurs in one bow
- One bow per pitch with good left-right coordination at a fast tempo
- Groups of two, three, and four notes on a single pitch at a very fast tempo
- Four consecutive up-bows at a moderate tempo
- Hooked up and down-bows at a fast tempo
- Spiccato at a fast tempo
- Sautillé stroke with even groups of notes (such as sixteenth notes in groups of twos or fours)

Advanced Level:

- Full-bow strokes at a very slow tempo with an even tone and perpendicular bow angle
- Slurs with more than eight notes in a bow
- More than four consecutive up-bows at a fast tempo
- Hooked up and down-bows at a very fast tempo
- Sautillé single notes per bow with good left-right coordination at a fast tempo
- Ricochet and other advanced bow strokes

FINAL THOUGHTS:

Midori gave a master class at an ASTA Conference in Reno years ago. A gifted graduate student beautifully played the first movement of the Barber Concerto, and the audience seemed to wonder, "What is Midori going to add to *that*?" Then Midori stood up and said, in so many words, "That was great; have you thought about playing it this way?" And our ears were opened to a completely new level of musicianship. Though her pitch and rhythm were impressive, Midori's overwhelming superior experience and musicianship were clearly conveyed through her tone.

Chapter 9

Intonation

As told by Yo-Yo Ma:

There once was a cellist who happened upon a genie, and the genie kindly offered to grant him a single wish. The cellist asked for world peace, and the genie replied that such a wish was quite impossible to grant, even for a great genie. So, instead the cellist asked for the ability to play perfectly in tune. The genie thought about it for a moment and then asked, "What was that first wish again?"

Yo-Yo Ma knows how difficult intonation is for string players, and knowing that it is a challenge for him makes the rest of us feel a little better about our own struggles. As string teachers we understand that it is difficult enough to get our own fingers to play "in tune," but getting an ensemble of young string players in tune is another matter entirely. That said, I want to let you in on a little secret that the world's best string teachers all know:

Student orchestras of any age can play *in tune*.

Believing this takes courage and a little faith. *Expecting* it requires uncommon discipline and perseverance, but it *is possible*. Here's how.

IN THIS CHAPTER:

- Barriers to Good Intonation
- Tuning and Cross-Tuning Upper-Level Orchestras
- Technique Problems That Impair Intonation
- Finger Patterns—Muscle Strength, Memory, and Velocity
- Changing Finger Patterns
- Fine Tuning Notes and Chords

- Upper-Position Technique
- Scales and Arpeggios
- Intonation Goal and Sequenced Objectives

We are what we repeatedly do;
excellence, therefore, is not an act, but a habit.

—Aristotle

It is the habit of expecting students to play well every day that will lead to better intonation.

Barriers to Good Intonation

Intonation is a complicated skill. School orchestra students must overcome the following problems before they can play in tune:

1. Students' strings are often still out of tune even after they just finished tuning, either because the student or the teacher did not take the time to tune the strings well, or the quality of the instrument is so poor it doesn't keep its pitch.

2. Students have poor instrument position or left-hand technique problems that impair their ability to play in tune.

3. Students have not developed a strong muscle memory for playing the different finger patterns accurately, especially at faster tempos.

4. Students do not have a clear understanding—in their heads or their hands—about the differences between all of the finger patterns or when to use them; this especially includes when the pattern changes from one string or position to the next.

5. Students don't understand how "in tune" truly sounds, and they do not adjust their fingertips to finely tune the pitch.

In the following sections, we introduce strategies and exercises to use during fundamentals time to teach students the skills they need to overcome these barriers to excellent intonation.

Tuning and Cross-Tuning Upper-Level Orchestras

We understand the importance of being in tune before we begin to rehearse or perform, but we also know that tuning a class of string instruments can be a real struggle for both students and teachers. Tuning time can easily become a mindlessly repetitive daily process in which students halfheartedly tune, so they require frequent reminders to pay attention and not stop before their strings are truly correct. It is up to us to maintain a standard of excellence in the classroom, tuning twice or more if necessary, because we know there is not much point in spending time and energy trying to get students to rehearse or perform in tune when their instruments are still out of tune.

Given a choice between tuning quickly and tuning well, always choose the latter whenever possible. The goal is always the same:

Students' strings *must* be in tune before rehearsal begins.

Expecting Good Tuning Mentality and Tone:

Too often we treat tuning time like an obligatory ritual, but it can be much more than that. It is a valuable opportunity to teach students to use the same part of the bow, same bow speed, weight, and placement to create a well-blended tone. The light, transparent "tuning tone" is the easiest type of tone to blend, making it the perfect time to teach students what it sounds like when notes are in tune *and* blending well. When we use tuning time to teach students to listen, blend, and finely tune their strings to other students' unisons, octaves, and fifths, we are taking the first steps in teaching them to blend and finely tune to each other when they are performing music.

Most students do not consider the importance of tone when they tune their strings, even when they are tuning to each other during a performance. As a result, students tend to play too loudly, making it difficult for everyone to hear the original tuning pitch. So if they cannot hear the tuning note, then what are they tuning to? Students must be taught—and then frequently reminded—to bow lightly at the tip and close to the fingerboard to produce a transparent "tuning tone." This will allow all students to hear the correct pitch over their own string. Tuning too loudly is a sign of immaturity—and also a lack of respect for others in the ensemble.

Chapter 4 contains strategies for teaching students to tune themselves. Even accomplished high school orchestras are still a little out of tune unless they go one step further and cross-tune after their initial tuning. After students take the "A" and tune their instruments, the student leader should then take the class through the following cross-tuning procedure.

Cross-Tuning for Students Who Are Able to Tune Themselves in Fifths:

1. Turn the tuner off. Then have everyone play the A string again, and continue to adjust until all of the A's agree perfectly.

2. Violins and basses continue to play the A string while violas and cellos tune the D string to the violins' A.

3. The players switch. Violas and cellos play the A string while violins and basses tune the D string to the violas' and cellos' A.

4. As the violins/basses continue to play the D string, violas/cellos cross over and finely tune the G string.

5. Players switch again. Violas/cellos play the D string while violins/basses tune the G.

6. As violins/basses continue to play the G string, violas/cellos cross over and fine tune the C string.

7. Violas/cellos play the A string, while violins tune the E string. Then violas/cellos drop out, and basses use harmonics to tune the E string to the violin. Basses can use harmonics throughout cross-tuning.

The hardest part about tuning our classes is not the tuning process itself; it's holding ourselves to the high standard of expecting our students' strings to be truly in tune—as in tune as we would want our own instruments, even when we are tired. We need to stay on top of the less-motivated students in our classes who balk at the idea of tuning twice. These are the same students whose instruments would probably benefit most from tuning twice.

Technique Problems That Impair Intonation

We must continually look at our students with fresh eyes to make sure they do not have hand position problems that undermine their ability to play in tune. Stiff right hands and poor bowing technique limit good tone production and hinder a student's ability to blend tone and intonation. The following technique problems must also be addressed whenever we see them.

Violin and Viola Left Hand:

- **The Flat Wrist** – When the left wrist caves in and supports the neck in the palm, the fingers are pulled back flat, making extended third and fourth fingers very difficult to reach.

- **The Sideways Wrist** – When students play on the upper strings without moving their elbow, the wrist is bent sideways, limiting mobility (especially in the fourth finger). Students should use the elbow to change strings and keep the wrist straight.

- Poor instrument position is a direct cause of tension and poor intonation. Without good instrument support, students grip and squeeze the neck, which hinders their velocity, their ability to shift properly, and their ability to finely tune fingertips after they land on the fingerboard.

Cello and Double Bass Left Hand:

- **Thumb** – Make sure cello/bass players do not squeeze, point their thumb up the neck toward the scroll, or push the thumb past the center of the neck.

- **First Finger** – When the first finger points down the fingerboard toward the bridge—a common trait of players who converted from violin—the "block position" is compromised, causing problems with extensions and general weight transfer to the string.

Use daily games and calisthenics (like those outlined in the chapters on instrument, left- and right-hand position) to reduce tension and improve technique. Continually assess student positions to catch and correct problems that hinder a student's ability to play in tune.

Finger Patterns—Muscle Strength, Memory, and Velocity

There is an athletic component to playing a string instrument. As a string instrument coach, our job includes helping students develop the muscles and muscle memory they need to extend their fingers far enough and fast enough to play the correct notes whenever the music demands it. This section outlines several strategies for developing the muscle strength, dexterity, and memory required to play finger patterns in tune. Before starting, though, we want to be clear that finger muscle development does *not* include the thumb, which must remain as relaxed as humanly possible throughout these exercises. Thumb tension is not just a barrier to finger accuracy and velocity, but it can cause hand injury. So remind students to polish and tap the neck frequently; keep those thumbs soft and balance the instrument well so the left hand has the freedom to move freely.

Tetrachord Etude:

The Tetrachord Etude (Example 18) is a short, effective technical study for introducing new finger patterns, reviewing finger patterns as a daily warm-up, and also targeting challenging patterns that show up in concert music. It works for every instrument on any string, in any position.

Example 18:

This specific etude from *Habits of a Successful String Musician* works well not only for the upper strings, but also for cello and bass students who need to spend more time learning how to shift between neighboring positions. In this etude, cellists practice moving between first and second position, and learn how extensions and non-extended finger patterns are organized between these two positions. Bass students learn how to shift and pivot to adjacent positions the way professionals do. After students learn the exercise in the Dorian mode, they can play it again in one of the other modes (Example 19).

Example 19:

After young students learn these basic patterns in their first two years of study, they need to be reviewed often. There is no better way to review all of the finger patterns in a more efficient and focused way than the Tetrachord Etude.

Velocity Etude:

When students learn a finger pattern slowly, they have time to listen and finely tune their notes, but patterns must be practiced at faster speeds if the students are going to develop the proper fast-twitch muscles to accurately perform fast technical passages in concert music. Without such practice, finger patterns lose their integrity at faster speeds, which is why sixteenth notes are often out of tune.

Velocity drills like this Sevcic-style etude (Example 20) can be practiced at any level to develop finger speed and accuracy in all of the modal finger patterns. Students can learn the major, minor, and Phrygian patterns slowly at first, and then gradually increase the tempo to develop finger speed.

Example 20:

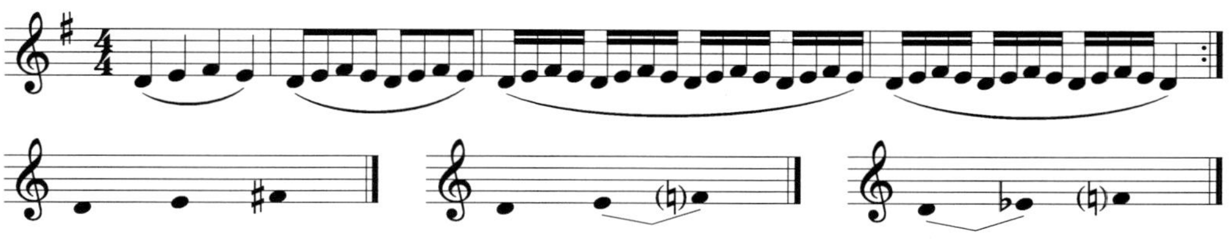

In the *Habits* method, this pattern is written for young players to start this etude on open D, for intermediate-level students, and for advanced cellos and basses learning thumb position. The violin example above can be learned in third position (or in second position to work on the fourth finger). Students must also practice different combinations of notes (Example 21) in all of the modal finger patterns above. Some patterns are more challenging than others, but learned together, these studies dramatically improve speed and intonation accuracy in students of all levels.

Example 21:

When studying velocity etudes, remind students to check their elbow placement and to relax their left hand and thumb. Tension will slow fingers down, and constant squeezing can create hand injuries.

Relaxation is a key component of velocity study.

Finger Tapes for Beginners—Yes or No?

In larger classes of beginning string students, especially elementary classes that may only see a teacher once or twice a week, finger tapes can and do truly help students learn hand structure finger placement. They can also help students learn the concept of whole and half steps on the fingerboard, and how they sound when performed correctly. Beginning students who receive only 35 minutes of instruction per week can learn to play very much in tune thanks in large part to finger tapes. Beginning students without tapes often spend much more time trying to figure out where their fingers go and much more time playing out of tune.

Whether or not you use tapes, it is important to keep singing with your students and encouraging them to listen for well-tuned octave "ringing tones." If taught correctly, they will no longer need tapes by the time they get to F- and C-natural.

Finger tapes don't impair student learning—*poor teaching does*. When used correctly, tapes can help students learn how the notes are supposed sound.

Changing Finger Patterns

Students make most of their finger pattern mistakes when the finger pattern *changes*, and these changes usually occur on the fourth and seventh scale degrees in major pieces. One way to address this problem is to practice the patterns in combinations. When teaching a pattern with extensions, for example, first isolate and practice the pattern by itself, and then combine it with previously learned patterns to practice moving into and out of the extension. Both the Tetrachord and Velocity Etudes described earlier allow you to isolate patterns first and then teach them in combination.

A second way to teach changing patterns is with dominant arpeggios, where finger pattern changes occur in close proximity (Example 22). Dominant arpeggios teach students the feel of a specific key better than the tonic arpeggio (1, 3, 5, 1), which does not include the scale degrees that need the most attention. Dominant arpeggios also teach students how to hear and listen for the changes that occur across the string.

Example 22:

In *Habits of a Successful String Musician*, dominant arpeggios like the one above are written out for every major and minor key. Set the tuner to drone the root note of the dominant chord (the fifth degree of the scale), and teach students to keep the seventh scale degree high and the fourth scale degree low. These troublesome notes are always the last sharp or flat in the major key signature and the natural note that would be the next sharp or flat in the key signature. When students can identify these notes from each key signature, their accuracy will improve.

Fine Tuning Notes and Chords

As teachers, we want our students to adjust their fingertips, but we need to give students more instruction and simple exercises to learn *how* to do this. Most of us already encourage students to match their pitches with their open strings when possible, and we use a tuner to provide pedal tones to improve their pitch center; but there is still more that we can do.

Tuning Canons (Example 23) give students the opportunity to listen and finely tune unisons and octaves first. Then, students can play the canon in two, three, or four parts—always listening, blending, and striving for perfect intonation. They should use a transparent tuning **tone** with little or no vibrato to help them listen, adjust, and blend their tone and intonation. This particular canon—also published in the Habits method in every key—accentuates the fourth and seventh scale degrees, teaching students to hear the leading tones and their resolutions.

Example 23:

Tuning Chords are progressions with a wider range of notes that are more challenging in scope than a simple tuning canon. They are the next natural step in teaching students to adjust and blend their tone and intonation. Students can learn to tune one chord at a time, starting with the lowest strings and then tuning the upper strings to the lower. The *Habits* method uses the same canons and chords for every key so students become familiar with how "in tune" sounds. Then as students learn more difficult keys, they can aim to maintain the same level of excellent intonation.

Tuning canons and chords give students the opportunity to learn pitch tendencies and how to practice "just intonation." When finely tuning a chord, begin with the root and the lowest octave. Once the root is in tune, add the students playing the fifth of the chord, which should be raised just slightly (about 2 cents) to achieve "just intonation." Then add the third of the chord (lowered 14 cents in major chords and raised 16 cents in minor chords). If the chord is a dominant seventh, the seventh is lowered significantly (31 cents). By understanding "just intonation," string players can play *more in tune* than a perfectly tuned piano.

Tuning Canons and Tuning Chords are good exercises to do at the start of class. When students are tuning their instruments, they listen and carefully tune their strings in octaves and fifths using a good tuning tone. The canon and chords add thirds and sixths to this natural tuning sequence. Performing the tuning canons and chords immediately after tuning also reminds you and the students about the importance of tuning well. If the class rushes through the tuning process, the out-of-tune strings show up immediately with the tuning canon and chords.

After studying tuning canons and chords, chorales are the next step of intonation development that will easily transfer to concert music. When introducing a new chorale, have students use a transparent tuning tone and build chords in the same way described above. When the students are in tune, have them add bow weight and project more, but not so much that their tone doesn't blend. Finally, incorporate phrasing, breathing, cueing, and musicianship into the chorale to make it a complete music learning experience.

Tuning canons, chords, and chorales can also be sung to improve students' aural acuity. Use solfege (*do, re, mi*), or scale degree numbers (1, 2, 3), or neutral syllables (*la, la, la*) to teach students to hear and focus on the correct pitch. Students almost always play a note better in tune after they have sung it. Demonstrate singing yourself; praise students who participate well and don't let reluctant students deter you. Great teachers make singing a common, non-threatening part of their everyday instruction.

Upper-Position Technique

In Chapter 6, we addressed left arm and hand technique, and introduced strategies for developing good general hand position, vibrato, and shifting skills. After shifting to the upper registers of the fingerboard, string players must make changes in their technique to reach the highest notes and to accommodate for the smaller spaces between notes.

In the upper positions on violin and viola, the thumb rests in the crook at the base of the neck and the wrist bends forward to allow the fingers to reach the highest registers. Advanced players should be careful not to spend prolonged periods of time in the upper registers, as the extreme flexion in the wrist can stress the tendons. After working in the upper register, allow students time to let their arms dangle at their sides to let the blood flow back into the wrist and hand, and to give the tendons and muscles a chance to rest.

Cello and bass players should also anchor their thumbs in the crook at the base of the neck, but only in the middle positions. Cellists keep the thumb there between fourth and seventh positions, and bass players do the same for fourth and fifth positions. This area is sometimes called the "transitional position" because it serves as a bridge between the lower position and thumb position. Lower string players cannot reach their upper registers without bringing the thumb up on top of the fingerboard—the technique known as "thumb position." This skill may feel slightly alien to upper string players, but it is not a skill that we can avoid teaching. Upper string players can take a couple lessons to learn the basics of thumb position, and there are also a number of good videos on the Internet that teach the basic principle.

In thumb position, the thumb rests on the string at an angle perpendicular to the string, and it is used like another finger to stop the string against the fingerboard. On the cello, the thumb actually stops two strings; the side of the thumb in the middle of the nail stops the lower string, and the side of the thumb just above the knuckle stops the upper string, typically the D and A strings, respectively. The thumb must be exactly perpendicular to both strings so they can be played as a double stop to produce a well-tuned perfect fifth. On double bass, the angle of the thumb is similar, but the thumb only stops one string at a time, and only with the part of the thumb between the bottom of the nail and the first knuckle.

When introducing thumb position, have students make a fist or ball with their left hand and practice playing perfect fifths with the thumb, starting on the A–D harmonics and then moving to stopped notes on other parts of the string. Young cellists and bassists will find thumb position uncomfortable, even a little painful at first. This is normal, and with practice a callous will develop to protect the thumb and reduce the discomfort. Make sure the height of the student's bridge is correct; when the string is too high, thumb position becomes much more difficult and more painful than it needs to be.

In addition to thumb placement, students must also learn the frame of the hand in thumb position, as well as how to include the thumb into the finger patterns. The hand should maintain its ball shape and fingers should remain curved, not flattened, when the fingers stop the string. The first finger should curve over the string so it stops the string with the tip of the finger near the nail.

On the cello, the thumb works together with the first, second, and third fingers to play diatonic tetrachords made up of whole and half steps, much in the same way that the four fingers of the violin do. The pinky is not generally used except in very rare cases. In thumb position, cellists can use the Tetrachord and Velocity Etudes to practice the four tetrachords and learn how those finger patterns sound and feel when the half step is in different places. The thumb on the lower string and third finger on the upper string produce an octave, which is the basic framework of the cello hand in thumb position. Use ascending and descending scales and arpeggios (Example 24) to strengthen and reinforce this basic framework and correct hand position.

Example 24:

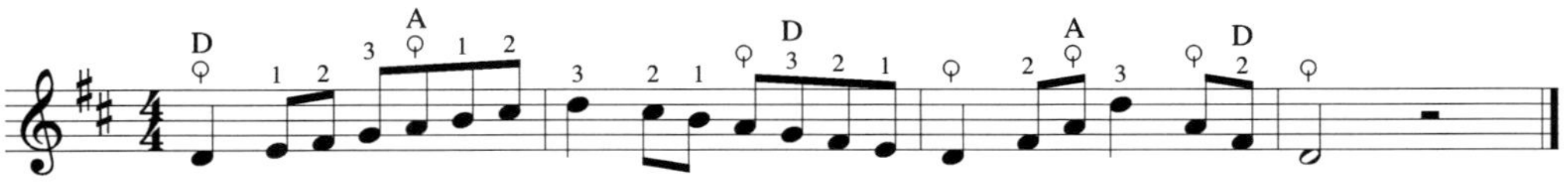

On double bass, players usually adjust the instrument position before the left arm can gain full access to upper registers at the end of the fingerboard. In lower registers, standing bass players balance the instrument in a position that is mostly vertical. To access thumb position, players step back and allow the bass to come back toward them so the neck of the bass rests near the neck of the bassist. Bringing the bass neck closer to the shoulder allows players to reach farther around the instrument and down the fingerboard. When returning to first position, bassists must return the instrument to the more vertical position. This instrument position transition can be practiced during the String Polishing Exercise described in Chapter 6.

The hand frame on the bass is similar to cello; however, the finger patterns are slightly different because the spaces are bigger. There are three basic finger patterns that bass players use in thumb position: Most start off by learning a chromatic finger pattern in which the thumb, first, second, and third fingers are all separated by half steps. A second commonly used thumb position pattern is chromatic, except for the whole step between the thumb and first finger. The first, fully chromatic position has the range of a minor third, and the second pattern spans a major third, which allows players to move across the string diatonically without having to shift. In the higher positions, the spaces are small enough for bass players to play a major tetrachord the same way a cellist would, with the thumb and first three fingers. Double bass requires so much shifting in lower positions that thumb position presents welcome advantages, and some schools of bass instruction send players up into thumb position early and often, even on the lower strings, to allow players to get around the bass without having to shift as much as they would in lower positions.

Our method book, *Habits of a Successful String Musician*, devotes a full section of the method book to alternate clefs and upper-position technique. This section has Tetrachord and Velocity Etudes in thumb position, scales and arpeggios like the one printed above, and common folk tunes for practicing thumb position, as seen in this cello example (Example 25).

Example 25:

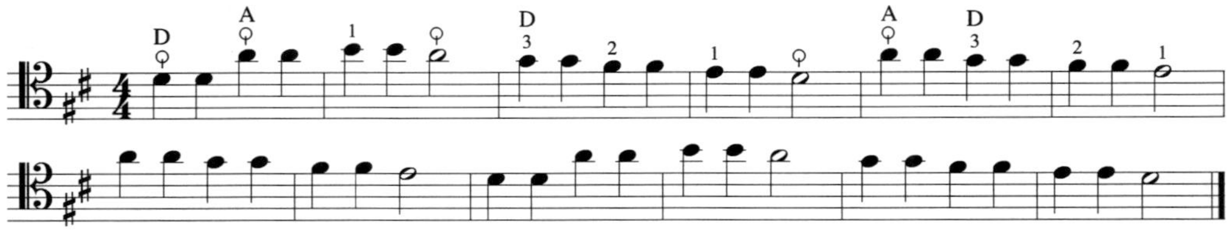

Scales and Arpeggios

As musicians, we study scales and arpeggios to learn the patterns and technique that different keys require. We also use them to help us synthesize many different performance skills, including changing finger patterns, shifting to and from a variety of positions, fine-tuning, and tone production in every register of the instrument.

When teaching scales, arpeggios, and thirds, use a method that allows students of different ability levels to learn and perform different numbers of octaves at the same time. We often see students of vastly different ability levels scheduled into the same orchestra class, especially at the high school level. Instead of expecting every student to meet the level of the method book, use a scale method that accommodates a wide range of student ability levels. The *Habits* method uses a format that allows students of different levels to study one-, two-, and three-octave scales at the same time.

When teaching multiple levels, have the students performing more octaves begin their scale first (Example 26).

Example 26:

Arpeggios can be taught the same way (Example 27).

Example 27:

Methods that allow for differentiated instruction can also accommodate the differences in difficulty of the instruments themselves. In a high school class, for example, violin students will likely be ready to learn a three-octave B-flat scale long before their lower string peers. Instead of asking the basses, or even the cellos and violas, to play a three-octave B-flat scale before they are ready, use a method that allows violin students to learn their three-octave B-flat scale while the rest of the students just play two (Example 28).

Example 28:

Introducing Scales and Keys

1. When first introducing a new key, start with a tuning canon and chords to help students hear the pitch center and learn the tendency tones and half steps of the new key (Example 29).

Example 29:

2. Set the classroom tuner to drone the note of the key, and have students play the scale slowly while listening and adjusting their fingertips to finely tune every note.

3. Have students play the scale in half notes, quarter notes, and so on.

4. Finally, add slurs to teach bow control and tone production. Begin with a slow tempo and increase the speed as mastery improves.

There are many components of performance students can study with scales. Instead of tackling all of them at once, focus on different performance elements each day. Drawing from a list of focus points like the one below creates daily variety in scale study, and it also ensures that we address all of the different elements scale studies can teach students.

1. Identify the key signature and all the leading tones.
2. Identify the finger patterns on each string and in each position.
3. Explain and perform the intervals of the shifts.
4. Perform with correct and relaxed hand positions.
5. Bow parallel to the bridge with the appropriate speed and weight to produce a good tone.
6. Use more weight at the tip to produce a strong, even tone.
7. Play close to the bridge in the top octave to produce a better tone.

8. Adjust the fingertips to finely tune pitches.
9. Perform the scale from memory.

Mary Wagner, former president of the American String Teacher Association, reminded me that scales and arpeggios are valuable teaching tools, but they are only as effective as the person teaching them. Students will play scales and arpeggios out of tune as long as the teacher allows it. It is up to us to listen carefully, especially to the leading tones, and insist that students pay close attention and correct their pitch every time it is out of tune.

Scale Theory

Scales can be used to improve students' understanding of how key signatures influence half steps, finger patterns, leading tones, and other important aspects of music theory. This is as easy as handing out blank staff paper and having students write the scale and arpeggio (going up and down) with the clef and key signature. Students can write in fingerings if and when shifts occur, and put a ^ between all notes that are separated only by a half step. Viola, cello, and bass students can also use alternate clefs when appropriate. Chapter 11 contains fingerboard mapping strategies that teach students to think cognitively about the elements in a specific scale that make it different from other scales. Students must figure out where the half and whole steps are in every position used, when to shift, what fingerings to use, and the names of the notes in every position.

Intonation Goal and Sequenced Objectives

The strategies in this chapter address the following goal and student performance objectives. When creating your unit plan, use the list below to help you:

- Select the objectives introduced in previous years that need *review*.
- Identify the new objectives you plan to *introduce* for the first time.
- Sequence the objectives you plan to teach in each course level into an order that promotes good technique and minimizes bad habits.

To help students learn the objectives they are expected to demonstrate, create a rubric with the objectives and have students use it to assess their own performance, evaluate the performance of their peers, and identify one or more goals for learning at home.

Intonation Goal:

Students use the correct finger patterns and best positions
to perform the notes in their music and
to adjust their fingertips to finely tune every note.

Position, Pattern and Fine-Tuning Objectives:

Novice:
Students will:

- Violin, viola, and cello – Find first position by tuning the octave created by the violin/viola third finger and cello fourth finger with the open string below it. All instruments, including bass, double-check first position by playing *Mary Had a Little Lamb*, adjusting the hand and fingers until they sound correct.

- Adjust fingertips to finely tune pitches, especially those that can be matched with open strings.

- Perform Beginning Finger Pattern #1 (open D, E, F-sharp, G, and A) on the D string and other strings with the correct whole- and half-step spacing and good left-hand position. Double bass students learn to play these notes and patterns using second and third position; cello students learn $2^{1/2}$ position.

- Perform one-octave D and G major scales and arpeggios, and study concert music that uses these keys, strings, and patterns.

- Perform Beginning Finger Pattern #2 (open D, E, F-natural, G, and A) on the D string and other strings with the correct whole- and half-step spacing. Perform this pattern by itself and in combination with previously learned finger patterns.

- Perform a one-octave C major scale and arpeggio in tune and the following major two-octave scales and arpeggios:

  Violin. . . . . G major
  Viola/Cello. . . . C major

Intermediate:
Students will:

- Perform a Backward Extended Finger Pattern (open D, E-flat, F, G, and A) on the D string and other strings with the correct whole- and half-step spacing. Perform this pattern by itself and in combination with previously learned finger patterns. Basses will call this "half position."

- Perform a Forward Extended Finger Pattern (open D, E, F-sharp, G-sharp, and A) on the D string and other strings with the correct whole- and half-step spacing. Perform this pattern by itself and in combination with previously learned finger patterns.
- Cellos perform all previously learned finger patterns in a variety of combinations in second and $2^{1}/_{2}$ positions.
- Perform first position double-stops that use one open string and one stopped string.
- Perform the following scales and arpeggios in tune:

  Violin. . . . . one-octave F major; two-octave A and B-flat major
  Viola/Cello . . . . . one-octave A and B-flat major; two-octave D and F major
  Bass . . . . one-octave F, A, and B-flat major

Proficient:
Students will:

- Produce a pleasing vibrato using a relaxed, consistent, and correct left arm, hand, and wrist motion.
- Use good shifting technique to execute same-finger and different-finger shifts in first through fifth positions. Cello and bass go to sixth and seventh positions.
- Perform all previously learned finger patterns in a variety of combinations using correct whole- and half-step spacing in third through sixth positions.

  Violin/Viola. . . . . second through fifth positions
  Cello/Bass . . . . . . third through sixth positions

- Perform two-octave scales, tonic and dominant arpeggios, and broken thirds in major and minor keys from three sharps to three flats.
- Perform first position double-stops that require two stopped strings.

Accomplished:
Students will:

- Use good shifting technique to bring the thumb and hand around the instrument when shifting to positions higher than sixth.

- Use the correct technique to perform all finger patterns in tune in higher positions.

  Violin/Viola. . . . . . . sixth position and higher
  Cello/Bass . . . . learn thumb position

- Perform three-octave scales and arpeggios in major and minor keys from three sharps to three flats; review all previously introduced scales, tonic and dominant arpeggios, and broken thirds with increasing speed, accuracy, and fluency.

- Perform double-stops in second through fifth positions.

Advanced:
Students will:

- Perform major and minor three-octave scales and arpeggios in keys with more than three sharps or flats; review all major and minor three-octave scales and arpeggios with increasing speed, accuracy, and fluency.

- Perform scales/arpeggios in thirds, sixths, octaves, etc., as appropriate for individual instruments.

FINAL THOUGHTS: THE DIFFERENCE BETWEEN WANTING AND EXPECTING

One of the toughest, most persistent challenges of teaching any level of string orchestra is the job of getting the students to play in tune. It is so difficult, in fact, that we easily give up on the idea that young students can play perfectly in tune. To protect our esteem, we often convince ourselves that the muddy, fuzzy intonation frequently heard in school orchestras is the best we can do.

I didn't know students could play in tune until I started going to concert festivals to listen to other teachers' orchestras. I heard some high school, middle school, and even elementary groups perform with highly refined intonation. Many groups also played out of tune, but when I noticed that the in-tune groups were taught by the same teachers, I came to a painful realization: *My orchestras play out of tune because I don't teach them to play in tune*. It was one of the most important teaching lessons of my life.

All string teachers want their orchestras to play in tune, but not all teachers actually *expect* it. This is harder than it sounds because we are required to expect many things at the same time. For students to be in tune, we must expect them to tune their strings perfectly, to perform with excellent left- and right-hand technique, to shift accurately, to correctly decipher the key signature's effect on finger patterns, and to listen and adjust their fingertips to tune to each other.

Our jobs are already hard. We put in long hours teaching multiple classes, sometimes at multiple schools. When we get tired of the daily grind, our high teaching standards and expectations easily slip. We start to give up on the belief that our students can play in tune, and pretty soon, those out-of-tune notes don't sound so bad—or we are just too tired to fix them.

So how do we get our student groups to play in tune? First, we must have a little faith and choose to see our tough job in a positive light: *If my students are playing out of tune, I know that I am the force in the classroom that can change this*. Then, we must continually remind ourselves that our students can play in tune; we do this by going to concert festivals and seeing school concerts of teachers that we most respect. Once we have a vision of what is possible, we can go back to our classrooms, listen honestly to our students, record them often, and begin planning strategies for improving their intonation.

Teaching intonation is a long-term process; it cannot be rushed. The best we can do is take it step by step, be consistent and *persistent*, and remind our students *every day* to pay attention to pitch and playing position.

Chapter 10

Pulse, Rhythm, and Rhythmic Literacy

Rhythm *feels good.* When we play in an ensemble, we move, breathe, and create music together, sharing our beautiful art form in synchrony with others in a musically expressive dance. For this reason, few activities are more intrinsically rewarding, both musically and socially, than dancing or playing music together with friends.

When we teach students the rhythm skills they need to read and perform music together, they get hooked on the joy of making music with friends, and they will come back to orchestra every day to get more. When they sight-read and perform music that is new for them, students get that elated "we did it!" feeling of success. Playing music *together* is fun, and no musical component is more responsible for the "together" part of music than rhythm. How well we teach rhythm will determine how well students read music and how much joy they experience with their instruments with their friends.

IN THIS CHAPTER:

- Rethinking How We Teach Rhythm
- Teaching Pulse
- Introducing Notation
- Teaching Students to Sight-Read
- Rhythmic Bowings
- Rhythmic Ensemble Skills
- Controlling the Tendency to Rush
- Pulse, Rhythm, and Ensemble Goal and Sequenced Objectives

Rethinking How We Teach Rhythm

If we teach rhythm the way we were taught—and many of us do—we use a method of counting or rhythm syllables to help us achieve a simple goal: to teach students how to recognize short rhythm patterns so when they see the patterns again, they recognize and perform them correctly. The traditional method starts with quarters and eighths (Example 30), and we learn to count "one, two, three &, four &."

Example 30:

Maybe you learned a different syllable system, such as Kodaly, Gordon, or Takadimi. Each of these systems progresses with increasingly advanced patterns containing dotted-quarter notes, then sixteenth notes, triple meter patterns, cut time, and so on. Once students have learned enough patterns, we hope they transfer the rhythm recognition to their concert music—and to a degree, many students do.

Even when using the methods described above, string students continue to struggle with rhythm because these methods do not go far enough. These syllable systems focus on rhythms contained within a beat, but most of the problems we see in orchestra occur in the long notes and rests—rhythms that last longer than one beat. In the example below (Example 31), the two places that will challenge students most are measures 4 and 7 because traditional methods do not do enough to teach students how to count through long notes and rests.

Example 31:

The rhythmic literacy strategies in this chapter are different because they are designed to teach string students not only to recognize short patterns (like the traditional methods), but also to know when to come in after long notes and rests. Our method also teaches both left-hand notes and right-hand bowing rhythm, and how to listen and adjust to other members of an ensemble.

Reading music together is more fun than plodding through class day after day, listening to the teacher explain notes and rhythms to each section of the orchestra. When we teach students to read well, they can experience the fun of sight-reading music with their friends, and more. When students read music faster, they spend less time learning notes and rhythms, and more time rehearsing musically rewarding elements like dynamics, expression, phrasing, and ensemble skills—that is, they spend more time learning how to *make music*.

Teaching Pulse

Think for a moment about that perfect principal second violin. We can rely on this student to perform syncopated and dotted rhythms accurately and never rush. This student listens and adjusts to other players in the ensemble and always knows exactly when to come in after long notes and rests. All of these rhythmic leadership qualities come from a strong sense of pulse, and when we spend more time teaching pulse, more of our students will possess the valuable rhythmic qualities we look for in our leaders.

Rhythm has two components:

1. The pulse
2. The rhythm that goes over the pulse

When we talk generally about "rhythm," we often include pulse as an assumed part of the equation. But when we *teach* rhythm, we should address pulse and the rhythm of the notes separately. There can be a pulse without a rhythm, but there is no such thing as good rhythm without a pulse. For this reason, it's important to teach pulse first. When we do, students gain a much better understanding of how different rhythms fit together, especially dotted rhythms, syncopation, long notes and rests. Said another way, if our students struggle with rhythms that last longer than a beat, it is a sure indication that they have not spent enough time learning and developing a strong pulse.

There are three important elements about pulse for students to learn:

1. Keep it steady.
2. Know how it is divided.
3. Learn to share the pulse with something or someone else, such as a metronome or another musician.

Use a strategy like the one below to teach pulse, division, and subdivision. As a general rule, teach pulse without written notation.

1. Set a metronome to a comfortable counting tempo (60 bpm) and turn it up loud enough for students to hear as they count.

2. Model how you want students to count with the metronome.

3. Using numbers, have students count to two ("1, 2, 1, 2...") or three ("1, 2, 3, 1, 2, 3..."), or four, etc., with the metronome. Then do the same without the metronome. Practice changing meters by holding up two, three, or four fingers and changing the number every few measures while the students count the correct number of beats with a steady tempo. Explain these groupings in terms of time signatures, like 2/4, 3/4, 4/4, 5/4, and 6/4.

4. Add divisions (1 & 2 &) and then subdivisions (1 e & a 2 e & a), and repeat Step 3. Have students march or clap the pulse while counting the subdivisions to reinforce the connection between the pulse and the subdivisions. Have students identify the note durations by ear: "Are these quarter notes, eighth notes, or sixteenth notes?"

5. Using an instrument, demonstrate how to play half notes, dotted-half notes, and whole notes with a bow on an open string while counting to two, three, or four, respectively; then have students do the same. Demonstrate different time signatures and ask students to identify them by ear.

6. Demonstrate how to play eighth or sixteenth notes with the bow on an open string while counting (and/or marching) to two, three, or four with a consistent pulse. Then have students do the same thing. Change the time signature and do it again. Can students identify the note durations and time signatures by ear?

7. Explore different tempos and the effects different tempos have on how quarter, eighth, and sixteenth notes feel. Discuss tempo markings (like Allegro, Adagio, Moderato, and Presto). Count off different tempos for students to echo, or have students take turns choosing a meter and tempo to count off for their peers to echo. Have students play different note lengths with their bows on an open string while counting to two, three, or four at different speeds.

8. To develop the listening and adjusting skills required in ensemble playing, slowly change the tempo of the classroom metronome while students perform the above exercises.

9. Look at time signatures and tempo markings in written examples, especially concert music and sight-reading examples, and ask students to count out a pulse that reflects the time signature they see. Be sure to include eighth and sixteenth subdivisions when counting slower tempos. Cover up the time signature and have students figure out what it is.

Introducing Notation

Once students have a good sense of pulse, and they understand how it can be divided, learning notation does not take long. The next step is to explain how rhythms look and teach students to decipher, recall, and perform written rhythms.

1. **Quarter, half, dotted-half, and whole notes** – Select a meter and instruct students to play quarter notes with their bow on an open string while they count to two, three, or four with and without the metronome. Then have students play half notes, dotted-half notes, and whole notes with their bows on an open string while counting to two, three, or four, respectively. Show the students what these rhythms look like, and then have them write down the rhythms they hear while you demonstrate those rhythms on an instrument.

2. **Eighth and sixteenth notes** – Have students march or clap a pulse with and without a metronome while counting eighth and sixteenth notes using a counting or syllable system. Then have students play eighth and sixteenth notes with their bows on an open string while counting and/or marching with a consistent pulse. Show students what these rhythms look like, and then have them write down rhythms while you demonstrate on an instrument.

3. **Syncopation, dotted, and tied rhythms** – In this category of rhythm, the dot, tie, or syncopation holds the note over a beat. These rhythms are easily explained visually by showing students the number of eighth or sixteenth notes that are contained in the rhythm. After showing the students what these rhythms look like, demonstrate them on an instrument and have students write down the rhythms they hear. When students play these rhythms, they must count out loud so they can hear the pulse contained in the dot, tie, or syncopation.

Symbolic association is a simple process of showing how a rhythm looks; it does not need to be over-explained with mathematical diagrams. For a deeper understanding of notation, have students listen to rhythms as you perform them, and teach them how to write the rhythms down using simple dictation.

Teaching Students to Sight-Read

Sight-reading is more than simple rhythm recognition. It is an extraordinary process that requires a person to read symbolic notation, immediately translate the images into sound, and then use a complex array of executive skills to perform on a string instrument the desired pitch, tone, style, dynamics, phrasing, and musicianship, all within a measured framework of time that we call "rhythm."

Earlier chapters address the development of technique, pitch, and tone. The following strategies will help students perform all of these skills while deciphering and performing rhythms within a pulse. To teach this, take students through a system of well-sequenced sight-reading exercises. We could, of course, practice sight-reading every time we take out a new piece, but resources that build the students' understanding through graduated exercises are both better for students and easier for the teacher.

Count the Pulse, Not the Rhythm:

To genuinely understand a rhythm pattern, students must keep a consistent pulse while simultaneously performing the rhythm. When teaching rhythm patterns (like we did in the previous section), we can use counting systems or syllables to highlight the differences between rhythms. But when teaching students to *sight-read*, students should count the pulse—not the rhythm of the music. Most performers use numbers to count through multi-measure rests and to measure the time passing throughout a "measure."

- Count whole numbers (1, 2, 3, 4) when sight-reading music with mostly quarter and half notes.
- Count the pulse and division (1 & 2 & 3 & 4 &) when reading dotted-quarter and eighth notes.
- Count subdivisions (1 e & a, 2 e & a, 3 e & a, 4 e & a) when reading dotted-eighth and sixteenth notes.

When we count the pulse, we are measuring time in increments (much like a ruler measures space). Numbers indicate the units of measurement, and smaller marks identify the divisions and subdivisions. Most rhythm syllable systems use the same syllable for each beat (like a ruler that has the number "1" on every inch or centimeter). A ruler without any marks is not much good for measuring the distance from one point to another. Similarly, when we stop counting, we stop measuring time and we lose the ability to discern how long to hold a note or when to come in after a long rest.

Students who do not count will wait to be taught by rote, or they will wait for their section leader or stand partner to count for them. School orchestras are full of followers, students who wait for someone else to count for them. Many of these followers actually have very talented ears; they learn their part after only a couple hearings. If we are not careful, we allow students with good ears to remain functionally illiterate for years, and by doing so, we unintentionally create students who become dependent upon the teacher or other players. It is our job to teach students to count for themselves—to be able to go home and independently figure out how to play their music. When we do our job well, we can turn a class of followers into leaders who listen, count, read, and learn music faster.

If we want students to count when they read rhythms—and there really is no other way to read and understand rhythms—then we must require them to *count out loud*. While this is impossible for vocalists and wind players, it is the preferred method for teaching string players to read and perform rhythms within a steady pulse, especially through long notes and rests. Students resent having to count because it makes them think and work much harder. They will say it's easier to count in their head, and that is because they temporarily stop counting. So, watch their lips and make sure they are counting out loud. It makes a difference. Students will learn to read much better when they count the pulse and divisions, especially during longer notes and rests.

Sight-Reading Strategy:

The following strategy teaches students to feel the rhythm in their bow as they count out a steady pulse.

It is the ability to read and perform rhythms correctly in our right hand while counting that makes string players strong leaders.

Set the classroom metronome to a tempo that is not too fast. Model the counting style you want your students to use during the sight-reading example. Then, while the students count the pulse out loud, have them perform the rhythm exercises with their bow.

1. Have students hold their bows vertically and air bow the rhythms in the sight-reading exercise. This allows you to see which students are performing the rhythms correctly. Students can feel the rhythm in their bow as they count the pulse out loud. Longer notes should be bowed with a slow, sustained motion. Watch lips to make sure students are counting, and watch bows to see which students are struggling.

2. After students successfully air bow the sight-reading exercise, have them count and bow the rhythm on an open string. Continue to watch students closely to make sure they count as they play. The students who do not count will not know when to come in after long notes and rests, and they will copy the players around them instead of internalizing the rhythm for themselves.

3. When they are ready, have students look at the key signature and the notes in the sight-reading exercise for 30 seconds to 1 minute. They should mentally practice, silently air bow, and put fingers on the string before the class plays together. This important step gives the non-readers with good ears a chance to practice reading without giving them the opportunity to listen to the person next to them.

4. Finally, instruct students to perform the sight-reading example. Teachers of younger students may want to take the intermediate step of counting and playing pizzicato before playing the notes with the bow.

Tricks of the Trade:

- **"Read My Lips"** – Watch the students instead of the score or sight-reading example. By watching the students' eyes and lips, it is easy to tell whom is reading while anchored in a strong pulse and who is not counting or feeling the pulse; they will look vacantly adrift in unmeasured time. Those students do not understand longer notes and rests; they are essentially cheating by copying the students around them.

- **Watch the Bows** – It is much easier to see one individual making errors than it is to hear that person within a group.

- **"Catch the Copy Cats"** – My favorite game for discouraging students from copying is to stand in front of the class and air bow with the students, and then on the long notes and rests, make intentional mistakes, moving the bow early and assertively to get the students who are not counting for themselves to follow. Students who have been copying for years will fall into this trap, and they are forced to redouble their efforts to focus only on the page in front of them while they count and air bow. This game is fun for the teacher and the students, and it teaches students to count for themselves.

- **Keep Reading New Material, and Avoid Repetition** – Don't let students get comfortable with a sight-reading exercise. Once the students with good ears have heard the example a couple times, they are playing by ear and no longer reading. Use a sequenced method with many different sight-reading examples, and constantly switch them up to get students to read. Our method book, *Habits of a Successful String Musician*, has ten pages of sequential rhythm studies, supplemented with over 130 additional sequenced sight-reading examples.

When you hand out a new piece, practice counting, air bowing, and reading straight through the piece. Keep gig books or sight-reading binders in your room so the entire class can sight-read together, or break up into chamber groups and read music on days when you have a sub. As students get older and continue playing into adulthood, the ability to sight-read will become increasingly important. Whether they are eventually reading chamber music with their friends, or performing at a wedding reception or with a professional symphony, classical musicians read music constantly. Remember, sight-reading music together is fun, and when we teach students to count, feel the pulse, and read well, they will learn music much faster and spend more time *making* music.

Rhythmic Bowings

Rhythm is motion, and practicing the motion of rhythms and bowings helps us learn to perform rhythms with greater economy, speed, and accuracy. In Chapter 8, we looked at a call-and-response strategy (Example 32) for teaching tone and articulations. This same strategy works equally well for teaching rhythmic bowings.

Example 32:

In the example above, the teacher models the rhythm/bowing on a five-note scale, and the students use the nine-note scale to practice the rhythms in unison or in canon. This exercise can be used to teach the rhythm patterns listed in variations 5a–5d above, or any other pattern the teacher can dream up.

Have students identify a challenging rhythm or bowing in their concert piece, and use the call-and-response strategy to teach it to the rest of the class. When practicing rhythms, make sure the students are in the correct part of the bow and the tempo is correct since the action of the bow can change dramatically with different tempos. Perform sixteenth-note patterns in the middle to upper half of the bow, keeping the upper arm still and opening the elbow like a hinge. When studying dotted rhythms, hooked bow patterns, and syncopated patterns, use a metronome to help students hear the beats and divisions contained within dotted rhythms. This is a good time to review and model flawless, tension-free bow hands because poor technique can impair rhythm as well as tone.

Overlapping Rhythms:

To develop deeper rhythmic understanding and ensemble skills, have different sections of the ensemble perform and overlap rhythm patterns to practice fitting different rhythms together into the same pulse. For example, violins can perform variation 5k, while lower strings perform variation 5m, and then they switch parts (Example 33).

Example 33:

Each group must listen to the other to perform the rhythms accurately together. Overlap dotted rhythms and syncopated patterns with steady eighth or sixteenth notes to help students hear how the rhythms fit together and perform them more accurately. In addition to overlapping complementary rhythm patterns, overlap competing rhythms to teach polyrhythms (like duple against triple).

Rhythm Transitions:

In concert music, problems frequently arise in the transitions between different rhythms. When changing from eighth to sixteenth notes, for example, it takes a moment (sometimes more than a moment) for students to get up to the correct speed. The same is true when changing articulations (like going from detaché to spiccato).

To practice challenging transitions, use a repeated five-note scale that alternates between two rhythms or articulations. For example, students can practice going back and forth between variations 5k and 5m above, or oscillate between eighth notes and triplets with a metronome. By pairing eighth notes off the string with sixteenth notes on the string, students can practice going from détaché to spiccato, a transition common in classical music.

Rhythmic Ensemble Skills

There are many components of ensemble skills that we will explore in detail in Chapter 12. When teachers talk about a group having poor ensemble, they are often referring to the *rhythmic* component of ensemble skills—the act of agreeing on a common pulse and playing rhythms together within that pulse. Rhythmic ensemble is connected to a specific human aptitude that helps us coordinate our movement with the moving world around us. In sports, we refer to it as *timing* or *coordination*, and we use it to catch a ball, swing a bat, or even fake out an opponent.

Coaches and music directors can attest to the fact that the ability to synchronize our body with something else is indeed a skill. Students with a greater aptitude will tend to learn this skill effortlessly. For other students, however, the ability to perform to the same beat can be difficult and frustrating for them, and for the director and the other people in the ensemble.

There are no magic strategies other than "practice" for helping students develop this skill. At the end of this chapter, there is an Ensemble Skill Sequence that you can follow to help your students learn rhythmic ensemble in steps. Some students will need more time than others to learn each step, and some will need to take smaller steps. Students who lack *timing*, *rhythm*, or *ensemble skills* tend to have more success synchronizing with music that has a clear and consistent beat or pulse. When the pulse is hidden in longer notes or legato lines of music, the students will need to internalize the pulse. Students will visibly bob their heads, breathe, cue, and move in tempo when they internalize the pulse well.

After students learn to synchronize with a consistent pulse, they will need to learn how to accelerate and decelerate together. This requires students to control their own tempo as they decide how fast or slow they want to go. Students who lack ensemble skills also lack the ability to control or adjust their tempo, and this makes them more susceptible to rushing or dragging.

At the highest levels of ensemble, students are doing much more than playing together rhythmically. They are listening to each other and the music, matching tone, intonation, pulse, style, dynamics, and more. Good ensemble is about paying attention to each other's musical ideas. Eventually, we want students to play together not like a machine, but more like a school of fish, breathing and moving together with precision, sharing in the expression of music, and letting each other finish phrases before beginning the next.

The Best Practice Assignment Ever:

The students who have difficulty with rhythm and ensemble are the same students who struggle with movement. They know they tend to stick out at the school dance, an opportunity for embarrassment they will often try to avoid. They say they "don't like to dance" but deep down wish that they could because it is a way to fit in—by being in a rhythmic human synchrony with their peers. They associate dance with embarrassment, and they need to overcome this association by doing their "ensemble homework assignment," which happens to be the best practice assignment ever. Here's what you tell your students:

> "Tonight, when you are tired of studying your books, close the door to your room, put on your headphones, crank up some popular music with a driving pulse, and dance. Move until your heart races, and maybe even until you break a sweat; then go back to studying with a refreshed focus. Do this every night. Your grades will go up and so will your sense of ensemble, and no one has to know your secret. If your parents ask, tell them you are 'practicing ensemble,' which is a fundamental skill for playing in orchestra. You can even tell them to e-mail me, and I'll explain that you are learning to find the pulse of the music and move with it."

Controlling the Tendency to Rush

Few things scare string teachers more than the prospect of having their students rush out of control at a concert. Students rush because of a natural human tendency to shorten time between notes. Young students seem especially prone to rush, and if we do not take steps to teach them how to control the tempo, the increased energy and adrenaline at concerts can trigger the catastrophic rushing we often see.

There are several strategies you can employ—in addition to prayer, that is—to help students learn how to control the tempo even when they are on stage. With maturity and musical experience, students naturally learn to control their tempo, but the following strategies can help even the youngest students develop an awareness of pulse and their ability to control it:

1. Identify a passage where students tend to rush. Students most often rush staccato notes, dotted rhythms, longer notes and rests, double up-bows, and string crossings.

2. Have the students play the passage with a metronome sounding out divisions and subdivisions. Then have them play with the metronome at different tempos. Changing tempo requires students to control their tempo.

3. Conduct the passage at a slow tempo, and expect students to follow you. Novice-level students may need to put their bows down and pizzicato as they follow you before they can do the same with their bow.

4. After they can follow a slow tempo, conduct the excerpt several other times at different tempos. Students will get better at following you as their ability to control their own pulse improves.

5. Once the students can follow you at different tempos, have them follow you as you gradually slow down and speed up throughout the excerpt.

6. Finally, change tempos just slightly when you rehearse the piece, and require the students to practice following you. When students become too accustomed to your usual tempo, they stop following and slowly they forget how to control their tempo.

Younger students forget to listen to other sections, and they come in early during long notes and rests. Use the overlapping rhythm strategies described earlier to help students learn to listen to the other sections of the orchestra and become more aware of how the other parts fill in the spaces between their notes. Even older students rush the ends of phrases; encourage them to wait for their friends to finish and then come in at the right time.

Remind students that they are responsible for paying attention and controlling the tempo. Step off the podium and have them play without you. If they feel the tempo getting away, they must take control. Have them play intentionally fast without you, and then intentionally slow. Help them find the musically convincing tempo in between those extremes that they can control themselves.

One final thought about rushing: The concert is not a good time to try and control students who refuse to follow. Occasionally when students rush on stage, directors will slow down their conducting as if to prove a point—that it's the students' fault for not following. The truth is, the game was lost before the concert began. So give in and make the best of it. Try to control the rushing as best you can, but don't let yourself get so far behind the collective beat that you confuse the students who are watching you. Remind students every day that mature musicians can add time between notes and phrases, and immature musicians tend to rush. "Now which kind of musician are you? Who among you is going to demonstrate control or lose control at the concert tonight?"

Pulse, Rhythm, and Ensemble Goal and Sequenced Objectives

The strategies in this chapter address the following goal and student performance objectives. When creating your unit plan, use the list below to help you:

- Select the objectives introduced in previous years that need review.
- Identify the new objectives that you plan to introduce for the first time.
- Sequence the objectives you plan to teach in each course level.

Pulse, Rhythm, and Rhythmic Literacy Goal:

Students read, independently decipher, and accurately perform rhythms within a common pulse and at a musically convincing tempo.

Pulse, Rhythm, and Rhythmic Literacy Objectives:

Students will read rhythmic notation, independently decipher, and correctly perform the following combinations of rhythms and time signatures.

Novice:

- Quarter notes and rests in 2/4 and 4/4
- Eighth notes, quarter notes, and rests in 2/4 and 4/4
- Eighth notes, quarter notes, and rests in 3/4
- Half notes and rests in 2/4, 3/4, and 4/4, plus the above combinations
- Dotted-half notes and rests in 3/4 and 4/4, plus the above combinations
- Whole notes in 4/4 and whole rests in 2/4, 3/4 and 4/4

Intermediate:
(pulse is divided into two and three parts)

Simple Meter (pulse is divided in two):
- Dotted-quarter notes/rests and eighth-note combinations in 2/4, 3/4, and 4/4
- Tied eighth notes in 2/4, 3/4, and 4/4
- Syncopation using tied eighth notes and quarters in 2/4, 3/4, and 4/4

Compound Meter (pulse is divided in three):
- Dotted-quarter notes and rests in 3/8 and 6/8
- Dotted-quarter notes/rests, quarter notes/rests, and eighth notes/rests in 3/8 and 6/8
- Tied eighth notes and syncopation in compound meter
- The above compound meter combinations in 9/8 and 12/8
- Combinations of triplet eighth notes and duple eighth notes in 2/4, 3/4, and 4/4

Proficient:
(subdivided pulse)

Simple Meter:
- Sixteenth notes in 2/4, 3/4, and 4/4
- Dotted eighth- and sixteenth-note patterns
- Tied sixteenth notes and sixteenth rests
- Syncopated eighth notes and tied sixteenth notes
- Cut-time (2/2)

Compound Meter:
- Sixteenth notes in 3/8, 6/8, 9/8, and 12/8
- Dotted eighth- and sixteenth-note patterns in compound meter
- Syncopated eighth notes, tied sixteenth notes and sixteenth rests in compound meter

Accomplished:
(irregular meter)

- Quarter, dotted-quarter, and eighth notes and rests in 5/8, 7/8, and 5/4
- Tied eighth notes and syncopated quarter notes
- Sixteenth notes and rests in combination with the rhythms listed above
- Syncopated eighth notes, tied sixteenth notes and sixteenth rests

Advanced:
(mixed meter)

- Alternate between 2/4, 3/4, 4/4, and 5/4 time signatures every measure or several measures with the same quarter-note pulse
- Changing meters with the same eighth-note division in 3/8, 5/8, 6/8, 2/4, 3/4, where the eight-note length stays the same
- Changing meters with the same pulse 2/4 to 6/8 where the eighth-note length changes
- Combinations of simple and compound meters, where the pulse and division change

Ensemble Objective Sequence:

1. Performing a pulse only:

   a. Perform and maintain a consistent quarter-note pulse.
   b. Perform a consistent quarter-note pulse with a metronome or other players.
   c. Perform in sync with others a quarter-note pulse that increases or decreases in tempo.

2. Performing a rhythm over a consistent pulse:

   a. Perform a rhythm as a group with a metronome or other players who are performing a consistent quarter-note pulse.
   b. Perform a rhythm alone with a metronome or other players who are performing a consistent quarter-note pulse.
   c. Perform a rhythm as a group in sync with other players who are performing a quarter-note pulse that gradually increases or decreases in tempo.
   d. Perform a rhythm alone in sync with other players who are performing a quarter-note pulse that gradually increases or decreases in tempo.

3. Performing a rhythm in sync with another different rhythm:

   a. Perform a rhythm within a group in sync with other players who are performing a different rhythm at a consistent tempo.
   b. Perform a rhythm alone in sync with other players who are performing a different rhythm at a consistent tempo.
   c. Perform a rhythm within a group in sync with other players who are performing a different rhythm as the tempo gradually increases or decreases.
   d. Perform a rhythm alone in sync with other players who are performing a different rhythm as the tempo gradually increases or decreases.

Chapter 11

Creativity and Tonal Literacy

Paul had been a student in my high school orchestra for three years before he felt comfortable enough to ask a question that had been bothering him for a long time. "I'm going to come right out and ask," he said. "What does that tic-tac-toe sign next to the note mean?" The class sat in silence, as stunned as I was.

"Well, Paul, I am so glad you asked," I replied. After all, I would have never known to explain what a sharp was unless he had asked. When I was a young teacher, I just assumed that my students could read music by the time they got to high school. Call it optimism, or maybe naiveté, but I never actually checked to see if they could read music; we were too busy rehearsing and performing music. I accepted my constant reminders to cellos about extensions as a part of normal school orchestra rehearsal, and I thought it was my job to repeatedly answer the students' daily questions like, "Is that a high or a low 2?"

What these types of questions are really telling us is that our students either do not understand what is on the page or they are not paying attention to what they are reading. In this chapter, we will look at strategies and activities that not only teach students to be more literate, but also get them excited about it. Literacy and creativity have been combined in the same chapter because they are naturally connected; most students instinctively want to create their own music, and they quickly learn that literacy helps them write down their ideas for others to perform.

Music theory, composition, and improvisation are each rich musical fields of study with enough content to fill many books and graduate courses. This chapter contains introductory ideas to allow orchestra teachers to infuse creativity and literacy into their class while maintaining the performing goals of their ensemble.

Instructional time is limited in every classroom, and if teachers have built programs around performing as many pieces as possible, then finding time for creativity or literacy can feel like a challenge. But we cannot deny that there is wholesome artistic value to creating well-rounded musicians who can read, create, perform, and speak intelligently and passionately about music. Indeed, when students read music better, they learn music faster; and when they have creative buy-in, they will participate in class with greater enthusiasm.

Literacy and creativity are not just part of being a well-rounded student musician; they also improve concert performance. With a better understanding of tonal literacy and creativity, your students will perform better, understand and derive greater value from the music they hear and play, and experience greater enjoyment from all the music they will create in your class.

How do we work tonal literacy and creativity into the orchestra classroom? The lessons in this unit fit perfectly in the first weeks of school, between concerts, after the last concert of the year, and on days when you have a substitute.

IN THIS CHAPTER:

- "High 2" Is Not a Note Name
- Fingerboard Mapping
- Improving Literacy by Writing Music
- Arpeggios Are Our Chords
- Creating Opportunities for Improvisation
- Tonal Literacy and Creativity Goal and Sequenced Objectives

---

"High 2" Is Not a Note Name

Let's begin by *not* assuming—like I did—that all students, even veteran players, know their note names. When they read music, students need to know the names of notes before they can truly know where to put their fingers on the fingerboard. Some students will try to convince their teachers that they don't need to know the note names because they still know where their fingers go. In reality, however, if they cannot identify the notes by name, then they also cannot identify the sharps or flats in the key signature or know which notes on the staff are sharp or flat—and *that* is a crucial part of knowing where one's fingers go.

String players don't have time to count lines and spaces before each note; they must be able to name notes *instantly*. To measure this skill, give students a *timed* Note Name Test (Example 34). The example below is the top staff of a system with three staves—one each for violin, viola, and cello/bass. Each line has 24 notes in first position mixed up randomly all over the staff, and students have *1 MINUTE* to write the names under the notes. If they do not get most of the notes correct, then they cannot identify notes fast enough to process the information they need to read music as they play it.

Example 34:

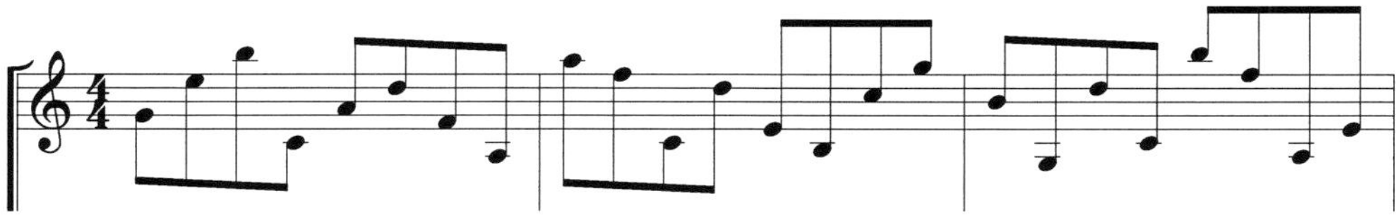

There are many online programs and worksheets for teaching note names. You can also use the music in your concert folder:

1. Turn on the metronome at 60.

2. Instruct students to read the note names in their concert music at a pace of one per second.

3. Split students into pairs (stand partners) and have them read the note names to each other.

Students must also learn how the key signature affects the notes on the staff. Most young students pay very little attention to the key signature, and instead of reading, they either guess the correct finger pattern or they ask the teacher: "Is that a high 2 or a low 2?" The correct response from the teacher should be, "You tell me! The answer is in the music. What is the name of that note, and where is it on your fingerboard?" Most wrong notes occur on the fourth and seventh scale degrees, primarily because students are not paying attention to the key signature's impact on finger patterns.

To teach students to pay attention to the key signature, find a line of concert music that has no accidental markings, or use the same Note Name Test described above.

1. Have students read the note names, *but change the key signature*, and have them read the notes with the new sharps or flats.

2. After they read the note names, have students play the exercise on their instrument with different key signatures.

Start with easy keys, and gradually add more sharps and flats; you will be surprised how quickly these exercises will correct most of your students' key signature literacy problems.

Dominant arpeggios like the one below (Example 35) also make excellent note name tests that teach students the relationship between the key signature and note identification. *Habits of a Successful String Musician* has arpeggios like this in every key.

Example 35:

Fingerboard Mapping

Learning the names of notes on the staff can be difficult for some students, but their biggest challenge may be learning where each note is located on the fingerboard. Most band students learn a chromatic scale, which helps them understand how all of the notes fit together and how to answer basic questions like the ones below:

- What are the notes one half step above and below A, B, C, D, E, F, and G?
- What are the notes one whole step above and below A, B, C, D, E, F, and G?
- Is the distance from C up to E the same as the distance from E up to G?
- What is the distance between B-flat and C-sharp?

Public school string students struggle with questions like these well into high school. They have severe difficulty answering questions about distances between notes, which is a terrible problem because without keys on our instruments, *distances are all we have*. We do not teach young students to perform a chromatic scale because it is complicated under the fingers. Instead, we use diagrams like the beginning D string finger pattern diagram (Example 36) to help map out the notes on the fingerboard.

Example 36:

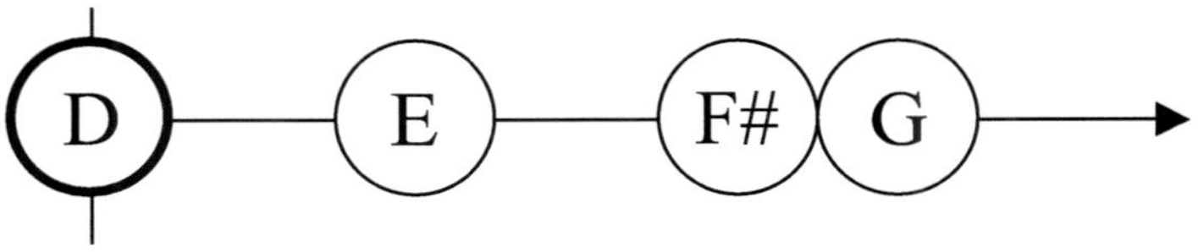

We teach beginners about half and whole steps and the note names, but we need to spend more time teaching them about *the notes they don't need to know right now*. The human brain is designed to subconsciously fill in gaps with hypotheses and extrapolations to help us make sense of things we don't completely understand. When given an incomplete diagram (like the one above), students subconsciously try to fill in the gaps with answers that make sense to them, whether or not they are right. Before you know it, you have students who think that B-natural and B-flat are the same note, and that G-sharp and A-flat are two different notes. Most string students do not understand the chromatic scale, and as a result, the note locations on their long fingerboard are something of a mystery to them.

Students need strong mapping skills to answer basic questions like, "What is a whole step above and below A, B, C, D, E, F, and G?" Cellists need to understand the difference between a major and a minor third before they can definitively say whether or not an extension is required. So it's important for us to leave as few gaps as possible as we teach students about how their fingerboards are mapped out, especially when they are first learning about finger patterns in their first few years of string instruction.

When students begin to see fingerboard maps in their method books, give them a worksheet like the beginning D string fingerboard map (Example 37) to help them correctly fill in the gaps.

Example 37:

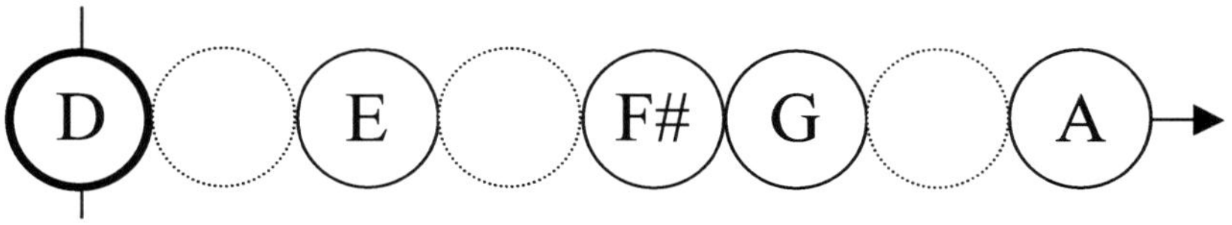

Explain that there are "other sharp notes" on the fingerboard that they will learn to play later. Keep it simple in the first year. Have students complete blank, first-year fingerboard maps (Example 38) using only natural and sharp notes. Then check their work to see if students are correctly mapping notes in their head. You might be surprised to learn how scrambled the mental maps of older students are, *especially those students with really good ears.*

Example 38:

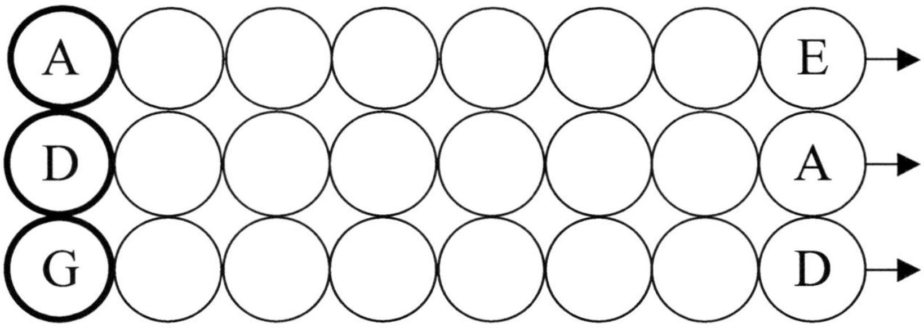

In the second year, introduce how flats work, and also explain enharmonic spellings. Most notes have two or more names, and this can be very confusing when we don't explain it completely. After students understand natural, sharp, and flat, they can solve larger, intermediate fingerboard maps (Example 39).

Example 39:

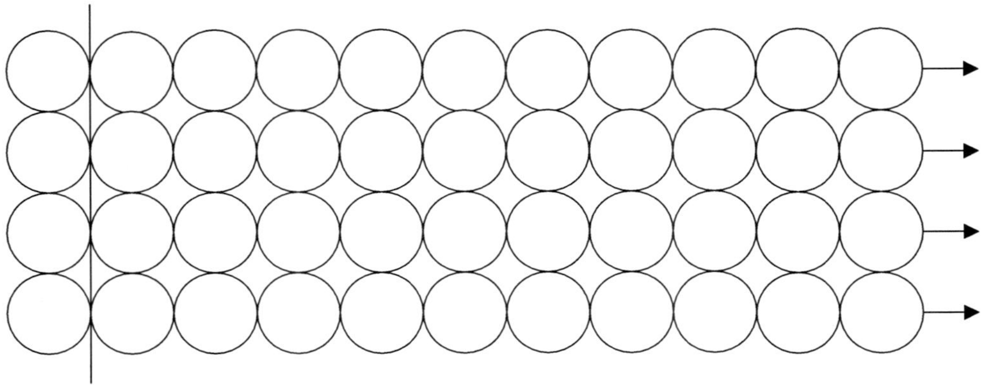

When introducing longer fingerboard maps, review some of the following idiosyncrasies that frequently trip up students:

- The notes E–F and B–C are *naturally* separated by half steps; there is no other note between them.
- All other natural notes are separated by a whole step—there is a "hole" between them. In each hole there is a sharp and flat note that have different names but occupy the same space.
- Each space can have two or more names, or *enharmonic* spellings. At the very least, students need to be able to define the terms *sharp*, *flat*, and *natural*, and understand how these symbols work.

To help students connect the fingerboard map to written notation, pass out blank staff paper and instruct students to complete the following note writing exercises:

1. Write an ascending and descending chromatic scale using only natural and sharp notes. Start on the lowest note of the instrument, go up two octaves, and then come back down. On the descending scale, be sure to use the natural sign to naturalize notes that were previously sharp.
2. Write an ascending and descending chromatic scale using only natural and flat notes. Start on the lowest note of the instrument, go up two octaves, and then come back down. On the ascending scale, be sure to use the natural sign to naturalize notes that were previously flat.

Tetrachords and Scales

Tetrachord patterns require students to transfer what they already know about the chromatic fingerboard map and apply it to the organized patterns they will see in their music. High school students should be able to complete Tetrachord Diagrams (Example 40) on their end-of-course test.

Example 40:

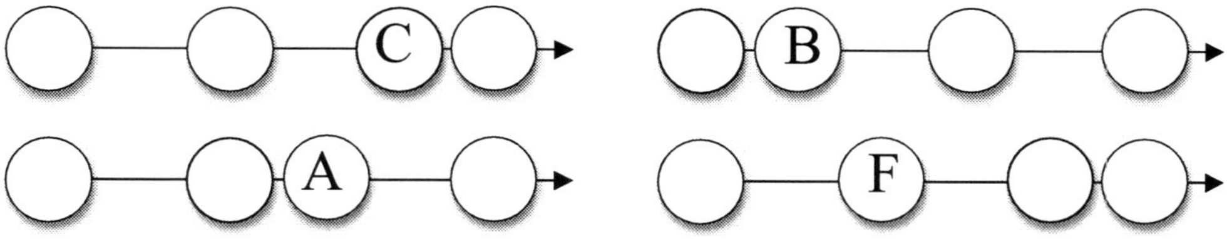

In Example 41, the circles are set up in the whole- and half-step pattern of a major scale. If we put a C in the first circle on the left, we can use this diagram to teach students the key of C and how the natural half steps occur between B–C and E–F. If we write G in the first circle, we can fill in the notes of the G scale and show students how F-sharp is a whole step from E and a half step from G. This explains why the key of G has an F-sharp. This pattern can be used to teach major key signatures for all keys.

Example 41:

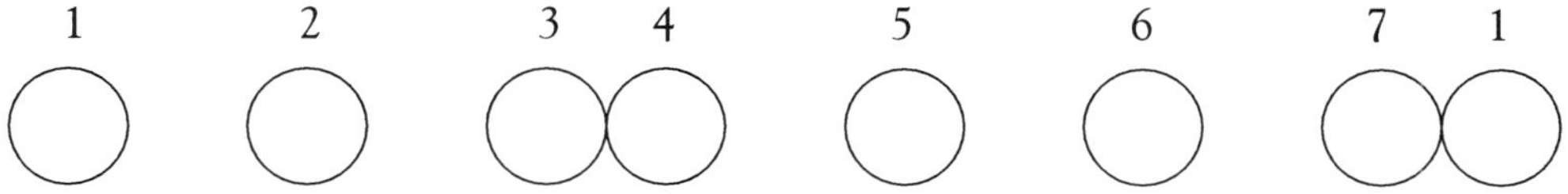

By putting numbers over each circle, we can easily teach students about scale degrees and demonstrate that the half steps occur between 3–4 and 7–1. Ultimately, scale degrees are an important part of our tonal language, and students should be able to answer questions like:

- What is the seventh scale degree in the key of D?
- What is the fourth scale degree in the key of F?

The final step in fingerboard mapping is teaching the relationship between the key signature and the notes and finger patterns that are to be performed. In the first year of string instruction, students should learn to write key signatures as they are introduced in their first- and second-year methods. They should also be able to determine the finger pattern by looking at the key signature. In Example 42 below, students can write their clef on the staff, followed by a key signature of their choosing. Then on the string map, they can draw in the circles and note names of the notes and finger pattern that agree with their key signature.

Example 42:

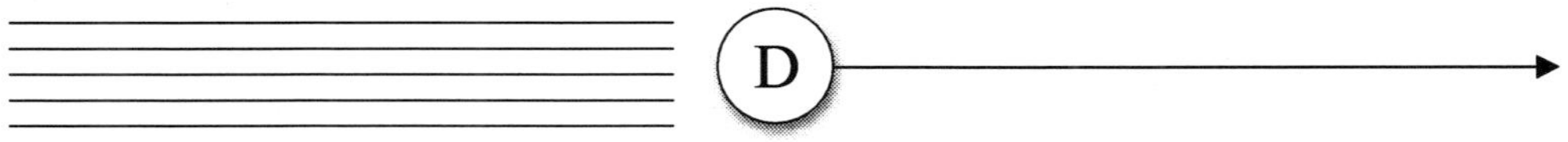

Students with a strong understanding of how the notes are mapped out on their fingerboards should be able to use a blank fingerboard map (Example 43) to plot the notes of a specific key or scale.

Example 43:

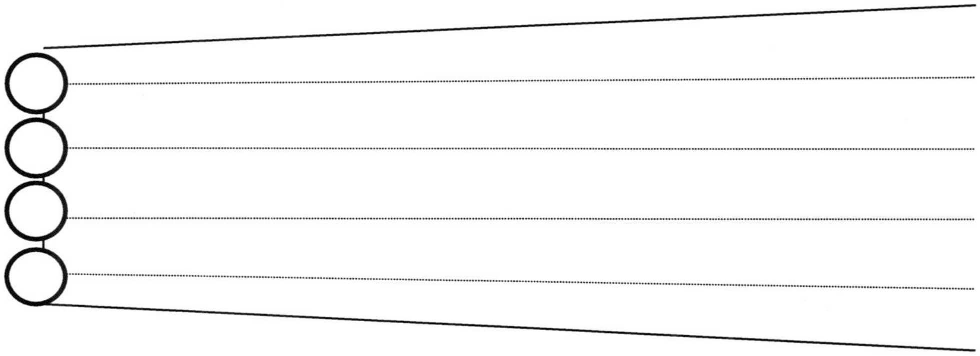

They would connect the circles separated by half steps, leave spaces between notes separated by whole steps, and line up all perfect fifths across the strings. It takes practice, but these mental mapping exercises will dramatically help students develop a clear connection between the notes on the staff and their corresponding locations on their fingerboard.

Improving Literacy by Writing Music

When teachers talk about music theory, some students' eyes glaze over, but when we ask the same students to write melodies, their brains come alive with interest and questions. Even in the first year of string instruction, students should be writing familiar melodies. It's as easy as handing out a blank page of staff paper. Start with familiar tunes (like *Twinkle, Twinkle Little Star* and *Mary Had a Little Lamb*) that are not too difficult, but are still rich with learning opportunities. *Twinkle, Twinkle* starts with a perfect fifth, and *Mary* begins on the third scale degree. Talk about stem length and direction, key signatures, time signatures, rhythms, resting, tones and much more.

1. Have students pick their next tune from a list (like *Hot Cross Buns, Frere Jacques, Go Tell Aunt Rhody, London Bridges, Deck the Halls, Jingle Bells*, or *Ode to Joy*).

2. After students write out their melody, have them swap papers with their stand partner.

3. Have them play each other's melodies and ask themselves, "Does it sound right when your stand partner plays what you have written?"

Students will laugh at their mistakes and still be motivated to figure out the answers to the puzzle of writing music correctly.

This activity is powerfully versatile, which makes it perfect in a class of students with varying levels of ability. Once students get comfortable with a melody, change the key and time signature: "OK, now write your melody in the key of B-flat, in 2/4."

If writing music comes easily to students, give them an extra credit assignment (like creating a good harmony for their melody). Or have them write the melody or harmony in another clef (like tenor or treble; violins can learn alto clef).

Arranging or Composition Project:

Once students are comfortable writing melodies, they are ready for a larger creativity project:

1. Find a melody, such as a holiday tune or cultural folk song, that is part of your heritage; the melody should be comparable to the length of *The Star-Spangled Banner*.

2. Using standard notation, write your melody in a key and range that lies well on your instrument.

3. Next, write a harmony or an accompaniment that will be played by at least one other instrument. Write out the arrangement so each instrument gets its own staff. Keep the harmonies simple, and if you want to write a bass line, limit it to 1, 4, and 5.

4. For extra credit, have the different instruments share the responsibility of playing the melody, harmony, or bass line. Students will perform their works

for the class; truly exceptional compositions may be selected for performance in the spring concert.

Arpeggios Are Our Chords

Arpeggios can look complicated to young players, but when students learn arpeggios by ear, one octave at a time, they make more sense. If you've never taught arpeggios by ear, you might add the following method to your bag of strategies. Demonstrate the following on your instrument, and have the students echo back on theirs.

1. Play a triad (1, 3, 5, 3, 1) on the D string, then the G string, and then the A string.

2. Play triads in different octaves and starting on other notes. Use triads to "discover" extensions.

3. In the key of the scale you are studying, play the first octave of the tonic triad; have the students echo back.

4. If your students can shift (or even if they can't), have them explore their instrument to find other octaves of that triad.

5. After the students have discovered the triads by ear, have them open up the scale book to learn the fingerings.

Once students learn how a triad sounds, explain that it is made up of the scale degrees 1, 3, and 5. It takes almost no time for students to learn the terms *root*, *third* and *fifth*, and that the root of the triad is also its name (e.g., a G triad is also known as a G arpeggio, and it's called a G chord when the notes are played at the same time).

When students learn that arpeggios can be built on each degree of the scale, the world of chords starts to open up for them. In the key of G, for example, play a G arpeggio and have students echo it back; then go up the scale one step to the A minor arpeggio, and repeat the pattern. By continuing on up the scale with a B minor arpeggio, C, D, and so on, you can explain how chords can be called by the letter name of the root, or by their scale degree (such as I, IV, V, and vi). This is enough to get students started on simple chord progressions and harmonizing their own arrangements. You don't have to delve into complex chord theory to have a little fun with triads, arpeggios, and chords.

Creating Opportunities for Improvisation

Most string teachers understand the important place improvisation has in American music, and we can agree that the ability to improvise is an important skill for musicians to have. The challenge of teaching this National Standard is that most of us did not receive formal instruction on how to improvise, nor have we seen how it should be taught in an orchestra class. Naturally, if we were not taught how to improvise, then demonstrating and teaching improvisation can be an uncomfortable, if not scary, endeavor for many of us. In this section, we offer some ideas that we hope will help you find ways to incorporate improvisation into your classroom. But our ideas come with a disclaimer: We don't believe improvisation can be learned from a book.

To learn how to teach improvisation, we recommend seeking out sessions on the subject at state and national conferences. The ASTA National Conference has numerous sessions every year on teaching jazz, fiddle, and improvisation. Ask the planners of your state conference to bring in improvisation clinicians. Though it requires some money, possibly the best way to learn how to teach improvisation is to invite a guest artist to your school, one who not only can improvise but who also has experience teaching improvisation to classes of string students. Most teachers will want to see a few sessions before they feel comfortable teaching improvisation.

Keeping it simple may be the most important ingredient to successful improvisation, especially for beginners.

1. To get them started, have students select a popular melody that they like and can play by ear.

2. Then have them experiment with the rhythms and notes to create their own version of the melody.

3. After they have gotten somewhat comfortable improvising over their own favorite melodies, teach them a melody to a string arrangement that contains improvisation.

Many of the string arrangements that have an improvisatory section within the piece use this idea of improvising on a familiar melody. So teach the melody by ear first, and give students time to practice improvising on the melody. Then give them the music, and let them experiment with improvisation within the context of a written piece of music. If you don't know any jazz string arrangements, ask your music distributor what is available. Over the last twenty years, a significant number of new jazz arrangements have been written for school orchestras.

Scott Laird introduced me to the idea of adding improvisation to pieces that were not originally designed for improvisation. Here's how:

1. If you have a good string arrangement of a popular song, find an eight-bar melodic passage where the melody can be easily repeated, and add repeat signs. This might be the "hook" or chorus, or it could be a verse.

2. The first time through, have a student play the melody as a solo while the other students play their parts pizzicato; then have the soloist play the melody as is or add as much variation as he or she likes.

3. Repeat the section and let other student soloists take turns developing this melody, improvising as much as they want over the chord progression.

4. On the final time through, have everyone play the music as written before moving on to the end of the piece.

Improvisation seems to happen more naturally and more comfortably in small groups of friends. Teach your orchestra a simple chord progression; then break them up into small groups and have them take turns improvising and accompanying. Play Pachelbel's Canon over the classroom sound system and have the students improvise over it. If you have any students who play guitar, encourage them to bring their instruments to help fill out the chords in the progression. Some students may even have effects pedals that can record a chord progression and then play it back over and over in a loop.

At the end of the year, have students create a cover of one of their favorite songs.

1. Divide students into small groups and select a popular, non-classical song with an easy, repeating harmony line and a fun melody.

2. After all of the students learn the melody and can play it together by ear, they can start to figure out which back-up parts are important and who will play the bass line, harmony, chops, and vocals.

3. For bonus points, students can pass around the melody and take turns backing each other up.

4. Groups can play their covers for each other, sharing what they learned and what they liked. Exceptional performances might be rewarded with a spot on the spring concert.

Improvisation is a skill that comes very naturally to some, and not so naturally for others. Students who don't have a lot of practice playing by ear will feel challenged, and students who hear well but read poorly will have an opportunity to shine. Improvisation is a different beast, but it doesn't have to be a scary one. We just have to think a little differently to create room for improvisation in our classically structured program.

Tonal Literacy and Creativity Goals and Sequenced Objectives

The strategies in this chapter address the following goals and student performance objectives. When creating your unit plan, use the list below to help you.

- Select the objectives introduced in previous years that need review.
- Identify the new objectives that you plan to introduce for the first time.
- Sequence the objectives you plan to teach in each course level.

Literacy Goal:

Students read and write standard notation and understand the relationships between the notes on the staff and the fingerboard.

Creativity Goal:

Students make musical, aesthetically sound choices to create original musical works, and arrangements and interpretations of the works of others.

Literacy and Creativity Objectives:

Novice:

- Complete a chromatic fingerboard map for all strings in first position using natural and sharp note names.
- Write and recognize the key signatures in the Level 1 method book and in concert music.
- Name the notes in the music at a tempo of one note per second.
- Recognize, write, and explain the differences between half steps and whole steps (major and minor seconds).
- Create and perform original interpretations of melodies from the book or another source.
- Listen and adapt the interpretations of other students to create your own interpretation.
- Create solos using the root, third, and fifth of a chord.
- Use traditional notation to write a simple familiar melody.

Intermediate:

- Complete a chromatic fingerboard map for all strings in first position using natural and flat note names. Review the sharp note names and define the term *enharmonic*.
- Explain how changes in key signatures affect the finger patterns on each string.
- Write an easy, familiar melody (*Mary Had a Little Lamb*, *Twinkle Twinkle*) in the keys of the method book exercises and concert music.
- Recognize and write major and minor thirds, and explain the differences between major and minor thirds in terms of major and minor seconds.
- Create solos using the root, third, and fifth of a chord over a two-chord progression.
- Write a melody that uses a formal structure, such as antecedent/consequent (*Mary Had a Little Lamb*) or ABA (*Twinkle Twinkle*).

Proficient:

- Complete a chromatic fingerboard map for all strings, from the open string up to the octave above the open string, including both sharp and flat note names for all notes that are not natural.
- Identify the scale degree of any note in the keys of the method book exercises and concert music.
- Recognize and write fourths and fifths, and describe them in terms of major and minor seconds and thirds.
- Explain and justify an interpretation of a performance.
- Create solos over a two-chord progression using the chord tones and the passing tones between the root, third, and fifth.
- Write compositions and arrangements for two or more instruments.

Accomplished:

- Recognize and write intervals larger than a fifth.
- Create interpretations that stay within the parameters of a style or aesthetic; for example, create an interpretation of a baroque, classical, or jazz melody without changing the style.
- Create solos over a three-chord progression using chord tones and the passing tones between the root, third, and fifth.
- Write compositions and arrangements for three or more instruments.

Advanced:

- Create solos using different scales over chord progressions.
- Write original structured compositions for four or more instruments.

FINAL THOUGHTS:

Creativity standards like composition, arranging, and improvisation can be challenging for classically trained musicians. Most of us have spent our lives practicing toward the goal of precision and flawless performance, and we teach the same way, working hard to get our orchestras to play every note in tune and every rhythm and bowing exactly right. We even tell students when to get louder, softer, how to shape their phrase, and how much vibrato to use. We can spend so much time teaching our orchestras to perform with synchronized precision that little time is left for developing individuality and creativity.

Creativity does not have to be at odds with performance. Quite the contrary, the creative process teaches students to bring greater expression, artistry, and understanding to their music. *Students want to be creative.* When taught correctly, creativity augments and energizes students about orchestra. And when students write music, they learn details about notation that they might otherwise ignore. By writing music, students become better readers, faster learners, and more well-rounded musicians.

Chapter 12

Concert Music and Ensemble Skills

A few years ago, I observed a young teacher slaving through a middle school orchestra rehearsal, pounding out notes and rhythms with her students. The class slogged along as each section of the ensemble learned their parts measure by measure, occasionally stopping altogether to practice a challenging skill. The faces and body language of the students and teacher revealed that this process was tedious and not enjoyable. This was orchestra, a *music* class, but I was not seeing or hearing musical expression, nor any of the joy that one hopes to get from making music.

As I watched, I recalled teaching orchestra the same way throughout much of my own career. I had believed the best way to inspire students was to give them challenging music and then spend weeks, even months, learning the notes and rhythms before the concert. There were many days that felt like I was working twice as hard as the students, teaching music as fast as I could, while they sat and waited to learn how the music was supposed to go. It was exhausting.

Looking back, I see now that I was making a number of common mistakes that led to unpolished concerts. When we ran out of rehearsal days before a concert, I would blame myself for not teaching better, and I would blame the students for not practicing enough. At the concerts, I would tell parents that the students were doing a "great job" given the challenges of such difficult music. And then after the concert, I would give the students a new challenging piece of music and do it all over again. As it turns out, there is a better way.

The recommendations in this chapter will make your rehearsals noticeably more enjoyable and musically rewarding, both for your students and for you. They may also improve your group's ensemble skills and the sound of your concerts more dramatically than anything mentioned in previous chapters.

IN THIS CHAPTER:

- Time to Teach Music
- The Goal and Objectives of the Concert Music Unit
- Seven Conducting Tips
- Teaching Ensemble
- Selecting Concert Music
- The Concert Performance

Time to Teach Music

The concert music unit is the most misunderstood unit that orchestra teachers teach, and this is unfortunate, because many orchestra directors teach nothing else. When we do not have an organized plan for teaching new performance skills during fundamentals time, we are left with no option but to try to teach new skills through our concert music. The inherent flaw with this plan is that most advanced string skills take longer to learn and polish than the eight to ten weeks that students typically have before a concert. Even if students got close to polishing the skills, we just spent eight weeks teaching and rehearsing new skills, and very little time teaching our students to *make music*.

Practicing notes, rhythms, and new skills is not making music. When we talk about the joys of musical expression or how fun it is to *make music*, we are talking about an experience that occurs *after* we have learned the notes and rhythms. When we sight-read, we are only making music after we have learned to read well enough to add musical style and interpretation to the notes and rhythms as we read.

Teaching students how to play notes and rhythms is not *making music*.

So how do we get students past the stage of learning notes and rhythms? How do we get through the mountain of string technique and literacy skills that our instruments require, and do it with music making still at the center of the class?

The answer is to use a separate time—*fundamentals time*—to teach and review new skills so concert music does not become the place where everything else must be learned.

Sequenced exercises and strategies for teaching skills in the proper order are the most effective method for teaching students how to:

- Play their instruments with good technique;
- Recognize and correctly perform new rhythm and pitch patterns; and
- Learn how to produce a good tone or perform new bowings and articulations.

Most music was written for the purpose of musical expression; artful music was not intended to be an efficient vehicle for teaching new performance skills. When we use concert music to teach technical skills, we never get to the higher-level ensemble skills—such as balancing and blending pitch and tone, matching rhythms, articulations, tempo, cueing, and breathing together. We also never get to the music-making skills—such as musical expression, shape, style, interpretation, emotion, and artistry. When we use fundamentals time to teach technical skills and we reserve rehearsal time for musical skills, we can teach both new skills *and* musical expression more effectively.

The Goal and Objectives of the Concert Music Unit

The goal of teaching concert music is not to teach students how to read and perform notes and rhythms, or how to play one's instrument "in tune" with a good tone and the right articulations. The goal of teaching concert music is to teach students how to perform all of these individualized skills *with other players to convey a clear musical idea, to make music TOGETHER with their instruments as an ENSEMBLE.*

The ensemble goal and objectives listed below should be taught to students of any age, beginners through advanced. Whether your orchestra is performing *Twinkle Twinkle* variations or a Tchaikovsky symphony, your goal as an ensemble is to agree on every musical element so the musical ideas that the audience hears from the ensemble are convincing and crystal clear. Students must agree on more than tempo, pitch, and rhythm; they must also agree on tone, style, dynamics, and phrasing. When students do not agree on the basic elements of music, the performance is marred by inconsistency and disagreement, and the resulting lack of clarity and focus obscures the musical message and ideas that the composer intended to convey.

Goal:

Students express clear musical ideas and styles
as an ensemble through the performance of orchestral music.

Ensemble Objectives:

Students must make the necessary adjustments in their individual performance to:

- Breathe, move, cue, and *perform together in synchrony* with other musicians.
- Perform accurate *rhythms* together within a synchronized *pulse* and a musically convincing *tempo.*
- Use the same bow weight, speed, and contact point as the other members of the section to create a well-blended ensemble *tone* and *timbre.*
- Finely tune one's own notes to be in tune with other musicians.

- Perform the same *bowings, articulations, and styles* in the same part of the bow as other members of one's section.
- Use a *volume* that blends with the section, that balances the importance of one's own part with respect to the parts of other sections of the ensemble, and that agrees with other players through the peaks, valleys, and points in between of all *dynamics* and *phrasing.*
- Convey clear and musically expressive ideas that go beyond the notes on the page; these musical concepts include character, style, interpretation, beauty, intensity, mood, and emotion.

In this section, students are taught how to apply the skills they learned as individuals and perform them together to convey clear and musically expressive ideas. They are taught how to:

- Pay attention to each other to play in the same part of the bow;
- Match their articulations and blend their tone;
- Listen and tune their notes to each other;
- Balance their respective volumes;
- Peak at the same time in their phrasing; and
- Agree on the musical characters, styles, interpretations, and moods that the music should convey.

In short, the rehearsal part of class is the time we devote to teaching students how to bring all of their individual skills together to make music as an *ensemble*—which, after all, is French for *together.*

Each of the individual performance skills that were previously learned during fundamentals time has a parallel ensemble objective. In the section below, we compare the individual performance objectives to their corresponding ensemble objectives to better understand the differences between the objectives we teach during fundamentals time and the musical rehearsal.

Technique:

In professional ensembles, a performer's technique is largely a personal issue. We don't usually comment about another player's technique as long as they are performing the music well. In teaching school orchestra, there is an ensemble element to technique that we can use to our advantage. During fundamentals time, the objective is to teach students to use a comfortable, healthy technique with the right combination of balance, breath, and movement that provides the best physical opportunity to perform the desired musical ideas.

In an ensemble, our technical objective is to breathe, move, and manipulate our instruments together in synchrony.

Cuing, breathing together, moving together is an integral part of a good ensemble. We can also use the ensemble to remind students what they learned during fundamentals time. Ask questions like:

- Is your stand partner's bow angle correct? Is the thumb squeezing?
- Are you breathing together before beginning that phrase?
- How are you going to cue that entrance?

Playing a string instrument is technique in motion. Cuing, breathing, and moving together is good ensemble, and as an ensemble, students can work *together* on their technique as well.

Tone:

Young teachers frequently misunderstand the goal of blending student tone within an ensemble. They try so hard to get students to play with a strong, full tone that blending seems counter-intuitive. After teaching individual students to produce a strong tone that projects well, we must also teach them how to blend because a well-blended ensemble tone resonates in a way that mismatched timbres do not.

During fundamentals time, we teach individual students how to correctly use bow weight, speed, and contact point to produce a characteristic string tone that projects well.

The ensemble tone objective is to teach students to use the same bow weight, speed, and contact point as the other members of their section to create a beautiful, characteristic tone that blends well with the section.

To do this, students must learn to pay attention and compare how their bow use is similar or different to other members of their section. We can help students pay attention to their ensemble tone by asking questions like:

- What kind of tone would be appropriate for this type of music? Airy, thick, scratchy, thin?
- How much bow is your stand partner using?
- Is your bow speed the same as your section leader?
- Are you digging into the string as much as your stand partner?
- Can you make your tone blend and disappear into your section's tone?
- What is the desired timbre, and how close to the bridge will you need to play?
- Describe the tone your section leader is producing. What are you doing with your bow to match and blend with your stand partner and section leader?

Use tuning canons, chords, and chorales to teach students to match bow speed, weight, and contact point, and produce volumes and timbres that blend well together. Blending can also be achieved with scales, arpeggios, and shorter note values. Also use bowing variations and one-octave scales to teach students to blend eighth notes and sixteenth notes.

Before teaching students how to blend with the entire ensemble, begin by teaching them to blend with their stand partner. Pair students up; give one student the task of playing with a good tone and the other student the job of blending with the first student. Teach students to "hide" their sound inside of the other player's sound: "See if you can make your sound disappear in their sound and then reappear." Start with the long tones, but also teach students to blend staccato, even spiccato, bow strokes. Once students learn to blend with their stand partner, similar strategies can be used to teach students to blend with their section.

Finally, for the entire ensemble to blend, we must pay attention to "balance," and so must our students. Ensembles are well balanced and sound best when the upper strings blend with the lower strings. This can be difficult in school programs where instrumentation is frequently heavy on violins. We must do our best to correct lopsided balance by having violin students make their tone blend in with the cello section. First violins must blend with the second violins, too. Young teachers often tell second violins to try and sound like the first violins, when in reality it is the job of the first violins to blend with the second violins.

Articulation:

During fundamentals time, we use open strings, bowing variations, and other exercises to teach students different types of attacks and releases in different parts of the bow. We teach students to develop a variety of articulations and bowing styles (like staccato, legato, spiccato, portato, slurs, slurred staccato, saltando, and more).

When performing music as an ensemble, the objective is to teach students within a section to perform the same bowings, articulations, and styles in the same part of the bow.

Students will learn to become aware of the part of the bow and the articulations their neighbor is using, and to make adjustments as needed to be in the same part of the bow and to use the same bow style.

Articulation may be the easiest category for introducing and teaching ensemble skills because bow use is so easy to see. The quickest way to fix articulation problems is to look up from the score and see if everyone is in the same part of the bow. We must pay more attention to our ensemble if we are to expect our students to pay more attention to each other.

Good ensemble articulation questions include:

- Did your section leader start up or down-bow? Where in the bow did your section leader start that note, and where did she release the note?
- What part of the bow is your stand partner using to play those sixteenth notes? You don't know? Why not?
- Violas, are the cellos playing those eighth notes on or off the string?
- Listen to the spiccato in the violas and then the second violins. Are their articulations the same or different? Which one do you like more, and why?
- Seconds, you have the same rhythm as the first violins. Why is your bowing different? Can you fix it without my help?

When teaching articulation skills during fundamentals time, encourage students to perform articulation warm-ups without music so they can look at the leader and use the same stroke and part of the bow. When the bowing styles are performed in the same parts of the bow, the articulation and style produced by the ensemble as a whole will be much more clear, clean, and well-defined.

Rhythm:

As individuals, students learn to read and perform rhythms correctly while keeping a consistent pulse. In an ensemble, students must listen and adjust to each other and agree on one pulse so all parts of the music can fit rhythmically together.

The ensemble objective for rhythm is to teach students to make the necessary adjustments to perform accurate rhythms together within a common pulse and a musically convincing tempo.

Most rhythm problems occur when students have not been counting and do not know when to come in after a long note or rest. An orchestra's sense of "ensemble" improves dramatically when students count together. It also improves when students learn to listen to other sections during their long notes and rests. Here are a few sample questions that would help ensemble rhythm:

- How are you counting that measure and a half of rest?
- Cellos, who are you listening to during your rest, and who are you coming in with after your rest?
- First violins, who is playing consistent sixteenth notes during your melody? Why is that important information to know?
- In which measures do we tend to rush? Where do we tend to drag? Why?
- The first and second violins have the same rhythm. Why aren't you together, and how are you going to correct the problem?

When students pay attention to the ensemble articulations, the rhythm of the group should also improve. While students are paying close attention to make sure their attacks and releases are in the same part of the bow, they will naturally and simultaneously make a similar effort to execute all of their attacks and releases *at the same time*.

As we mentioned in Chapter 9, students can inadvertently change their tempo when they change rhythms, bow strokes, and dynamics. Tempo problems are especially common in classical works (like Mozart divertimenti), which require articulation changes (on then off the string), going from eighth notes to sixteenth notes and back again, and sudden changes in dynamics. Using a metronome, practice transitioning from one bowing/rhythm/dynamic to another to improve tempo consistency between the sections of the orchestra.

Intonation:

When we are playing our instrument alone, we aim for our strings to be in tune with each other and our fingers to be in tune with our strings. In an ensemble, playing in tune means students are playing in tune *with each other*. When they tune their strings as an ensemble, they must tune and cross-tune together to make sure their unisons, octaves, and fifths agree. When they play music together, students must listen to each other's notes and tune to each other's unisons, octaves, fifths, fourths, and thirds the same way.

In an ensemble, the intonation objective is to teach students to make the necessary adjustments to finely tune their own notes to be in tune with other musicians.

What questions can we ask to help students learn to listen and adjust?

- Your F-natural is not correct. Can you tune it to your stand partner's F?
- Violas, your C-sharp is not in tune with the cellos' A. How are you going to tune your note to theirs?
- You are tuning very loudly. Can you hear the tuning note?
- Are you in tune with your stand partner, with your section, with the other sections of the orchestra?
- To whom are you listening, and to whom are you tuning that note?

In Chapter 8, we looked at strategies for tuning chords with tuning canons, tuning chords, and chorales. To improve intonation within fast-moving concert music, slow down the group significantly (half speed or even slower) so every note can be heard, performed in tune, and blended together. Instruct students to use a good *mezzo piano* tuning tone so everyone can hear themselves *and* each other.

Then, after the ensemble can play the excerpt slowly with blended pitches, gradually increase the tempo. Aim for continued blending even for fast notes. Pay attention to problem notes, typically the fourth and seventh scale degrees. If students' fingers are still not landing in the correct place, use the strategies in Chapter 8 to improve finger patterns, velocity, and moving from one pattern to the next. If you do not have time to do all of this to get your notes in tune, then the music you selected is too difficult.

Sometimes students sound out of tune because of an ensemble problem with tone and blending. At the 2009 National Orchestra Festival, Dr. Robert Gillespie worked with my chamber orchestra after their performance. I had two all-state bass players who were both extremely skilled, but I could not get them to play in tune with each other, even after working with them for years. Dr. Gillespie quickly picked up on the two hotshot bass players who could not agree on pitch; he immediately asked them to play a little softer, listen to each other's tone, and blend their tone. The pitch problem disappeared immediately, and Dr. Gillespie said rather matter of factly, "And that is how you fix that."

Dynamics, Balance, and Phrasing:

Soloists use contrasts in volume to convey a musical idea by accentuating different aspects of the melody and phrasing a melodic line. For phrasing and expressive dynamics to be clearly heard in an ensemble, performers must agree on the following objective:

In an ensemble, the objective is to perform the same dynamics through the peaks and valleys of their phrasing, to use a volume that blends within their own section, and to agree upon the volume that balances the importance of their own section's part with respect to the parts of other sections of the ensemble.

Use some of the following questions to help students agree upon their dynamics and phrasing:

- Where is the top of the phrase, and how loud should your section be there?
- Where is the bottom of the phrase? Is the change sudden or gradual?
- Who has the melody? How important is your part in that measure?
- How would you sing that phrase?
- Did you taper the cadence at the end of that phrase, or did you accent it? Why?
- When the phrase repeats, should we play it louder or softer? Where are we going with that?

Chorales offer an excellent opportunity to teach students that artful music is always doing one of three things:

- **Building** – leading up to the top of the phrase
- **Arriving** – fulfilling the top of the phrase
- **Relaxing** – gradually releasing and resolving the energy

Phrasing is initially learned by first exaggerating the dynamics and then allowing them to ebb and flow naturally. Chorales can be used to teach students to use more weight at the tip, make smooth bow changes, and avoid unintended decrescendos or accents.

Musical Expression:

What are the musical concepts that transcend the notes and rhythms on the page? What are the ideas, character, and emotions that the composer was trying to convey?

Our ultimate goal is to teach students about musical self-expression. Music gives us an opportunity to move beyond the rehearsal vocabulary of "shorter-longer, louder-softer, faster-slower" to more musical terms and descriptions designed to elicit a musical response. After all, music is a form of musical communication, a language in and of itself.

- Use "mood" words to establish emotion, intensity, style, and character.
- Tell a musical story. Assign different words to entire musical phrases to help convey variety in each phrase's meaning and purpose.
- Give purpose to phrase beginnings and endings. Encourage students to "breathe" in between phrases so the musical ideas do not run mindlessly together.
- If a line is repeated, perform it differently the second time. Determine the direction of the music and use the repeated line to take the music in that direction.
- Find tension and release points. Discuss dissonance and resolution, suspensions, and tapering a cadence.
- Listen to the way notes begin and the way they enter into sound from silence. Listen also to the way they end and return from sound back into silence.

Chorales can be used anytime to teach all musical components, including tone, intonation, phrasing, and musicianship. Teaching these components in a concentrated chorale setting will help students improve these components and develop a musical understanding that will transfer naturally to the concert music.

Seven Conducting Tips

I taught three levels of middle school orchestra as I earned my conducting degrees, and during that time I learned that public school students were very capable of following a conductor. The list below is four years of graduate conducting condensed neatly into seven bullet points— my conducting teacher believed in small gestures, so I know he would be proud.

1. Stop counting off. Just raise your baton, wait for the students to put their instruments up, and cue students in with a "click, prep, play."

2. Keep your conducting pattern simple. Make small, clear beats with a firm wrist, and eliminate all loops, jerks, and hitches between the beats.

3. With your left hand, conduct musical lines, not beats. Don't let the left hand mirror the right.

4. Teach your students to follow you by regularly changing gestures and tempos. The more you are the same, the less relevant you become.

5. Lead and expect students to follow your tempo; don't follow the orchestra. The conductor is the driver, not a passenger.

6. If your students don't understand a gesture (such as a crescendo), teach them what it looks like and then have them practice following and performing it. This includes your gesture for "stop playing."

7. Record yourself with a video camera and then watch the video. If you don't like what you see, consider your students who have to watch your conducting every day. Work on your technique, record yourself again, and you will improve quickly!

Public school orchestra teachers work very hard to polish their group's performance by practicing concert music over and over the same way to get it "right." When we conduct a piece the same way, day after day, students stop paying attention to us, and eventually their ability to follow us will atrophy. Repetition also teaches students to be inflexible. When we do the same thing, day in and day out, students learn only one way, and they become easily confused if you try to change course or do something different.

One of music's most powerful and interesting attributes is the variety of ways we can interpret a single phrase. We can enjoy music even more when we create different interpretations, and we can teach students to stay aware and flexible by doing things a little differently every day. Change it up; the variety will keep rehearsal more interesting for everyone, and with a little practice, students will learn to follow you.

Teaching Ensemble

How do we teach students to:

- Count for themselves?
- Pay more attention and listen to each other better?
- Be in the same part of the bow as their section leader?
- Become better leaders and take greater ownership in their orchestra?

The answer to all of these questions may well be to stop conducting.

Rehearsing and performing without a conductor is more than a gimmick or performance trick for dazzling audiences. It may be one of the most effective tools in your arsenal for teaching students to listen, watch, move, and breathe together.

Lower the conductor's podium or remove it altogether. Have the violin and viola students stand up so they can see each other and their section leader and concertmaster. Then, instruct the group from outside of the ensemble and teach them to cue, breathe, and move together like they would if they were playing in a string quintet. Students will begin to take more ownership and feel more responsible for correcting notes and bowings. It's a little like giving them the keys to the car; you are still in the car teaching, but they are in charge of driving.

An additional benefit of not conducting is that it is easier to focus completely on the ensemble, which is where the focus should be anyway. Teachers see more, hear more, and teach more when they are not staring at the score and thinking about their own gestures and cues.

Silent Simon Says:

When first teaching students how to watch, cue, move, and breathe together, play "Silent Simon Says."

1. Stand in front of the group and hold a violin in playing position.

2. Then raise the scroll while you inhale, and expect all of the violins and violas to mirror exactly what you do. Cello and bass students can also gently lift their heads and inhale together.

3. Practice breathing and cueing at different tempos, and then add the bow.

4. Without making any sound, put the bow at the frog, then middle, then tip, and expect students to put their bows in exactly the same place.

The beauty of "Silent Simon Says" is that no one "says" anything. It teaches students to communicate without speaking and to pay attention to the leader, the people around them, and what part of the bow they need to have on the string.

After students master the silent game, do a similar exercise with sound.

1. Cue and play an open D.

2. Instruct students to mirror you, raising their scrolls, setting their bows, inhaling, and playing a D. Students should reach the ends of the bow at the same time as you do. Slowly accelerate or decelerate the bow speed, and challenge students to follow different tempos.

3. Next, teach students to lead. Demonstrate cues with an instrument from the podium several times, and then have students try it.

It requires a little practice, but they'll catch on quickly. Some students have more natural ability than others, and it's important in a chamber orchestra to place students who are comfortable with leading the group in front of the sections. When cuing entrances, students must learn to cue in tempo, which leads to a natural discussion about how fast the music should go and how the students are going to start together.

Teaching Students to Move:

When leaders cue their section, all other students in the section should *reflect this cue*, moving just like the leader. This promotes awareness and movement from all players. When using full bows, have students move side to side. Encourage them to move with the music. Some students may be a little stiff or reluctant to move, but movement helps the body relax. By watching videos of great student and professional orchestras who move, students will learn that great symphony orchestras move because moving helps them stay together and perform better. Movement can bring more joy to the audience, too, because it is much more enjoyable to watch relaxed, expressively moving students than it is to watch a bunch of statues.

To see and move better together, students should lower their stands enough to see each other's faces. When they are paying attention to the people around them, begin to ask questions like:

- What part of the bow is your section leader using? Are you in the same part of the bow?
- Second violins, do the firsts have the same rhythm as you? Why are you using a different bowing?
- Who has the melody at letter C? So what adjustments do you need to make?

Using questions promotes student buy-in and gets students thinking deeply about what they are doing. The classroom discussion that comes out of chamber orchestra rehearsal is much more rich than the traditional procedure of a conductor barking orders and students silently obeying.

Of course, a conductor becomes more necessary in larger ensembles, and everyone sits to better see the conductor. The late Michael Allen was a strong believer in teaching even larger student orchestras to move. Watching him work with one of my orchestras at a festival in New York, I learned that students can still move in their seats, reflecting the cues of their section leaders and moving together as they play, just like they would if they had no conductor. When students over-rely on us and stop paying attention to the ensemble, we can step off of the podium and ask them to play without us to help them refocus their attention on the ensemble.

The image below teaches students that orchestra (and life) is about paying attention to more than one's self.

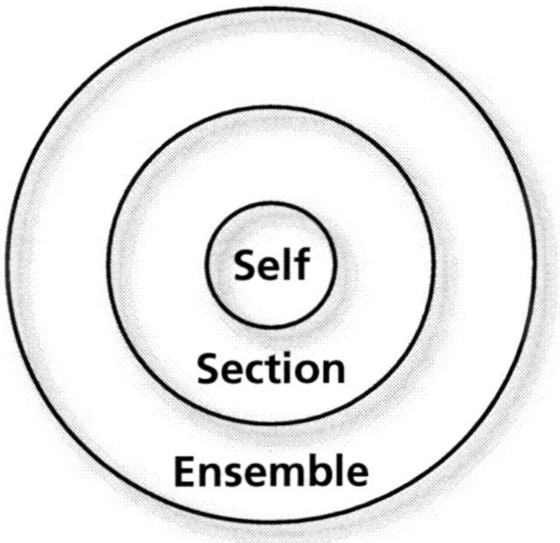

Ask students:

- Who do you include in your circle of attention?
- How many people can you really see in your section?
- To whom should you pay the most attention?
- Can you include the whole ensemble?

The non-musical lessons that students can learn in an ensemble are just as important as the musical skills. Teaching ensemble fosters greater ownership, leadership, and awareness of each other, and all of these qualities promote learning, mutual respect, citizenship, and positive morale. When the students know their music moderately well, have them play the Smiling Game:

- "While you are playing your part, look around, find someone to look at who is looking at you, and smile at them, and see if they smile back at you."

The smiles start bouncing all over the classroom, and laughter and joy immediately follow. We teach so many things through the development of our ensemble, but maybe the most important of all is teaching our students to share in the fun of making music together.

Section Leader Problems:

Strong section leaders can be very helpful in rehearsals and performances, but if we are not careful, we can easily over-rely on section leaders in a way that can be detrimental to the group. Some leaders will try to play *for* their section by playing louder than everyone else in an effort to get their section to "follow" them. Some will lead by playing way in front of the beat, jumping in early before the rest of their section. Or some will take it upon themselves to slow down and play behind the beat if they perceive the group to be rushing.

Leaders must learn that being a good role model doesn't mean playing *for* the section. A leader's job is to model and be the first to perform what everyone else is supposed to do. In the end, every student, including the leader, must learn to blend, and the students in the section must learn to play with a strong tone and to count and sight-read for themselves.

Selecting Concert Music

The task of selecting the right music for our ensembles is one of the most important things we do—and one of the most difficult. Our first impulse is to select the music that we love, possibly titles that made us want to become music teachers. We want to share with our students the music that inspired us when we were young. While it's very important to select music that speaks to us, good teachers select music that is appropriate for the students' musical development.

Our second impulse is to select music that we think our students will like, but trying to predict what students will like is a slippery endeavor. Instead, it's better to trust your professional instinct and experience, and if you need recommendations for selecting appropriate music, ask a colleague whom you trust.

Selecting Music of the Correct Difficulty Level:

The difficulty level of the music will largely determine how polished the performance will be, how much music your students will make, and how much enjoyment the students will get from the experience. There is so much riding on this decision that the next few paragraphs may be the most important paragraphs in this entire book. Over and over, teachers make the same mistakes when selecting their concert music, and they do so completely unaware of how damaging their mistakes are.

One of the most common and detrimental mistakes orchestra teachers make is programming music that is too difficult for their students.

Of course, we want to challenge our students to learn and grow, and we want to challenge ourselves, too. But choosing difficult music is not a good way to challenge our students, technically *or musically*.

Challenge your students by giving them tough exercises and etudes; use fundamentals time to build their technical skills and stretch their limits. New finger patterns, positions, rhythms, or bow strokes can all be taught more efficiently with exercises designed specifically to develop these skills. Etudes and exercises save time that can then be allocated toward teaching great music—and making great music with repertoire that the students already have the technical skills to play well.

When we select concert music with newer skills that students do not solidly have under their fingers, we are choosing to devote more of our concert music rehearsal time to learning notes, rhythms, and skills, and less of that time to learning how to make music. Since concert music is not designed or written for the purpose of skill development, we must address these new skills as they come up in the music, one section of the orchestra at a time, while the rest of the orchestra sits and waits. These skills are not in a pedagogical sequence, so we must also fill in holes and supply ad hoc exercises to teach each new skill, which slows down progress even more. Music that is too difficult slows the progress of the class, and sometimes the rehearsal grinds to a halt while the students in one section learn a measure or two. The slow pace begins to bore the advanced students who we intended to challenge. In an effort to keep students interested and get them prepared by concert time, we race to teach the disorganized skills as fast as we can, while telling the less-skilled students—those who may not have private teachers and who most need good pedagogical classroom instruction—to practice more.

When we spend too much time inefficiently teaching randomly sequenced skills, we are not spending enough time teaching the students how to *make music—which was the main reason we took this job AND the reason they signed up for the class*. This mistake sets students up for an unpolished performance at the concert, which is not only artistically unrewarding for everyone involved but also an embarrassment that can lead to teacher frustration, lower group morale, and higher attrition.

Teachers make the mistake of selecting music with difficult technical skills with good intentions of wanting to challenge their students, but they are failing to take into account the skills or rehearsal time required to perform their repertoire *musically*. They forget, ignore, or significantly underestimate how much time it will take to teach all of the end-game skills (such as blending pitch and tone; agreeing on tempo, balance and phrasing; matching rhythms, articulations, attacks, and releases; watching, cueing, and breathing together; and most importantly, conveying clear and musically expressive ideas).

When selecting music, we must remember the concert music goals and objectives listed earlier and ask ourselves, "Will this piece require students to spend more time on notes and rhythms than they will spend on ensemble and musical objectives?"

What is the most important thing to look for when selecting music? The answer may well be the one musical element we cannot see: *TONE*. If we want students to sound good at the concert, then we need to consider if they have the skills to play the music with good tone. We cannot look at music difficulty in terms of notes and rhythms, because when we do, we tend to forget about tone. Without good tone, students cannot finely tune their notes, or play with clean articulations, or focus on the other ensemble objectives. If we do not put tone first when selecting concert music, then we set up our students for a bad-sounding performance.

So how do you know if the music is too hard?

If you have to teach the notes and rhythms measure by measure, then the music you picked is too hard.

When you first hand out a piece of concert music, the students should be able to roughly read through the piece. If, after one rehearsal, the students cannot hack through a piece of music, collect all the parts and try a different piece. Also look for works that are relatively consistent in their level of difficulty. Consider the size and relative strength of each section of your orchestra, and look for music that is a good match.

If you are going to make mistakes in your music selection, it is best to err on the side of picking music that is too easy. "Easy" music gives us the opportunity to expect our students to perform with better technique, beautiful tone, finely tuned chords, and gorgeous phrasing. That's not such a bad mistake at all—not nearly as bad as the alternative.

Looking for High-Quality Music:

Many great works have been written for orchestra over the past 300 years, but not every piece that gets put to print is a great piece of music. In fact, there are quite a few duds out there as well. Whether you are a new teacher or a veteran looking for new material, the best way to learn about good-quality concert music for your orchestra is to seek out great teachers who teach the same level of orchestra as your own and ask them for a list of their favorite teaching pieces. Ask them what they are taking to concert festival; go and listen to groups at concert festival; and write down the titles used by teachers you trust and admire. Listen to the new release CDs that publishers send out, or go to publishers' websites and listen to recordings of the pieces they are selling. It is critical that you also look at the score to see the keys, finger patterns, and shifting the piece may require. Sometimes, I will buy the score first to make sure the piece is a good fit for my group before I purchase parts. I also make time every year to visit the music distributer booths at the state or national conferences. With my phone, I take pictures of the title pages of scores that look promising, and when I get back home, I listen to recordings and purchase the best music online.

Music Appropriateness:

Not all music is appropriate for every occasion. Good teachers consider their audience and the time of year when selecting music.

- Are you performing for parents only, or also for adjudicators?
- Is this music for a holiday concert, spring concert, or graduation ceremony?

All of these factors go into making the right decisions about music selection.

For many teachers, the winter concert is the first big concert of the year. The appropriateness of religious music in the string curriculum is a tricky issue, partly because opinions, local customs, and cultural norms vary widely from principal to principal, and from region to region. In the south, for example, Christmas music is not only permitted in December, but it is almost expected by parents and even some administrators. Further north and west, however, teachers use much more caution when programing religious music, and they often avoid it altogether. Since it is a grey area, ask your principal what is appropriate for your school. If you decide to do a unit on holiday music, make sure to study the holiday music from a variety of religions and cultures.

For adjudicated performances, one expects to hear orchestral arrangements or original works from baroque to twenty-first century "classical" styles. Recently, folk and jazz fiddle have become more serious in nature and arguably more acceptable at concert festival. While the range of what is considered acceptable at adjudicated festivals may be growing, most would agree that we expect to hear music that is written "for music's sake," which does not typically include novelty, patriotic, or religious music written for movies, TV shows, or religious holidays.

The last concert of the year is a good time for finale-style productions and for doing something fun and different. The spring concert is a good time to be thinking "outside of the Bach's." Movie themes, Broadway music, festive orchestral works are all appropriate at the end of the year. Look for string works that incorporate jazz or rock influences in a way that is both authentic for string playing and convincingly musical. Encourage students to find or create their own works, such as the creativity projects discussed in the previous chapter; have the class vote on the best student creations to perform at the spring concert.

Finally, it is the teacher who determines *what music* the students will play at the concert, and also *how polished* the music will be at the concert. When selecting music, carefully consider the skills your students have and the types of concerts they are going to perform, and then write down some titles of enjoyable and educationally valuable pieces of music. If your list looks easy, you probably listed repertoire correctly. Of course, you will want your students to be able to play harder music, too, and over time, they will. Use these challenging works to inspire you to plan and teach during fundamentals time the skills students will need to play more advanced literature well.

The Concert Performance

- Are your students happy when they play?
- Are they moving to the music they are making?
- How many people are in the audience and what is the intensity of the applause?

The answers to these questions are important. We spend months preparing for concerts, so not only do we want the audience to be impressed, but we also want our students to leave telling their parents how great the performance was and how much fun they have in orchestra. We want our school concerts to be more than a seasonal event where the parents and siblings of our students come together and politely listen to sounds that only a mother could love. We want our students to make music, and we want the audience to truly enjoy the musicianship of the performance.

The concert performance is the parents' window into our classroom. Parents form their opinions about us and our professionalism by the way we present a concert, how well the students perform, and how good the students feel about the performance. Concerts require a lot of work and planning, and if we are not careful, we can be so tired and stressed by the time we get to the concert that we are not at our best when we are most visible to the public. This is why it is important to think ahead and plan how we want our concerts to look and flow. The best concerts are for a packed house that leaps to its feet and cheers after hearing a crowd pleaser. What can you do to make that happen at every concert? Create your vision of the ultimate concert, and start planning for that dream to become a reality.

You and your students put months into learning a concert program; how many times will they perform that program? The more they perform, the better they get at performing. Could your students perform each program once for the school, once for the parents, and once out in the community? Perform for the students and parents of the schools that feed your program. Make a yearly trip every December to perform at a local retirement community, or at the mall, or at an arts festival. Ask yourself, "Where can my students perform?" If you live near a professional orchestra, maybe your students could play in the foyer before going in to hear a symphony concert.

Much of my extended family lives in the wonderful town of Maysville, Kentucky. During a recent visit, I was walking downtown when I came upon the Maysville auditorium. On the marquis, I noticed that the high school orchestra and chorus had an entire concert series there in the town auditorium—from classical concerts, to holiday concerts, to productions of the school musical and guest performances with Mark Wood. If you don't live near a professional orchestra, make your orchestra part of the arts center of your town. Why not? How many small towns in our great country have no orchestra at the center of it? Together, we can change that!

FINAL THOUGHTS:
ON BEING A MEMBER OF AN ENSEMBLE

At the Midwest Clinic in Chicago, I once saw a group of 50 string students rehearse Tchaikovsky's *Serenade for Strings* with a great conductor. Within about two minutes, I realized that this ensemble was better than my orchestra—but not for the reasons you might think. As soon as the conductor stopped, no one played an extra note—*no one*—because everyone was paying attention—*everyone*. Time after time, I heard the students start together, end together, attack and cut off together, breathe together. But there was one more thing, probably the most important thing: They all seemed to share the same purpose of making music together, and this one thing governed everything else they did perfectly together.

Teaching students to be an *ensemble* includes teaching them to agree on the purpose of making music *together*. It includes teaching them to start and end *together*, and do their level best, *together*. What impact does one person who is not paying attention have on the rest of the ensemble? In an ensemble, one person can impair the group's overall progress and performance.

I make a point to say to my students, "Are you ready to show up and be a member of this ensemble, united with us in mind and purpose? Are you willing to start with us, end with us, and do your level best to make great music together with us during our limited time together? If you want to be part of this great ensemble, then I welcome your presence, your commitment, and your effort. We are so very fortunate to be able to participate in something as enriching as making music together. Show me what your best attention and effort is for the next 45 minutes, and we will learn together, perform together, be present and purposeful together, with every minute of the next small part of our precious lives that we are going to spend together. So, join me, join us, and let us make music, *together*."

Chapter 13

So What's the Plan?

Our lives would be a little easier if someone just told us what our students should learn by the end of each year. The reality is that there are simply too many variables in string education for a universal curriculum document to work well. Some classes are full of students with a strong family foundation; others are full of students who have immense challenges at home. Some classes meet every day for 50 minutes; others meet only 35 minutes a week. Some teachers have more financial and administrative support than others; some are simply more skilled than others, or they work harder, or both. All of these different factors help determine how much students learn. A curriculum that is designed for one program may not work at all for another.

Instead of identifying minimums to describe how far teachers *should* get in their different levels of orchestra, this resource was written to help you identify what *your* students need and what is appropriate for *your* specific program. Each of the previous unit chapters lists skills, goals, and objectives to help teachers assess what students know and what they need to learn next. In this chapter, we organize all of the objectives, assessments, and teaching strategies into understandable and teachable units, outlining how to incorporate these units into a long-range plan that is meaningful for you and your students. The planning that you do up front makes your job easier and more enjoyable in the long run, and it also makes your teaching more efficient and effective for your students.

IN THIS CHAPTER:

- There Is a Reason We Struggle with Planning
- What's the Objective?
- Organizing Your Teaching into Units
- Orchestra Units Are Different
- Selecting Unit Objectives for Your Program
- The Importance of Reviewing Previously Introduced Skills

- Assessment
- Selecting Material for Teaching the Objectives
- The Unit Timeline
- Teaching Strategies
- A Few Words About Standards
- Unit Format
- Finalizing Your Long-Range Plan

There Is a Reason We Struggle with Planning

Before you get in the car and start driving, it's a good idea to know where you are going. Once you have established your destination, the next step is to have directions for getting there. Before we start teaching objectives in class, it's a good idea to know where we want the class to be by the end of the year. After we have established our goals, the next step is to organize the student objectives in a pedagogical sequence for achieving those goals. This sounds easy, but it is not.

Can you answer these three questions for yourself and your students?

- What do I expect my students to learn by the end of the year?
- What is my pedagogical plan for reaching our end-of-year goals?
- How does my lesson plan for today help students reach our end-of-year goals?

You would think the answers to these questions would be basic knowledge for every string educator, but the reality is that these are some of the hardest questions we have to answer. Why is it so difficult? Part of the reason is the sheer number of skills we are responsible for teaching.

Long-range and daily planning is harder for orchestra teachers than it is for most academic teachers. In math, for example, the teacher is responsible for teaching every student in the class the same skill. String teachers are responsible for simultaneously teaching a new notational language and different skill sets to violin, viola, cello, and bass students—and that's if they are all reading the same music. Orchestra students are often performing different parts, making the number of different skills that students are performing in front of us increase exponentially—and that's just for one class. Unlike the typical math teacher who may teach the same material several times a day, we often must plan for multiple levels of orchestra (or other classes like general music and guitar), and that's before we begin planning our fundraisers and field trips. Our job is extremely demanding, even for veteran teachers.

You may already be so busy right now that you are saying to yourself, "I can't do any more!" The prospect of writing a long-range plan can stir up feelings of anxiety, especially if you are reading this chapter three weeks before concert festival. If you are in the middle of your busy year of teaching, keep reading this chapter, but don't try to organize your material until you find a better time.

Most of us do our deepest thinking and planning during the summer. Also, a long-range plan is an evolving document, so don't try to write the perfect long-range plan in one sitting, or even in one summer. Just start writing your ideas down, and keep documenting, reflecting, and improving what you do. If you start to feel overwhelmed, take a breather. The better you organize what you do, the better your teaching will be.

What's the Objective?

Naturally, students learn best when they understand what they are expected to learn. They are also more motivated to learn new concepts and skills when they understand *why* they are learning them. Students want to know what is going to be on the test and why they need to learn it. This is why administrators expect teachers across all disciplines to articulate the learning objectives of the day's lesson and explain the lesson's relevance within the scope of the class, and possibly even the student's life as a whole.

As music teachers, that is what we are *supposed* to do, but we don't do this very well, if we do it at all. Instead of explaining what students are expected to learn, we tend to go over the day's agenda, telling the students what they are going to do. "Today, we are going to do this scale, then we will practice these exercises, and finally, we will rehearse this piece." But telling students what they are going to *do* or *rehearse* is not the same thing as explaining what they are expected to *learn*.

When we are clear about what we expect students to learn, we do a much better job of targeting efficient teaching strategies, selecting appropriate learning materials, and developing assessments to measure student mastery. When students have a better understanding of what they are expected to learn, they practice more efficiently and make faster progress.

Students are more motivated to learn a lesson when we explain *why* they need to learn it. Most students sign up for orchestra because they are hungry to make music on string instruments. An important part of our job is to inspire students and keep them hungry for music. Remind students why orchestra is great fun, and then show them the skills they need to learn next. Remember to explain the relevance of learning new skills, and encourage students to ask why. If you can't explain why students need to learn a new skill, then maybe they shouldn't have to learn it.

All of this sounds easy, but identifying clear learning objectives in orchestra is more difficult than it sounds. Before you can tell your students what they are expected to learn next, much less why, you must have an idea about what the students already know and how that fits into the sequence of all that they need to learn. In a nutshell:

You cannot figure out today's objective or how it fits within your long-range plan until you have a clear long-range plan.

If we don't have a useful long-range plan, then we resort to faithfully following the exercises in the method book. Or if we teach older students, we select a piece of music that is in the ballpark of what we think the students should be learning, and then we try to teach the skills as they come up in the music. We teach without a long-range plan because we haven't figured out a better way—but there is a better way.

Organizing Your Teaching into Units

This chapter was written to help you create a useful long-range plan that is individually tailored to meet the specific needs of your program. Our aim is to help you organize all of your lessons, materials, and strategies into one plan so you can refer to it, improve it, and share it with your administrators and colleagues. The previous eight chapters are organized into the skill-centered units listed below:

1. Instrument position
2. Left-hand skills (including position, vibrato, and shifting)
3. Right-hand position
4. Tone and articulation
5. Intonation
6. Pulse, rhythms, and rhythmic literacy
7. Tonal literacy and creativity
8. Ensemble skills and concert music

Your unit plans will make up the heart of your long-range plan. They are towers of content, each with their own distinct set of skills, objectives, assessments, sequences, and materials.

The names of your units and how you organize your material will depend on you and your program. For beginning string classes, you will likely want to keep instrument and left/right-hand positions divided into separate units, the way they are listed above. For more advanced students, you might prefer to combine instrument and hand position into one larger review unit. Or you might prefer to group the right-hand position with tone production, and the left-hand position with finger patterns. There is no "right" way to organize the material. Our goal is to help you organize it in a way that is most useful for you.

The purpose of a long-range plan is not to create more work, but to organize the work you already do, to make a place for everything, and to put everything in its place. Long-range plan units can include the following sections:

1. Pedagogically Sequenced Objectives
2. Goals for How Much Students Will Learn (at each level)
3. Assessments
4. Teaching Materials—Exercises, Etudes, Music
5. Teaching Strategies

Orchestra Units Are Different

Orchestra units are not the kind of units we are used to seeing in other classes. In American History, for example, we learn about the Civil War, reconstruction, the industrial revolution, and World War I. Like most of our academic classes, history units are taught one after another in succession. Orchestra units are different; we teach our units side by side at the same time. We introduce them separately, and then we use exercises and music to teach students how they overlap.

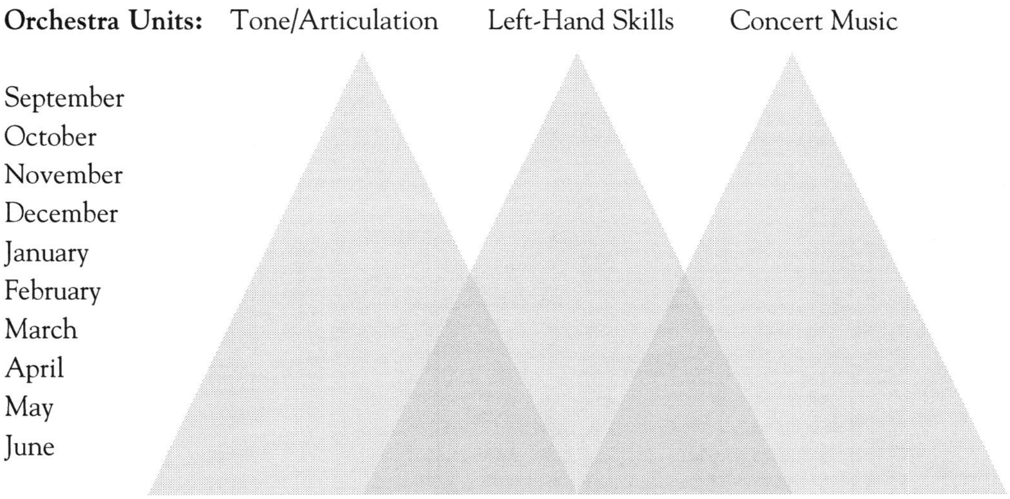

Orchestra units also last longer than a year. Hopefully, they last a lifetime.

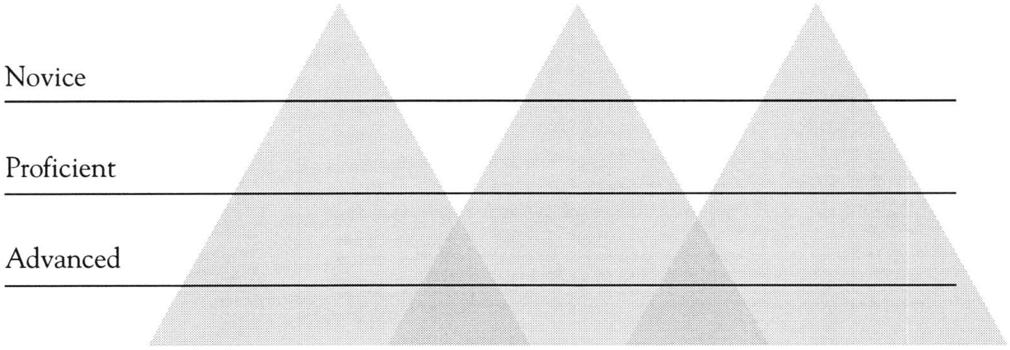

Goals, Objectives and Standards:

Each of the unit chapters in this book has one to two over-arching goals and a list of specific teaching objectives that support those goals. The units on tone, intonation, rhythm, literacy, and creativity list many objectives that are intended to be taught over many years. To help you organize your plan, the objectives have been divided into 5 levels that align very closely to the 5 levels used by the National Association for Music Education (NAfME) and the American String Teacher Association (ASTA):

1. Novice
2. Intermediate
3. Proficient
4. Accomplished
5. Advanced

While the skills and objectives are listed in increasing order of difficulty, there is no timeline or schedule that ties benchmarks to any specific grade. You must determine which objectives are grade-level appropriate in your program.

The goals and objectives in this book address many state and National Standards. It would be counterproductive for this book to recommend specific teaching standards, especially since each district and state writes or adopts their own. Many teachers have mixed feelings about standards, and that may be putting it nicely. Standards can feel both uselessly vague and frustratingly confining at the same time. They can be difficult to interpret, and they don't always fit what we want to teach. Even so, standards are important for several reasons. They remind us—*and our administrators*—that music education is larger than one teacher in a school that may or may not support music education. We are part of a professional community of hundreds of thousands of past and present music teachers, and the importance of sequential, comprehensive music education taught by highly qualified teachers is recognized at the national level.

Most administrators cannot tell us what our state or National Standards are for music education, much less how to organize sequential lessons around them. Nonetheless, they do expect us to figure it out as part of our job. When we address the standards in our long-range plans and classroom instruction, our administrators take us and our profession more seriously—though it may not always feel that way to us. Despite the fact that we became teachers to teach students *what we wanted to teach*, standards help us make sure we are teaching them everything our professional leaders have determined they need to know and be able to do. This is important because one person, especially a young adult, cannot be expected to inherently know all that our profession expects of us.

So familiarize yourself with the standards you are expected to teach and determine which units best address each standard. Every standard will not be addressed in every unit, but it is important to make sure you address each standard adequately during the year.

Selecting Unit Objectives for Your Program

The previous eight chapters sequenced objectives for each unit. Select a unit that you would like to organize first. Then create a Word document similar to the template shown in Example 44.

Example 44:

Unit Title: ______________________________

Novice Level

Review Objectives:
1. ______________________________
2. ______________________________

New Objectives:
1. ______________________________
2. ______________________________

Intermediate Level

Review Objectives:
1. ______________________________
2. ______________________________

New Objectives:
1. ______________________________
2. ______________________________

Proficient Level

Review Objectives:
1. ______________________________
2. ______________________________

New Objectives:
1. ______________________________
2. ______________________________

The first step in writing a unit is to identify the objectives you would like to introduce at each level and to determine which objectives your students need to review. Think of review objectives as previously *introduced* objectives—not previously *learned* objectives. If you teach more than one level of orchestra, you will need to determine which new skills to address at each level. The new objectives from one level will likely be review objectives in the next level. As the levels of orchestra become more advanced, there will be fewer objectives in the new column and more objectives in the review column. Continue to review objectives until you decide a skill no longer needs formal review.

Only list review objectives when you plan to devote class time and strategies to teaching those objectives. It is not necessary to include in your long-range plan every skill you want to see your advanced students demonstrate. For example, advanced-level classes hopefully don't need lessons on basic note reading. While you should certainly keep an eye out for students having literacy issues, it would not be a good use of time to teach the full lesson to the whole class when remedial help or tutoring could help the few students who still need it. So if you don't plan to spend class time on it, don't list it in your objectives.

Our template lists places for only two objectives, but your actual objective lists may be longer. Feel free to add your own objectives to the ones provided in our unit chapters. If you are using a sequenced method book in your class, identify the objectives that are addressed by the exercises in your method book. Method books can help teachers guide their long-range plans.

The Importance of Reviewing Previously Introduced Skills

Two music professors from the local university visited my school and performed Beethoven's Cello Sonata in A Major, among other works. After the performance, a young student raised his hand and asked, "How long did it take you to learn that?" The pianist smiled and said, "About forty years."

Long-range plans are usually structured around the new objectives that are introduced in each class level; as a result, we tend to pay less attention to how we review concepts after they are introduced. The inherent problem is that musicians spend relatively little time learning new skills compared to the time we spend reviewing and improving music and skills that were previously introduced.

Review is an extremely important part of all string classes that is too often downplayed or overlooked altogether.

While the concept of ongoing review is nothing new to musicians, the greatest challenge for teachers—even veteran directors with decades of experience—is incorporating all of the review we do into a long-range plan. This task of planning a thorough, sequential review is especially difficult when planning the advanced middle school and high school levels because older students have more to review.

Well-planned review helps students remember skills that are forgotten over the summer. Furthermore, it gives teachers the opportunity to identify students who have missed content or skills in past years and help them catch up. In this way, skill review helps get every student more or less on the same page, a strategy that is especially important in upper-level programs where significant disparity between older and younger students can exist.

As you create units for left-hand skills, scales, bowing skills, etc., consider new skills that are introduced in that class level, and then create a plan for reviewing the important skills and objectives that lead up to the new material. Much of the review can be done at the beginning of the year, revisiting skills that were introduced in previous years. You can also review skills throughout the year. For example, before teaching students how to shift, it would be valuable to review instrument and left-hand position to make sure their left hands are free to move around the fingerboard. It would also be wise to review finger patterns in first position, which will help them find their patterns more easily in higher positions. When teaching ongoing units like scales, you can continually review hand position, intonation, and tone production skills, even as the scales increase in difficulty throughout the year.

Assessment

After identifying the new and review objectives you plan to teach, the next step is to give some thought as to how these objectives should look and sound when students have learned them well. By creating assessment tools, such as rubrics and checklists, you can get a clearer idea about your teaching goals and what you want students to be able to do. There is also another benefit to creating assessments first: You can include them in your teaching process. When you give students the rubric for what you expect them to learn and do, then their learning and practice tend to become much more efficient.

In this section of your unit plan, write a clear description of what you expect students to do on their test. This description is called a *performance task*, and the more details you can include, the better. For example: "On Wednesday, April 24, the student will perform a two-octave A major scale in eighth notes slurred in two-note groups at a tempo of 60 bpm." Then, include the rubric or assessment tool you will use to evaluate the student on each performance task. The rubric should include specific descriptions of excellent performance to give students the information they need to know if they have learned the objective. The next chapter contains strategies for building rubrics and other types of assessments.

One of the beauties of organizing your material into skill-centered units is that your rubrics for unit assessments will look a lot alike. In a "Scale and Arpeggio" unit, for example, your rubric for the C scale will be similar, if not identical, to your rubric for a G scale. Using the same rubric for each scale test helps the students learn the rubric and what they need to focus on specifically from one scale test to the next.

Furthermore, the rubric you create will describe the characteristics of mastery that you want to see in each scale, and those characteristics will look very similar from one class level to the next. If you teach one-octave scales for the lower-level class, two-octave major scales for the middle level, and two-octave minor scales for the upper level, your rubrics will also look very similar. Units keep the objectives, assessments, and teaching strategies all organized by content, which makes your teaching more organized, focused, and effective. It makes your job easier, too.

Selecting Material for Teaching the Objectives

After selecting the objectives you plan to teach, and the assessments that describe student mastery for those objectives, the next step is to create or identify the exercises and other material you will use to teach the objectives and assess student mastery. Decide what material and music you will use, and write it in this part of your unit plan.

While assessments may look very similar from one class level to the next, the material the students are playing in each class level is usually different. Unless you are planning to combine classes at your spring concert, you are probably going to select different music for each group to play. It is equally likely that the students will study different scales, left-hand exercises, and bowing exercises throughout the year. Much like your lists of new and review skills for each level, your choice of material will help you identify distinct differences between the levels of orchestra you teach. It will help you define the scope of your entire program, from the beginning level to the most advanced.

A sequential method book is the primary material for teaching skills to classes of young string students. There is an abundance of material for teaching students in their first few years of orchestra. Sequential method books are less effective for upper-level orchestras for a couple reasons. First, in high school, students of wildly varying levels of ability and experience are often scheduled into the same class, and sequential method books have difficulty accommodating students of varying ability levels. Second, upper-level orchestras focus on repertoire, and the skills required in the concert music rarely coincide with the schedule and order of skills taught in a sequential method.

Habits of a Successful String Musician was written to accommodate the needs of high school programs and students. Students of many different levels can simultaneously learn the skills appropriate for their individual level. Instead of trying to get every student to fit the skill levels addressed in a book, we created a method to meet the students at their individual skill levels. The *Habits* method is not sequential like most traditional method books. It is divided into unit chapters.

1. Tone and Articulation
2. First Position Finger Patterns
3. Shifting
4. Upper Positions and Alternate Clefs
5. Scales, Arpeggios, and Thirds
6. Chorales
7. Rhythm Charts
8. Sight-reading

Directors of upper-level orchestras can select the exercises for the unit and skills they want to teach, and also apply exercises to the music they are playing. Whether or not you use the *Habits* method, it is important to remember that the teacher—not the method book—determines the content of the class.

The Unit Timeline

After selecting the material you will use to teach the unit's objectives, the next task is to determine the timeline. Write a general calendar, either by months or quarters. Then, write the names of the unit performance tasks in the quarters or months that you plan to assess those objectives. Using the performance task name only on your timeline keeps your timeline easy to read and easy to edit if you decide to move your performance task to a different time of the year.

When planning your timeline, consider how long it will take to introduce a skill and prepare students for their performance task. Also determine the amount of time that should exist between one performance task and the introduction of the next objective; this could be a few days or a few months. The unit timeline is a flexible guideline; do not write in actual dates. They need to be determined closer to the assessment date.

Teaching Strategies

Great teachers have many strategies floating around in their heads waiting for just the right moment to be used. We are proud of the strategies we keep in our "bag of tricks" because, unlike goals and objectives, the creative strategies we know and use are the very things that define us as teachers. String teachers teach similar skills, but *how we teach those skills is what makes each teacher unique.*

In our unit plans, we can group strategies with the skills they address. When we write down our strategies, it helps us to remember them from year to year, and it also allows us to methodically keep track of strategies that work and revise ones than don't. The longer we teach, the more strategies we can add to this section. Master Suzuki teachers have a hundred different ways to teach *Twinkle, Twinkle* to students with different learning styles.

So what teaching strategies do you use to teach left-hand position, vibrato, tone, spiccato? Start writing them down in an organized way in your unit plans. The previous chapters introduced sample strategies that teachers can adopt and include in their own plans. The goal is to adopt, create, and use strategies that work best for you. The more strategies you have in your bag, the better.

Unit Format

So much of what we teach is circular, so when we try to write down what we do, our plans have a tendency to become repetitive. One of our goals when writing units should be to use a format that streamlines the plans and groups similar content and material together to reduce repetition. Here is one example of a unit format:

1. Unit Title
   - Standards Addressed
2. Objectives
   - Review Objectives
   - New Objectives
3. Performance Tasks and Assessments
4. Teaching Material
5. Timeline
   - Quarter 1
   - Quarter 2
   - Quarter 3
   - Quarter 4
6. Teaching Strategies

In the format above, objectives are grouped together, as are the assessments, material, and strategies. Units can also be organized so assessments, strategies, and material are grouped specifically to each objective:

1. Unit Title
   - Standards Addressed
2. Objective #1
   - Performance Tasks and Assessment
   - Teaching Material
3. Objective #2
   - Performance Tasks and Assessment
   - Teaching Material
4. Timeline
   - Quarter 1
   - Quarter 2
   - Quarter 3
   - Quarter 4
5. Teaching Strategies

Write each unit in a format that makes the most sense to you. The format you choose will depend on the similarity of the rubrics, material, and strategies you use.

Finalizing Your Long-Range Plan

To organize your instruction within several units into one long-range plan, map out the performance tasks on a chart (Example 45) to help you determine how the units will fit together. Divide the year into quarters, and decide which music, left-hand skills, scales, etc. to assess in each quarter.

Example 45:

1st Quarter			
Left-Hand Skills	Scales	Literacy Skills	Concert Repertoire
2nd Quarter			
3rd Quarter			
4th Quarter			
Final Assessment Skills:			

Mapping out your long-range plan allows you to plan when skills will coincide and also determine how to stagger the weeks when you introduce new skills. The year-long overview also helps you plan around months like December, March, and May when students may need to focus more on polishing concert music.

Most teachers concentrate technical skills in the first semester because students have more patience for skill building earlier in the year; and when done right, this skill building investment pays big dividends in the spring.

The last thing you may want to add to your long-range plan is an introduction containing course descriptions and a brief description of the units taught in your course. This introduction might also include program goals, a mission statement, and lists of your accolades and achievements from recent years.

FINAL THOUGHTS:

Writing units and merging them into one year-long plan requires practice—maybe years of practice—so be patient and forgiving. Too often, we think of writing a long-range plan like we are etching the year in stone. Your unit and long-range plans are living documents that evolve with you from one year to the next. They will evolve and grow along with you, and by the end of your career, you will have a book of masterful plans that you can share with younger teachers. To make this evolutionary process easier, save your long-range plan at the beginning of the year as a new file called "Next Year's Long-Range Plan." Then as you teach and follow the plan throughout the year, write notes for next year's plan that can be reviewed later.

Do you remember the three important questions introduced at the beginning of this chapter? How would you answer these questions for yourself and your students?

- What do I expect my students to learn by the end of the year?
- What is my pedagogical plan for reaching our end-of-year goals?
- How does my lesson plan for today help students reach our end-of-year goals?

We have a professional responsibility to articulate what we expect our students to learn.

Why? Because we teach better when we have clear goals, well-sequenced objectives, and teaching strategies for reaching those goals.

Once we answer these questions, our lessons and instructional delivery will have more direction and purpose, and our job will become much more clear and enjoyable.

Chapter Checklist:

Do the following for each class level you teach:

- ❑ Identify the review and new objectives that students should learn in each level of orchestra class in your program.
- ❑ Create performance tasks and assessments for the objectives.
- ❑ Select the material—exercises, etudes, and music—that you will use to teach the objectives.
- ❑ Sketch out a timeline describing when the performance tasks will be completed.
- ❑ Write down the strategies you will use to teach the objectives.
- ❑ Map out how the performance tasks of different units will fit together over the course of the year.

Chapter 14

Assessment

Begin with the end in mind.

—Steven Covey, from *Seven Habits of Highly Effective People*

We often think of assessment as the last thing we do in a lesson. After planning the lesson and teaching the students, we create and administer a test to measure how well students learned the objectives. In this chapter, we will look at a variety of effective assessment tools and testing strategies, but we will also suggest a different approach to assessment. When we create the assessment *before* we teach the lesson, we develop a clearer picture of what we intend to teach; and if we present the assessments to students early in the lesson, we give our students a clearer picture of what they need to learn, which helps them practice more efficiently and learn faster.

IN THIS CHAPTER:

- Helping Students Learn What Is Expected of Them
- Assessment Formats and Strategies
- Homework and Practice Habits

Helping Students Learn What Is Expected of Them

Clearly stating what students are to learn is an integral part of helping students learn material and do well on their tests. Students want to know what is going to be on the test. They want to know what we expect them to learn. If we introduce the performance task and assessment as part of the lesson, and use them to explain the objectives that will be tested, we give students a clear goal and a fair shot at working and practicing toward their target grade.

Performance Tasks:

Before creating a rubric or checklist, the first step is to define the "performance task" that explains exactly what the students are expected to do on the test. When assigning a two-octave scale, for example, students need to know specifics. When is the test? How fast are they expected to play the scale? With slurs or separate bows? What is being graded—tone, pitch, rhythm, technique? Will students be playing by themselves or in small groups, live in front of the class or in your office? A well-written performance task provides details that help students understand exactly what is expected. A performance task for a two-octave scale might look something like this:

Test:
Wednesday, March 30

> Perform a two-octave D melodic minor scale and arpeggio in class from memory, using separate bows in eighth notes with the metronome at quarter note = 80 bpm. Use the correct fingerings, good technique, and play in tune with a strong tone in both octaves.

This performance task is the goal. Students will learn the scale better when you explain the goal as soon as you begin working on the scale. Understanding what they are expected to do on the test is just the beginning, however; students will also want to know how they are going to be graded, including your definition or description of how a successful performance looks and sounds.

Performance Assessments:

Performance assessment tools (like rubrics and checklists) help students learn what is expected by describing a performance that is learned well. Well-written performance assessments are easy to understand, and they clearly identify the criteria used to evaluate the students. When your students can use a rubric to accurately grade themselves, the rubric becomes the test and you can frame yourself as the helper instead of the grader. This perspective encourages students to come to you for help to learn how to perform the skills at the level the rubric and the music demand.

To create a rubric or checklist, make a list of the characteristics that define a successful performance. In the case of the two-octave scale, what does this scale sound and look like when it is learned and performed well? You want students to play the scale in tune, with good tone, good technique, and fluently, without pausing or stumbling. So these are the skills your rubric needs to measure. The better you describe the traits in the rubric, the better you can articulate the objectives for your students.

This sample assessment tool (Example 46) is a hybrid of a checklist and a traditional rubric. It is easy to read and mark. The bold key words help the teacher and students navigate the rubric and quickly underline criteria that are not being met. This saves time writing comments, which is very important with large string classes.

Example 46:

<table>
<tr><th>Category</th><th>Few correct
0–4</th><th>Some correct
5–6</th><th>Most correct
7–8</th><th>All correct
9–10</th></tr>
<tr><td>Hand, Body Instrument Position</td><td colspan="4">❑ Body and instrument position are correct, relaxed, and well-aligned
❑ Left hand: elbow, wrist, thumb, and finger shape and placement
❑ Right hand: thumb, pinky, fingers, knuckles, and wrist are fluid and placed correctly</td></tr>
<tr><td>Rhythm and Preparation</td><td colspan="4">❑ Rhythms and tempo are correct and consistent; no rushing
❑ Fluency: no stopping, stumbling, or dragging
❑ Memorized: exercise is performed from memory (if required)</td></tr>
<tr><td>Intonation</td><td colspan="4">❑ Notes are consistently correct and in tune, especially fourth and seventh scale degrees
❑ Fingerings are correct; shifts are well executed: relaxed, fluid, and accurate
❑ Fingertips adjust quickly refining the pitch after finger placement
❑ Upper octaves and lower octaves are in tune</td></tr>
<tr><td>Tone and Articulation</td><td colspan="4">❑ Bow speed and weight are balanced and produce an excellent tone that projects well
❑ Contact point is the correct distance between the bridge and fingerboard
❑ The bow angle is perpendicular to the string and rotated correctly
❑ Slurs/articulations are correct and performed in the correct part of the bow</td></tr>
<tr><td>Total</td><td colspan="4">Comments</td></tr>
</table>

The drawback of this type of rubric is that it doesn't describe varying degrees of success the way a traditional rubric does. Ultimately, you must design clear rubrics that are easy for you to use and for your students to understand.

Assessment Formats and Strategies

In this section, we will look at the benefits of different types of assessments tools and strategies. There are a variety of ways to assess students, and not all of them end with a grade. The goal is to select a format that best measures what you want to assess, whether or not it is graded.

Self-Assessment:

A good rubric can help students learn how to assess their own playing, which is a critical skill for students to practice productively at home. When teaching a lesson, distribute a copy of the performance task and rubric to the students. Give students time to review the rubric, and instruct them to perform the assessment task for themselves in class. Then have them assess their performance using the rubric and write down their goals for that evening. Over several days, have students describe the skills that have improved, as well as areas in which they still need to grow. Students can also share the strategies they used for fixing the problems.

Peer-Assessment:

Students learn and remember skills best when they teach the skills to someone else. Pair students up with their stand partner or a friend, and have them use the rubric to evaluate each other. Simply performing for someone else helps students to think critically about their performance, but it also helps them to learn the performance task and the objectives of the assessment.

Pair up students by stand, and have outside players perform while inside players listen; then have inside players perform while outside players listen. At the end of the activity, have students tell each other all the positive things they heard in their partner's performance plus one thing to work on. Over several days with the same partners, students can follow up to see/hear if their partner has corrected a problem identified on a previous day. To foster good feelings in class, have students share with the class any improvements they heard in their partner's performances.

Large Group Performance Assessment—Concert Festival:

In the months leading up to an adjudicated performance (such as a concert festival), record the students and teach them to use the state assessment rubric to evaluate their own performance. This activity produces rich musical discussions about goals, shortfalls, and solutions—and that's not all. It teaches students to collectively work together as a team to solve group problems and achieve group goals.

Audio/Video Tests:

As technology becomes more affordable and ubiquitous, digital audio and video recordings are growing in popularity with students and teachers as a standard testing format. Many students are now able to record tests on their smart phones or home computers, and then they e-mail the file to the teacher. Large files can be shared by e-mailing a link connected to YouTube or another file sharing site.

Digital tests are a win for students who prefer to perform their tests at home instead of performing in front of the class. Recording is also a better learning process for students. When students record their tests, they can listen to their performance, assess it, and practice more before they decide to submit the final version. When they turn in a poorly performed test, the teacher can give it an accurate grade and use the recording to explain the grade to the students and their parents.

Furthermore, digital files don't have to be graded during class, which preserves class time for rehearsal and instruction. They can be graded almost any time and anywhere you have access to your e-mail. They can also take less time to grade because there is no stopping and starting between students that can slow down live tests. Digital tests are especially helpful for big jury tests or final exams when a teacher may want to listen to recordings more than once. In the case of chair auditions, the teacher can go back and compare the recordings of close students, or ask another music teacher to break a tie.

Live Assessments:

Live solo assessments are good for testing scales and technical exercises that help teachers evaluate technique, intonation, and tone. Students can perform shorter assessments in front of the class. To save time, have students put their name on the test and collect them in the order in which the students will be tested. Then turn on the metronome, and proceed down the rows quickly.

Live group tests are a fast way to measure how well students are practicing and learning their concert music. When students play one to a part in trios or quartets, they must count, listen, and perform their own part without hiding behind another section player. Ensemble tests can be done in front of the class, which allows students to see, hear, and appreciate who is learning their music. It also inspires students to practice. Select excerpts that allow you to assess every student in the group.

Pass-Offs and Achievement Programs:

Pass-off tests help students understand that certain skills must be completely right, or they are wrong. They can be a powerful motivator for students who enjoy the sense of accomplishment they get from passing off a skill. A list of pass-fail skills might include tuning the instrument, holding the bow correctly, looking at a key signature, and performing the correct finger pattern. Even certain important scales or etudes can be made pass-fail. Some teachers use pass-off programs that award colored tags or ribbons, like martial arts belts, for graduated levels of accomplishment.

The biggest benefit—and drawback—of self-paced achievement programs like this is that students can learn at their own speed. While self-motivated students will peck away at the pass-off list as fast as they can, other students will need teacher assistance to pace themselves before the end of the nine weeks. Teachers also need to determine how many times the student can take the test over, and also how long they have to wait before taking the test again.

Written Tests:

Though multiple-choice questions cannot be used to evaluate a performance, they can be used to measure much more than just musical terms. Take a look at the sample questions below, and think about how these questions require higher-level reasoning. What would your students need to know to be able to answer these questions correctly?

1. The distance from E down to C-sharp is ______________.
   A. one half step
   B. two half steps
   C. one half step plus a whole step
   D. two whole steps

2. Which answer best explains the difference between the time signatures of 3/4 and 6/8?
   A. 3/4 has more eighth notes than 6/8
   B. 6/8 has more eighth notes than 3/4
   C. 3/4 is divided into three equal parts, and 6/8 is not
   D. There is no difference once you reduce them

3. In which answer below do the tempos go from slowest to fastest?
   A. Andante, adagio, allegro, allegretto
   B. Adagio, andante, allegretto, allegro
   C. Allegretto, allegro, adagio, andante
   D. Allegretto, adagio, allegro, andante

4. In a D major scale, the half steps are located between F-sharp–G and ______________.
   A. B–C
   B. B–C-sharp
   C. C-sharp–D
   D. C–D

5. In the example below, how many B-flats are there in the four notes under your instrument name?
   A. 0
   B. 1
   C. 2
   D. 3

Sometimes the best way to have students learn a concept or skill is to ask them open-ended questions, and then help them figure out the answer. For example:

- On a piece of staff paper, write *Twinkle, Twinkle Little Star* in common time and in the key of F. Include the key and time signatures; make sure each measure has four beats in it, and the stems are going the right direction. When you are done, write it again in a different key of your choice.

- Your stand partner holds his bow like a baseball bat. Write out what your partner needs to do to form a good bow hand. Your answer should include the most important points about the thumb, pinky, fingers, knuckles, and wrist.

Homework and Practice Habits

How many times have we heard teachers say, "If only my students practiced their music more"? The good news is that teachers can take concrete steps to improve the practice habits of their students. Developing a strong homework ethic takes time, but the extra teacher effort pays off in the long run by extending instructional time to the home hours and increasing student accountability for the work they do in class.

Getting students into the routine of practicing may be the hardest part. Once they start practicing every day, they grow more accustomed to the idea of practicing tomorrow. Consistency is a big part of making practice enjoyable for students, so give them frequent and small assignments to help them learn to practice a little every night. Don't give up if you don't see immediate results. Learning to practice and liking to practice can take time.

We need to be mindful that tests are a measurement tool, and while they can be a powerful motivator for some students, tests are not meant to be a form of extortion to force students to practice for their grade's sake. When we teach students to practice for their grade, we set them up to stop practicing (and playing) when they leave the class. Ultimately, we want students to practice for the right reasons so they continue enjoying their instruments and making music for the rest of their lives.

Let's look at how we assign homework and identify ways to help students understand what they should learn and how to practice assignments effectively.

1. Clearly explain what you expect students to learn.

Students need more information than we typically give them; it is not enough to tell students, "Learn mm. 27–43 for tomorrow." When first teaching students to practice, start with small assignments that establish a clear goal. For example: "For tomorrow, perform mm. 27–43 at a tempo of 136 without stopping. Play the correct rhythms, bowings, and finger patterns with a good tone."

Write the homework assignment and objectives on the board before class begins, and make sure students write down the assignment before leaving class. Be conscious of how much time students will need to complete the assignment well.

2. Teach students how to learn music at home.

Naturally, students will learn more at home if we teach them *how* to practice and learn the excerpt or exercise before we assign it for homework. Students who are armed with strategies to learn an assignment at home will not only accomplish more, they will also feel successful at home. Students who do not have enough information to learn an assignment are more likely to get frustrated and begin to associate practice with feelings of frustration, failure, or boredom. Can you blame them for not wanting to practice?

- Break up the assignment into small, attainable goals.
- Help students identify the hardest measures or problem spots.
- Give students practice strategies for learning the specific objectives.
- Give students a rubric so they can identify their trouble areas and evaluate their progress.
- Give students a clear idea of how the excerpt sounds when it is "learned" or at an "A" level.

3. Explain how homework will be graded.

In addition to specific homework objectives, students need to understand the criteria for evaluating their performance of these objectives. The easiest way to do this is to give students the playing test rubric and have them practice using the rubric during class and at home.

- "Let's listen to the first violins play the assignment; use the rubric to identify what they need to improve, and give them a sample grade."
- "Everyone play from B to D. Now, look at the rubric and identify the things you need to work on most."

4. Grade fairly.

After creating an assessment, ask yourself: "Does this test measure what I want it to measure? If a student gets an A or an F, are they earning this score for the right reasons?"

When students believe the grade they received was not right or fair, they lose trust in the practice-yields-success model of learning. Ideally, students should be able to score their own performance using the rubric they used to help them learn the assignment, and the grade they give themselves should be close to the grade they received from the teacher. The closer these two grades are, the more students will believe the grade they received was fair.

Give honest grades and genuine encouragement to students who perform poorly. Tell them, "Learn tonight's assignment, and you'll do better on tomorrow's homework check. You can do it; I know you can!" Some students will not begin to practice until their grade begins to fall noticeably; so let those students' grades go down, and encourage them to start working at home to learn their assignments.

Before a homework check, warm up the students with a scale or rhythm exercise, but be careful not to spend too much of the class practicing the music before the homework check. Doing so negates the need to practice at home!

FINAL THOUGHTS: THE DIFFERENCE BETWEEN ASSESSING AND GRADING

A principal walks into the orchestra room and says to the teacher, "I just got off the phone with the parent of one of your students, and she is upset because she doesn't understand how her son can get a 93 in intermediate orchestra and still not qualify for advanced orchestra next year. If earning an A is not good enough to get promoted, then what is? And did you communicate this to the parent?"

We assess students to measure how much they know. We *grade* students to let them and their parents know how well they are learning what they are expected to learn. Grades help parents understand whether or not a student is doing a "good job," and parents want to know this. When grades do not reflect how well the student is doing, then the teacher is not doing a good job of communicating with the students and parents—and this can cause problems.

Accurate grades foster trust. "She's a tough teacher, but at least I know where I stand." Students take grades personally, but it's very important that students and parents understand that it is not personal for the teacher. Young teachers tend to be compassionate, and can even feel apologetic about grades. Don't be sorry. This is business; keep it positive: "If you want a better grade, this is what you need to do on your next test."

Chapter 15

Characteristics of Great Teaching

Throughout this book, teaching strategies have been organized by unit content. This chapter contains important general teaching and rehearsal strategies that great teachers use to inspire their students to work harder and learn *more*. Since you may already use many of the following strategies to motivate your students to practice and learn, use this chapter to reflect on what you do already, and on what you might still want to improve.

IN THIS CHAPTER:

- The Nature of Rehearsal and Practice
- Inspiring Students to Learn
- Questions Teach Students to Think for Themselves
- Characteristics of Great Teachers
- How Great Teachers Use Sequential Method Books
- Additional Best Practices

The Nature of Rehearsal and Practice

My principal did an unannounced observation of me not too long ago. The rehearsal my boss observed was our first and only combined rehearsal the day before our fall concert. Afterwards, my boss said, "The good news is that they sound great, they had fun, and it was a well-run rehearsal; the bad news is that the teacher evaluation rubric that all principals in the school district are required to use defined your teaching as 'ineffective' because you didn't teach anything *new*." I should add that my principal is an accomplished pianist, and I could tell from her smile and tone that my abilities and job performance were not in question. I feel lucky to have a boss who understands the value of rehearsal and who sees the flaws in our district's observation rubric. In previous jobs, I have had many well-meaning administrators who simply did not understand.

In schools where so much focus is placed on teaching large amounts of new material, we must remind ourselves (and politely help our administrators understand) that *fine arts classes are different*. Students spend more time reviewing and refining skills in our classes than they do in most other classes.

The practice of review, refinement, and pursuit of flawless artistry is one of the main traits that make arts education a valuable component to a child's overall development.

To explain and justify what orchestra teachers do, we can refer our administrators to the four stages of learning, sometimes called the *stages of competence*. These stages remind us that learning is not instantaneous; it is a process that requires time, practice, and some awareness of where were are on the path toward mastery.

1. Unconscious Incompetence is the stage of not knowing what we cannot do.
2. Conscious Incompetence is the stage of knowing what we cannot do.
3. Conscious Competence is the stage of being able to do something when we think about it.
4. Unconscious Competence is the final stage of being able to do something even without thinking about it.

When we first introduce a skill, we understand that the introduction is only the beginning. The deepest learning occurs not when a concept is first introduced, but when we are reviewing, practicing, and refining the skills with our students. There is a saying among Suzuki teachers:

Practice can only begin *after* the skill has been learned.

It is this practice that enables our fingers to reach "unconscious competence" so we can focus more on phrasing, musicianship, and artistry. Our students can *make music* only after they have practiced enough so they do not have to think about the hundred other skills that go into playing a string instrument.

It's one thing to explain the value of practice to our administrators and students. Convincing students to do the practice in rehearsal and at home requires a completely different set of skills. Most teachers use and rely upon testing and grading students to measure learning and incentivize practice. Assessments are designed to measure learning, not inspire it. So how do we get students to *want* to take their instruments home and do the work? How do we inspire students to *want* to rehearse and practice for the love of music, and not just because they want a good grade?

All teachers *want* students to learn.
Good teachers *require* students to learn.
Great teachers *inspire* students to learn.

Inspiring Students to Learn

Inspiring teachers increase the students' desire to learn and encourage them to become accountable for their own learning and successes. They motivate students to rehearse well together and practice hard at home. Is there anything teachers do that could be more important than developing a student's hungry desire for learning and performing music?

It takes time, patience, and persistence to develop an inspired work ethic, but the investment in the following strategies pays off in the long run. And there's one more benefit: Inspired students are a genuine joy to teach, and they tend to inspire their teachers right back.

1. Tend to your own fire first.

Many of us became music teachers so we could share with future generations the same love and excitement of music that we experienced when we were young. One of the hardest parts of public school teaching is keeping this passion for music and music education front and center through all of the planning, grading, paperwork, meetings, fundraising, field trips, and phone calls. The fatigue and stress of our jobs can diminish our own joy of teaching music and, consequently, the optimism and effectiveness of our daily instruction. This is important because we cannot light a fire in our students when our own spark has burnt out; so the first step to inspiring students is keeping our own fire burning brightly.

If you are feeling burnt out, make time to rekindle your love for music; continue to play and enjoy your own instrument. Take time to listen to good performances of the music you are teaching. Before the start of your day, remind yourself why you became an orchestra teacher. Your own happiness and optimism are more powerful and inspiring than anything else you may do. When your fire is burning brightly, you can tap into it for reference as you teach style, dynamics, and tempo to your students. Ask yourself, "How would I play this if I were going to perform it myself at Carnegie Hall?"

Teachers who have forgotten their passion for music may still be good at teaching technique, discipline, and good behavior, but what good are those things if the students do not have a desire to play music for music's sake?

2. Share with your students the joys of performing well.

How do musicians like Yo-Yo Ma or Itzhak Perlman awaken the desire in us to be better musicians ourselves? Some teachers talk about technique, and they may require and expect good discipline and musicianship from their students. But when teachers share their love for playing music, students become inspired to pick up their instruments and practice. When we see other musicians reaping enjoyment from performing well, we want to experience that joy ourselves and we are inspired to work for it.

The love of music is truly the most inspiring quality great music teachers possess. To inspire your students, show your students how fun it is to play music with beautiful tone. Bring in guests, especially older students, to show younger students how much fun they have playing music at an advanced level. Show videos of great youth orchestras and professional orchestras, or take them to a symphony concert in town or on your next field trip. After showing students inspiring performances, speak immediately about the skills the students need to learn next, and explain *why* they need to learn those skills. When you demonstrate why students need to learn a skill, they will be more inspired to practice hard enough to learn it.

3. Expect students to establish their own goals.

As music teachers, we talk a lot about our goals for student learning. This part of our job often overshadows the importance of having students establish goals for themselves. When we ask students what they want to accomplish on their instruments, we give them ownership in their future and education. Students generally work harder to achieve goals they have set for themselves. Talk to your students about their goals, and have them write down goals of their own. Then speak to them in terms of what *they* want.

Of course, you will have goals for your students, too. When explaining your goals for student learning, explain them in terms of class goals. "By the end of the year, our goal is to be able to…." This is a natural extension of what orchestra players already do: they learn the music individually to the best of their ability so their own performance contributes positively to the group's performance. Set goals with your students, and expect them to set goals for themselves. Then, offer your help and make yourself available to help your students achieve their goals.

4. Create opportunities for students to succeed, and then celebrate their success.

Everyone wants to succeed and be a member of a successful group. Inspiring teachers cultivate and fuel this desire by creating a learning environment in which students are rehearsing and practicing for their own achievement and success—not for their grade or the approval of the teacher. Students will have many different motivations for doing work, including grades, peer pressure, and teacher approval. But those motivators are all secondary to the satisfaction and pride students feel about their own accomplishments. When delivering praise, focus on the success of your students and how it makes them feel. Encourage them to be proud of their accomplishments.

Give students frequent, if not daily, opportunities to demonstrate their successes.

Make small, achievable goals that give students the best opportunities to celebrate their own success. Give students group projects to learn together—as a section, in quartets or other small ensembles—and then let them perform for the class. Go down the row and give praise to the students who perform the assignment well. Before state auditions or similar high-caliber performances, have students perform their audition or solo for their peers, either in a concert setting or as a mock audition. Go out of your way to recognize the achievements of students who demonstrate good practice efforts, and help students identify what to improve next. If you give a grade for these performances, it should not overshadow the main goal of giving students an opportunity to demonstrate their successes.

Acknowledge and encourage students to celebrate their accomplishment of learning homework assignments. Showcase students who learned their assignments, and have them demonstrate their successful learning so students can hear what "learned" sounds like. Encourage other students to share what they liked about a peer's performance. Call or e-mail parents to praise a child. This parent contact is worth the time; if a student begins to do poorly later, then you can call again and say, "I know Frank is talented because he did so well last month. He is not learning his assignments as well this month, and he might need your encouragement to set aside a time to learn his homework."

Success is not only contagious, but it is also addictive. It is the kind of addiction that inspires us to work hardest in the face of adversity.

5. Improve performance without belittling the performer.

Be careful not to belittle any student, especially the 50 percent of students who perform "below average." Every student has a different amount of experience, talent, and support from their home environment. The playing field is *not* equal, so it is important to minimize student competition.

This does not mean you should sugar coat poor performance, nor imply that it is acceptable when students play poorly. Students see right through false praise, and to them it is the worst kind of insult; it means the teacher does not believe they have the ability to play any better.

So what should you do when students play poorly? First, keep it positive. When students need to improve, you can say, "I believe you can play better than that; I've heard you play better than that!"

Second, talk to the students about their *performance* and *sound*—not about the students themselves. For example, it would be better to say, "The tone was a little scratchy, and the notes were out of tune," and not "*Your* tone is scratchy and *you* are out of tune." Talking about the students themselves not only makes things personal, but it also puts you and your students on opposite sides of the problem. When you talk with a student about a performance, then you and the student are on the same side looking at the problem and searching for solutions together.

A good rubric can reinforce this positive relationship by giving students the information they need to evaluate themselves. When your rubric defines good performance, then you can work together to help your students learn the expected skills. You can let the rubric be the "bad cop" so you can be the encouraging "good cop."

Furthermore, when you put students in charge of evaluating and improving their own performance, you can use questions to coach them to solve their own problems.

- "What was your assignment?"
- "Are you happy with your performance?"
- "What do you think is the next thing to improve?"
- "What is the best way to do that?"

Students won't always reply with correct or thoughtful answers to these questions, but the process of using questions to identify solutions is more important than the answers themselves.

Chair Auditions Do Not "Inspire" Students

We know that chair auditions can motivate students. We also know that not all forms of motivation are equal, nor are they all necessarily good for students. We want our students' motivation to practice to come from a desire to develop their musical skills, but chair auditions inspire students to practice to protect their image or status. Most teens are already extremely sensitive about where they fit in social circles. Chair auditions exacerbate these anxieties and fears because they highlight how students' abilities and deficiencies affect their rank within the orchestra. Getting a poor grade is a private embarrassment; getting a "poor chair" is public one, and that is quite a different thing.

We understand that sometimes auditions are the only solution to a difficult problem. When implementing auditions and announcing results, always use great care, be extremely consistent, and emphasize the importance of good leadership, no matter where a student sits. Even when handled well, the mathematical reality is that there is only one "first chair." At the end of the day, chair audition results almost always create more unhappy students than happy ones; they can damage the same team spirit we want to foster in our ensembles.

Now more than ever, parents are sensitive about their child's happiness and self-esteem, and when a child goes home upset about a chair placement, teachers often find themselves on the defensive. Students privately compare themselves enough to each other, and parents fall into the same trap by comparing their child to others.

We can help parents, students, and ourselves by focusing solely on the students and avoiding comparisons to other students whenever possible.

Have students rotate chairs and share leadership responsibilities. Good orchestras have strong student musicians spread throughout the ensemble, from front to back and around the room. If you must have chair auditions, then include the following paragraph at the top of the results page:

Notice:

> Students are expected to find happiness in their encouragement of everyone's success and musical performance, and to make self-improvement goals based upon their own technical and musical skills. Students are discouraged from making a competitive sport out of seating auditions, from wishing others to play worse than themselves and from creating personal goals based on where they sit. Such practice is poor leadership, and it impairs group performance and morale. Do your best every day, and encourage everyone else to do the same. You may not be able to choose where you sit, but you can choose the kind of leader you want to be from any chair.

Questions Teach Students to Think for Themselves

In the professional circuit, rehearsal time is very limited, and conductors are expected to efficiently pull an orchestra together in several rehearsals. In school orchestra, performance is important, but the goal is education. Telling students what to play and how to play it is easy and efficient in the short run, but giving students a steady stream of answers gives students no reason to think. Over time, students become dependent on the teacher's instruction, instead of learning to think for themselves. In the information age when answers to nearly every question are just a click away, the questions are more important than the answers. When we speak in questions, we teach students how to ask the right questions, and how to think and solve their own problems. So instead of telling students how to play the notes, rhythms, and dynamics, ask them questions like the following examples:

Finger patterns:

- "What are the names of the notes under your fingers?"
- "Do those note names agree with the key signature?"
- "What is the finger pattern?"

Intonation:

- "Does that note match your stand partner's note?"

Articulation:

- "What part of the bow is your section leader using, and are you in the same part of the bow?"
- "What bow stroke is the section leader using, and are you using the same bow stroke?"

Ensemble:

- "Is your cue clear enough for others to follow?"
- "Is the leader's cue clear enough for you to follow?"

Tone:

- "Describe the timbre we should use here."
- "How do you create that timbre?"
- "Are you using the same timbre as your stand partner?"

Phrasing:

- "Where is the top of the crescendo?"
- "How loud should that be?"

Questions can be used to teach students to rehearse, practice, and solve their own problems:

- "Which measure is giving us the most trouble?"
- "What skills in that measure are causing the problem?"
- "What exercises from our book would help us learn these difficult skills?"
- "Is there an exercise that you could create to help you develop these skills?"

Questions may also be the answer to teaching students self-discipline. Delivering orders—"Do this, not that"—does not require students to think about what they are doing wrong; their only requirement is to be mindlessly compliant. The Flippen Group is an educational firm that teaches parents and educators to use "Four Questions" to foster self-discipline in young people. Ask these questions in a nonjudgmental tone whenever your students need to be thinking more about what they are doing:

1. What are you doing?
2. What are you supposed to be doing?
3. Are you doing it?
4. What are you going to do about it?

Most students simply need a reminder, and this sequence of questions is the best way to help students remember what they are supposed to be doing without getting negative or punitive. For example:

1. "Joey, what are you doing?" *I'm going to get some rosin.*
2. "What are you supposed to be doing?" *I'm supposed to be tuning my instrument with the rest of the class.*
3. "Are you doing it?" *No. Sorry.*
4. "What are you going to do about it?" *Stop rosining and tune my violin.*

These four questions can be used for almost anything! For example:

1. "Jane, what part of the bow are you using?" *The tip.*
2. "What part are you supposed to be using?" *The lower half.*
3. "Are you doing it?" *No. Sorry.*
4. "What are you going to do?" *I'm going to play in the lower half.*

Questions are also good for enforcing classroom rules and expectations, even those that require consequences on the first offense. For example:

1. "Jeffrey, what are you doing?" *I'm coming into class.*
2. "What time are you supposed to be coming to class?" *8:30*
3. "Are you on time?" *No. Sorry.*
4. "What is the consequence?" *Lunch detention.*
5. "What are you going to do about it next time?" *Get to class on time.*

In most schools, students are expected to follow a teacher's reasonable instructions, and students who disruptively refuse to follow instructions are removed from the classroom. When students repeatedly refuse to follow instructions, the question veteran teachers know to ask is, "Are you refusing to follow instructions, and are you choosing to be removed from the classroom?"

When we ask students questions, we give them the power to determine their own future. Questions teach students one of life's most important lessons:

Students are responsible for their actions and their own learning.
Once they get that straight, students are much easier to inspire and teach.

Characteristics of Great Teachers

Busy string teachers have little opportunity to visit other schools, hear other programs, or get an accurate sense for how well students in programs like ours can really play. This is a *big* problem because our peers and mentors play a big role in our own development. It is impossible to learn in a vacuum, and in the absence of seeing the product of our peers, teachers tend to stagnate and entrench themselves in mediocrity.

This job is too difficult to learn without guidance from colleagues. They help us establish the standards and expectations we hold for our students, and they help us find solutions to the myriad challenges that string teachers face. Being the social creatures we are, we tend to become more like the people who surround us, so...

1.
Surround yourself with great people.

This is one of the most important characteristics great teachers possess. Here are a few others:

2.
Great teachers have a clear vision of what they expect their students to learn, and they do not allow this vision to become clouded by fatigue or other distractions.

One of the hardest parts of our job is maintaining high standards throughout the whole year, especially as teachers and students become tired. As teachers repeatedly see and hear imperfect performance in their groups, the tendency is to gradually notice the problems less and less. Eventually, the problems become so much a part of the students' performance that the teacher has difficulty noticing the problems without help.

Great teachers bring in mentors and peers to listen, evaluate, and give them honest feedback. Invite a guest artist to conduct your students while you listen and critique from outside the rehearsal. Have the mentor speak to your students to reinforce what you have been telling them. In private, ask if the mentor noticed anything you might change to improve the results in your classroom. Even on days when you do not have guests, you can counteract the natural tendency to overlook problems by doing the following:

- Stand in the back of each section and listen critically; look for things you've missed; be honest about what your students are doing well and what needs improvement.

- Record and/or video the class so you and your students can watch and listen critically to how they really look and sound.

- Learn the score at home so you can carefully watch your students and listen to the group in front of you—*not the one in your head.* Teachers who sing or play along with their students are audiating what they want to hear instead of listening to the actual performance.

- Finally, keep asking yourself questions: "Is that bow hold really correct?" "Was that G really in tune?" Always hold students to high standards, and expect them to perform no less than their very best.

3.
Great teachers keep their vision separate from what the students actually demonstrate.

While we must take into account what students can do before we begin to teach them, great teachers do not lower their expectations to meet their students. Teachers who are clear about both their expectations and the true level of student accomplishment can identify what skills the students have yet to learn *and* what areas the teacher can improve upon next year. Grade your students only on the skills that were addressed in class, but continue to seek better strategies for getting your students to reach their full potential.

Great teachers also keep their vision separate from their own history and teaching ability. Teachers naturally and habitually tend to teach what they know best. A common example of this is the young bass player who is often left alone to figure out bass fingerings. Avoid shying away from the skills that are less familiar and continually seek out new answers and strategies from peers, mentors, or method books. Seek ways for your students to surpass your own abilities.

4.
Great teachers hold themselves and their students accountable.

It is too easy to pin the blame on the students' previous orchestra teacher, scheduling problems, or the endless list of things your program may lack: funding, private teachers, planning or class time, parental support, or student practice. Every teacher faces challenges like these, and great teachers find ways to either lessen the effects of these problems or resolve them altogether. Ask your peers and mentors how they handle these problems, and always look for better solutions to the challenges your students and programs face. Hold yourself accountable and remember that the most powerful and influential force in every classroom is the teacher.

Students will play as poorly as the teacher allows; they will perform their best only when the teacher gives them absolutely *no other choice*.

5.
Great teachers are always learning and improving their craft.

Make every effort to seek and listen to the finest student groups in the country. Go and listen to the groups at state and national conferences. Go to concert festivals and hear the performances of other orchestras. Occasional pangs of jealousy, frustration, even inadequacy, are normal; they provide you with an incentive to improve your game. Turn these pangs into inspiration, and identify the skills that the students in superior programs possess; then create a curriculum to develop those skills in your students. Base your decisions about what your students should demonstrate at the end of the year on real information that you gather from other teachers and programs—this is too important to make up on your own.

How Great Teachers Use Sequential Method Books

Our string education community—including college methods classes as well as the method book publishing industry—has addressed the needs of the middle school string class better than any other age group. Beginning and second-year method books and supplementary materials are plentiful, and teachers should take full advantage of the wealth of resources available to them. Do a little research and find the method that is right for you. If you don't know which one to choose, seek out a highly successful middle school program in your state and ask the director what method they use. Or, spend a few hours at the exhibit booths at your next state conference and find a method that more closely suits your teaching preferences and goals.

Method books offer many benefits, and the greatest of these is thoughtful sequence of exercises that helps teachers organize their daily and long-range lesson plans. There are a variety of method books on the market, and each uses different exercises, strategies, and pedagogical philosophies to teach basically the same things:

- Instrument and Hand Position
- Finger Patterns and Tonal Literacy – Organization of Half and Whole Steps
- Rhythms, Rhythmic Literacy, and Bowing Mechanics
- Articulation and Volume
- Musical Terms and Facts about Cultural/Historical Connections

Sequential method books are designed to be easy to read, visually appealing, and pedagogically sound. They are created for the student and teacher to move seamlessly from one exercise to the next in a natural progression that is extremely easy to follow and teach. They are so easy to use that one hardly has to think to open up the book and go through the exercises.

As helpful as method books are, they create several powerful illusions that can divert an unknowing teacher's attention away from teaching deep, meaningful skill development. Understanding these illusions, like understanding mirages in the desert, can help us keep our focus on how the skills and knowledge should be organized, taught, and assessed. To be clear, the problem is not with the method books themselves, but in the way we use them and how we allow ourselves to believe that the following illusions are real:

Illusion #1: Learning new skills is more important than review.
Illusion #2: Learning a string instrument is as easy as 1, 2, 3.
Illusion #3: Our job is to teach the skills in the book.

Illusion #1: Learning new skills is more important than review.

The skills in all method books are introduced in a thoughtful pedagogical order. The authors understand the importance of review, but they are also pressed to address as many skills as possible within a certain number of pages. As a result, the natural focus of every method book is the introduction of new skills; review is mentioned in most books, but the job of review is left to the teacher, not the book. This creates an unintentional illusion that learning the next new skill in the sequence is more important than review. In string education, nothing could be further from the truth.

This illusion leads to a sort of treadmill syndrome. The seamless, sequential structure of a well-written method creates a natural momentum and desire for pushing forward to the next exercise. It is very easy to move from one exercise to the next because it requires absolutely no planning to say, "OK, class, let's do the next one." After a while, we begin to think in terms of exercise numbers with little regard for the skills that each exercise addresses. We mindlessly press forward with a plan of doing 3 to 5 exercises a day, whether or not the students understand and learn the skills!

Great teachers understand that review is a fundamental principal of learning any instrument, and in a sequential method, it is up to the teacher to frequently halt that forward momentum and review what the students just learned. Set the method book accompaniment to play and repeat 5 to 10 previously introduced exercises, and as students play, travel around the room helping students improve technique. Great teachers also identify important scales, melodies, and exercises throughout the method book, and use them as review anchors. On review days, instead of playing every exercise, just have students review the important anchors that are exceptionally effective for addressing the skills you want to review. As students learn more skills, review becomes increasingly important and should take longer amounts of time.

Illusion #2: Learning a string instrument is as easy as 1, 2, 3.

A good method book makes learning a string instrument look easy, and we consciously support the illusion because we want our students to be excited about playing a string instrument, not overwhelmed by it. The only problem with the simplification of playing a string instrument is that after a while, we begin to believe it, too. We *want* to believe it's easy because thinking about objectives, strategies, and assessments that support the method book exercises is complicated.

The danger of this illusion is in the way that it dulls our awareness and understanding about all that goes into playing a string instrument. We easily forget that the material in a student method book is just the tip of the iceberg—actually, many tips of the many icebergs we now recognize as units on tone production, hand position, intonation, rhythm, and musical expression. The mountains of content that took us years to learn are slickly simplified and smoothed into a nice easy path. As we minimize the depth of each content area, we eventually forget the unit objectives, strategies, and assessments that support the concepts in the book. Instead, we just skim effortlessly over the top, touching briefly upon each skill before moving on to the next exercise.

Great string teachers make a clear distinction between the content they plan to teach and the method book they use to teach it. They derive their content, not from the method book alone, but also from their own education and the development of unit goals, objectives, strategies, and assessments discussed in previous chapters of this book. When great teachers use a method book, they analyze the exercises, identify the skills that each exercise addresses, and *focus on teaching and assessing the skill, not the exercise*. They use a variety of teaching strategies, games, and material to teach each skill from a deep understanding of unit goals, objectives, and assessments that are associated with that skill.

Method books can help teachers with sequencing and material, but they cannot make string instruments any easier to play. String instruments require the same skills and the same hours of practice that they always have. It is our job to understand that a method book is just a tool to help us teach the content we want our students to learn.

Illusion #3: Our job is to teach the skills in the book.

If our eagerness to over-simplify skills fuels the second illusion, then our eagerness to over-simplify our job fuels the third. Being a string teacher becomes a little easier if we believe that our job is to teach the skills in the method book. When we are busy or overwhelmed—as we frequently are—we want to believe that if we finish teaching everything in the method book and play some concert music, then we have done our job. This may be the illusion responsible for the lack of music making going on in many string classrooms.

Method books are great for organizing strategies and exercises, and concert music can be fun to perform, but neither type of material can teach the artistic processes of *creation*, *expression*, and *reflection* that are central to music and music education. When we get busy, we reduce our job to teaching notes, rhythms, and skills, but there is so much more to music making.

Great teachers ask students to play a method book exercise with different interpretations. In a single-line exercise, they ask where the top of the phrase is, and they ask about the character of the melody. They work improvisation and composition into their lessons on beginning tetrachord patterns. They research the background of the method book folk songs, and tell students the historical relevance of the melodies. The NAfME standards and the ASTA *Curriculum* remind us that there is more to music education than teaching the skills in method books and music.

Additional Best Practices

Sometimes the littlest things can make the biggest difference. The seven best practices listed below do not require enormous effort or preparation. They are small, but significant, habits that make instruction effective for your students.

1. Develop an effective warm-up routine.

A good warm-up routine is a teacher's best opportunity to correct the technical issues that are the root cause of other problems (like poor tone and intonation). To keep warm-ups from becoming mindlessly repetitive, give the warm-up a pedagogical focus. For the sake of variety, it is good to rotate between several different warm-up exercises.

Violins and violas should stand during warm-ups to promote better performing position. Standing also makes it easier for the teacher to isolate and correct position problems without leaning over the student. When the warm-up routine is led by a student, the teacher can freely move around the room, provide one-on-one instruction, and hold every student to a high standard of tension-free posture, balance, and hand position. The warm-up routine gives teachers a chance to remind students how relaxed looks and feels. If done convincingly and respectfully, students will learn good technique from the teacher during warm-up.

2. When you are conducting, look at your students and not the music.

Look at your students 80% of the time and your score 20% of the time, instead of the other way around. The first thing you will discover is that your students play just the same or better when you look at them instead of your score. Secondly, and more importantly, you will immediately see, with painful clarity, all of the things your students still need to learn. Look! Are they using excellent left- and right-hand technique? Are their attacks and releases in the same part of the bow? Are their heads also in their music, or are they looking and paying attention to the other members of the ensemble—bowing, breathing, and cuing together?

3. "Show me!" Assess every student every minute you teach.

If a skill is important enough for you to spend time and energy to teach it, then it is also important enough for you to spend some time making sure your students understand what you have taught. Good teachers assess student understanding during and after every concept taught. When teachers do not assess or correct their students, the students naturally conclude that they are doing it right, whether or not they are. Effective, ongoing assessment is as simple as saying, "Show me." For example:

- "Use a marcato stroke at the beginning of that measure; now, show me."
- "Vibrate every half note; show me how you'll do that in m. 3."

- "Violas, listen to the sixteenth notes in the second violins; now, show us how you are going to play your off-beats with them."

There is an important corollary to this lesson:

**If the concept is important enough to teach,
it is also important enough for the students to write it in their part.**

"Show me your pencils" should be the first four words of every musical rehearsal. After you ask the students to make a correction in the music, give students the time and a reminder to write it down.

- "First violins, shift to third position on that D. Play it for me...Good, now mark the fingering in your part."

4. Aim to engage 100% of the students 100% of the time.

Though it is not always possible, engaging every student should be one of your main goals. One of the biggest differences between teachers is the amount of time their students sit in class and do *nothing*. Great teachers create ways to keep all of their students actively learning for large amounts of class time. Young or unprepared orchestra teachers expect their students to sit and wait for long periods of time while their attention is focused elsewhere in the room.

Record a class and time how long students are actively learning or how long they sit and do nothing. The more time students spend actively learning skills in class, the more they will learn. When one student or a small group needs special instruction, use the teaching opportunity to review the needed skill with the entire class. If the violas are playing a C-sharp out of tune, include everyone in the review of playing C-sharp. If the cellos have a tricky rhythm, see if other sections have the same rhythm elsewhere, and teach everyone the rhythm at the same time.

5. Sing.

Singing is a state and National Standard that will help students improve their intonation. The better students sing, the better they play, especially on a string instrument. Sing note names, numbers, solfege; hum or sing on *la*. Sing alone, in groups, with and without the tuner or the CD player. Just SING! Teachers who are uncomfortable singing in front of students are *the perfect role model* for those students who are also uncomfortable. Teachers who do not sing allow their own fears to hold themselves and their students back. Get over it, and sing.

6. Model great playing *for* the students, not *with* the students.

Music is an aural discipline, so you must constantly give your students aural examples. Modeling reaches both visual and auditory learners simultaneously. Good teachers model tone quality, articulation, intonation, and dynamics, and they expect students to echo on their instruments every aspect of the teacher's fine playing.

Great teachers play *for* the students constantly, but as a general rule, they refrain from playing with the students, which can impair their ability to watch, listen, assess student progress, and plan the next steps in the students' development. Great teachers also sing *for* the orchestra, and they have their students sing back; but they don't sing *with* the orchestra. Teachers who hum along with the group are not actually listening to the group in front of them; they are instead listening to the one in their head.

It was once common practice to teach all music classes, including strings, from behind a piano. Playing the piano distracts the teacher and covers up the students. If a piano is required for a concert, begin rehearsing with the piano a couple days before the performance. Until that point, give 100% of your attention to the students and the sound they are making without accompaniment.

7. Teach students to do the work.

The more you do for your students, the more they learn to depend on you. Dependent students will run teachers ragged with all of their problems and questions. If you feel like you are working harder than your students, then it is time to expect students to do the work. In well-managed classrooms, the students are doing most of the work, including distributing music, leading the tuning and warm-ups, giving the teacher time to take care of the few problems that require a professional's experience. Figure out ways for students to do the work, and give them the time and encouragement to work it out themselves.

When students learn to start class, it frees up the teacher to take attendance or resolve emergencies (like fixing a slipped peg or broken string). You can take care of problems while your class moves forward on task. Students are not capable of teaching themselves, and you must be present to guide students and hold them to high standards, or the beginning of class will decay into mindless repetition. That said, you will be a happier, healthier, and more energetic and powerful teacher if you are not facilitating all of the opening routines that students could be doing themselves.

Part of your job is to teach students to be more independent, and when students learn to motivate themselves in class, they are more likely to do the same in other classes and during their practice time at home. This practice fosters ownership and leadership, and teaches students to get themselves ready for class, both physically and mentally. The goal is to guide students and encourage them to take leadership roles and more responsibility for their ensemble and their own education. Furthermore, on the days when you have a sub, you can rest assured your students will be able to get class up and running without you.

Chapter 16

Working with Parents

People who are parents know that the job of parenting isn't easy. Parents face many different challenges, and most are doing the best they know how to do with the time, resources, and parenting skills they have. This caring will go a long way as you help their children endure the challenges of learning a string instrument and performing in an orchestra. Parents also want to know that you support *them* and you appreciate the many difficult challenges of parenting.

Young teachers may have trouble relating to parents. In their first few years of teaching, learning how to communicate with older adults—and dealing with the ramifications of not communicating well—can be one of the hardest elements of being a young teacher. But we can all treat our students the way we would like our own children to be treated by their teachers.

IN THIS CHAPTER:

- Understanding Parents
- Angry Parents—A Survivor's Guide
- Communicating with Parents
- Parent Organizations—The Role of the Booster Club
- Planning a Booster Budget
- Field Trips

Understanding Parents

Dealing with angry parents is one of the worst parts of our job. It can be stressful and very time consuming for you *and your principal.* Just as beekeepers must learn to collect honey without upsetting the bees, teachers must learn to teach students without upsetting their parents. Following the three rules below will greatly reduce misunderstandings, headaches, and emotional anguish for you, your boss, and your students and parents. If parents are angry with you, it is very likely you broke one (or more) of these rules:

Rule #1:
Communicate with parents frequently and in a positive and non-threatening way.

Go out of your way to keep e-mails and information letters positive and encouraging, especially when you are communicating rules or expectations. Today's parents expect to be informed, and they do not like being surprised. Make sure your information is easy for parents to access. Put it in your handbook, on your website, and send home e-mails with information about upcoming events. Above all, though, keep the information consistent and positive, even caring and encouraging, and your parents will not only appreciate your tone, but they will more likely develop greater trust and will be less likely to react to you with fear or anger.

Rule #2:
Create fair and enforceable policies and procedures, and enforce them with *everyone* equally.

State your policies and procedures clearly in your handbook, and make sure your principal understands and supports them. Your policies should follow school rules and school board's policies as closely as possible. It is equally important that your policies are *enforceable* and that you enforce them consistently and fairly. Enforceable rules do not discriminate; they are the same for everyone. Following rules simply comes down to students or their parents making a decision about consequences.

Many parents won't even notice or care about your policies until it applies to their child. All of a sudden, when you least expect it, Perfect Parent A would like for you to bend the rules for little Lisa because she has been the top fundraiser for the last two years. Avoid making exceptions because students and parents talk to each other, and other parents will soon ask for you to make exceptions for them. When you start making exceptions, your job becomes very complicated very quickly. If you believe your policy is not fair to an individual, don't make an exception to the policy; *change the policy*.

Rule #3:
Communicate that you support and encourage the uniqueness of every child, even though they are learning the same curriculum and following the same rules as everyone else in your orchestra.

Schools and classes have a preset amount of content that students are expected to learn, and rules must apply to everyone. Your challenge is to recognize and appreciate the unique needs and learning speed of each child while teaching every child the same curriculum and treating everyone equally and fairly. Students naturally learn at different rates because they have different:

- Amounts of experience and skills already under their fingers;
- Strengths and weaknesses (some students learn much faster than others);
- Learning styles and levels of work ethic; and
- Parental and financial support.

The best way to handle this apparent paradox is to frame everything in the positive. Teachers and parents should make a habit of approaching their students from the perspective of how full their glass is, not how empty. It's the same child either way, so encourage the child and build the child, supportively, to be the best he or she can be. This means we should set student goals for growth, not based on how others are doing, but based on what the student has learned already and what he or she needs to learn next. There will always be students with more skills and students with less, and it is important to remind students and their parents that it is natural, and even okay, for students to learn at different speeds.

Angry Parents—A Survivor's Guide

Some parents are naturally temperamental, stressed, or have a hair-trigger response. Sometimes teachers do make mistakes that set off parents, but sometimes it's not the teachers at all. Parents may have doubts and fears based on their own experience that may include you, or maybe not. Your job is to recognize that parent frustration is usually about miscommunication and not about you, your qualifications, or how much you care about their children.

The first and best way to calm down parents is to listen to their concerns. Like all people, parents raise their voices when they believe their fears or concerns are not being heard. So listen—without taking offense or taking it personally. You can listen without having to respond; just listen and let the parents know that you hear their concerns.

If you don't feel comfortable responding, then learn when to say, "Let me get back to you." Especially when we are tired, parents can drive us to do things that we know we shouldn't. Being professional includes being professional even when we are stressed or tired, so pay attention to your ability to cope. If a parent approaches you at a bad time, have the professional wherewithal to tell the parent that you will get back to him or her as soon as you can. This is always better than losing your cool—or worse, your job.

Along the same lines, when you get an angry e-mail, always wait before you respond. Never, ever, reply when you are angry; you will regret it every time. If necessary, wait

24 hours. Then when you do respond the next day, keep it short and positive. If your e-mail is longer than three brief paragraphs or if your words could be misconstrued as negative, it's better to stop writing and call the parent or set up a conference.

Be aware of the *location* in which you discuss student issues. Never allow a student or parent to begin an important discussion in any other location than your office. If a parent approaches you during or after a rehearsal, simply arrange a time to talk about the matter in your office. If you ever feel that a conference is going to be unusually confrontational, schedule the appointment with an administrator present, or schedule the appointment in the school conference room.

When you encounter a parent who is truly unreasonable, it is important to document everything you do. If you had to defend your decisions to the school board, would you have enough documentation to prove your case? Write down dates and times, keep recorded messages and threatening letters, and keep hard and soft copies of e-mails. It may be necessary to keep several years' worth of records if you have a particularly disruptive student. Most of the contentious issues that drive parents to their most vehement arguments are the same issues that should be clearly spelled out in your handbook and must be clearly enforceable, which is why your handbook is so important.

Teaching music can be a very difficult job; but remember, it's just a job. It's not personal. You put everything into this job—your heart, soul, everything—and it feels personal to you. It *feels* personal to all great teachers, but when we *make* it personal, we diminish our professionalism.

One more thing:

No matter how great your teaching is,
there will always be crazy parents.

You must decide if you are going to define yourself by what they say, or define yourself by what you do. Administrators learn very, very quickly to let the comments of crazy parents roll off their backs. They wouldn't survive a month if they didn't. So be more like an administrator: *listen to parents, but don't let them define you.* Define yourself.

Communicating with Parents

The most important rule is to communicate frequently and positively with parents. There are different types of information we need to communicate, and different ways to communicate each type. In Chapter 3, we looked in detail at the Orchestra Handbook and the policies and expectations that we communicate to parents. Let's look at some of the other ways we communicate with parents.

The biggest problem with communication
is the illusion that it occurred.[1]

We are in the middle of the "information age," and the way we communicate with students, parents, and administrators is evolving so quickly that it can be difficult to keep up. Since younger people tend to adapt more quickly than older generations, the generation gap tends to produce a communication gap. For example, parents check their e-mail, but many students don't. Instead, students text or communicate by messaging through the latest hip social media platform, which seems to change every three to five years. Younger teachers tend to be technologically savvy, but they do not communicate as formally as their principal or the older parents of their students. Conversely, older teachers are resistant to building websites and using text blasts, which is a problem in a world where these have become primary modes of communication.

In the information age, people expect to be able to find any information easily, and they become quickly frustrated and impatient when they cannot find information when they want it. We must be clear with our students and parents about how we plan to communicate. This is usually done at the Fall Meeting—which is, itself, a valuable form of communication.

Fall Parent Orientation Meeting:

Every meeting with parents is an important one because parents form an opinion about their child's experience in your program based on their experiences with you. Parents want to know that you are organized and efficient. When parents come away from the first parent meeting feeling excited about the orchestra program, then they will keep the climate at home a positive one.

At your orientation meeting, parents will want to know how you will communicate with them and how they can communicate with you. They also need to know how to find the calendar, policies, and various forms on the website. Be sure to include required materials and concert dress, practice expectations, and anything else you want parents to know. Finally, explain why it is important for the students' orchestra program to have parents' support, and how parents can help by volunteering for jobs or being on the booster steering committee.

The Orchestra Website:

Websites are great tools for communicating information that stays constant throughout the year, including performance calendars, grading policies, rules, and procedures. Parents will go to your website to become familiar with the general expectations and requirements of your program. Your website is also an important recruiting tool because it is the first place the parents of prospective students will go to see if they want their child in your program. So make sure it looks sharp!

---

1 This quote is commonly attributed to George Bernard Shaw, but the actual source is unclear.

Teachers are often expected to keep a teacher webpage on their school website, but you may want to create a separate professional-looking website for your orchestra program. Below are some information topics and pages you might include on your orchestra website:

- Calendar of after-school rehearsals, concerts, trips, and important deadlines
- Grading and attendance policies; information about promotion and auditions
- Postings for auditions (including rules and links to excerpts)
- Testing rubrics and practice records
- Spring trip information (including links to forms and deposit slips)
- Fundraising materials and sponsors
- Instructions for paying fees (with links to online payment services)
- Private teacher contact information
- Summer camp information (with links to local camps)
- Information about local scholarships
- Awards, special student recognitions, and photos
- On-line webcasts of performances
- Orchestra booster by-laws, booster e-mail directory, job descriptions, and parent profile forms
- Archived newsletters and booster meeting minutes
- A letter from the director and the director's bio
- Why music? Advocacy statements about arts education
- Frequently asked questions
- Parent testimonials about the virtues of the program for their child

A professional-looking website is worth its weight in gold. Be sure to include pictures of smiling students happily playing their instruments and enjoying the orchestra family. Don't use the website for communicating time-sensitive information that will become quickly outdated; people don't check the website for updates, and nothing kills a website faster than old, outdated information. Newsletters and e-mails are a much better tool for sending out timely concert details and reminders.

Information Letters and Newsletters:

Gone are the days of handing pieces of paper to the students and hoping that the information gets home. Information letters about concerts, field trips, and fundraisers are now sent home in e-mails, and parents are thankful for this. As a rule, e-mails longer than 3 paragraphs work best when they are written in a separate document and sent as an attachment. You can review "handouts" with your students on the Smartboard and then e-mail the handouts to parents. Always make a few hard copies available for students whose parents don't have e-mail or a printer.

The monthly newsletter is an excellent vehicle for reminding parents about events coming up in the next month, including more details than one might find on a standard calendar. Details about fundraisers, concert attire, reminders about field trip payments are just a few examples. Newsletters are also great for seasonal information, like reminding parents in November that it's time to start thinking about summer camps and scholarship auditions that usually come up in the early spring. Newsletters don't have to be fancy. You might even find a parent who can help you with your newsletters.

E-mail Blasts and Positive E-mails:

Short e-mail blasts can serve as a great weekly reminder about upcoming events. Keep them short, three paragraphs or less, if possible. All e-mail correspondence is dependent upon a teacher's ability to get every parent's e-mail address at the beginning of the year. Put an announcement on the cover of your handbook telling parents to e-mail you with their best addresses so you can communicate with them about upcoming concerts and field trips.

E-mails are easy, but they do have their drawbacks. If you find yourself spending a lot of time constructing a long e-mail, especially to a parent or your boss, then you probably should call them instead. If you receive an angry e-mail from a parent, the best thing to do is step away from the computer, give yourself enough time to cool down—possibly 24 hours—and then pick up the phone and call the parent. Never, *ever* send an angry e-mail; it may release stress at first, but angry e-mails are both inflammatory and unprofessional. We are better than that.

Positive e-mails, on the other hand, are a powerful motivational tool. Create a plan at the beginning of the year to ensure that all parents in the program receive a positive e-mail or personal postcard praising their child.

Text Messaging:

Currently, the best way to communicate immediately with students is through texting. There are excellent free texting services (like *Remind*) that allow you to text short blasts to all of your students or one class at a time. You can send out reminders about upcoming events or homework assignments from your computer or phone, and they use a filter that allows you to keep your number confidential. If you want to send students more information than a text will allow, send them a text that refers them to an email or a webpage.

Facebook:

Once considered taboo for employees, many school districts now use Facebook to communicate with parents. My parent organization created a public and private Facebook page for our orchestra, and it has been a great tool for sharing concerts, field trip pictures, and all kinds of news with parents. As an older educator, I completely underestimated the powerful impact Facebook could have on our program. Students and chaperones share pictures of smiling kids, and it has greatly enhanced orchestra morale and a sense of community. If you are not a Facebook fanatic, give the job to a parent who loves Facebook and the orchestra.

Communications Chair:

Effective communication is so important and multifaceted that you may want to consider appointing a new person to your booster board who holds the title of Communications Chair. This person should be someone who loves the program and supports you. The communications chair can send out multiple communications with quick-hitting bits of information about upcoming rehearsals, performances, concert dress, fundraisers, notes to volunteers, and so on. Find the right person to make the program tick and keep all parents happy and informed.

Phone Calls and Parent Contact Logs:

The rapid increase in communication platforms hasn't stopped people from miscommunicating and misunderstanding each other. Sometimes it is still best to pick up the phone or meet face to face.

My principal is fond of saying, "The phone is your friend, unless it is ringing." In other words, use the phone to reach out to parents before they get upset and start calling you. Keep a file on your computer that has a place for date, time, student name, parent name, and subject matter. Any time you talk to a parent, whether about a positive or negative situation, notate it in your parent log. This will give you a record of how you are doing with parent communication. If everything on your log is about negative situations, start making calls several times a week to parents letting them know how well their child is doing in orchestra.

Parent Organizations—The Role of the Booster Club

Briefly look at "The Life of an Orchestra Director" (Appendix B) and review all of the jobs and responsibilities you have. Then ask yourself, "Would I rather spend my time managing administrative duties or musical ones?" We cannot dodge every administrative duty, but delegating even some of the responsibilities to parents allows us to spend more of our time on music-making issues. Plus, when parents are actively involved in the orchestra program, their endorsement of the program gives us credibility in their children's eyes. One of the best ways to create a positive culture among your parents and students is to start a parent booster organization.

There are a few things to do before you put a booster program in place. First, get yourself and the needs of your program organized. For parents to follow your lead, they must first trust your organization and vision. Second, make sure everyone understands this fundamental premise:

The orchestra director handles music/orchestra issues.
The booster club president/committee chairs handle booster club issues.

When a booster club is running smoothly, both sides can work on their own issues, though there will be times when you will need to be more involved in the booster club decisions.

The first step in creating a booster organization is to define, in as much detail as possible, the jobs that would benefit the orchestra most. Using Appendix B, make a list of the jobs that only you can do, and another list of jobs that can be done by someone else.

Next, find out your parents' interests and skill sets; some parents have no time or interest to serve on the boosters. Learn about parents' skills and interests using a Parent Profile Form (Appendix E). Hand out the Parent Profile Form at the first parent meeting of the year, and encourage parents to sign up and become active. This form should list of all the jobs you would like parents to do. Parents should have a place on the form to identify the skills they have that could benefit the orchestra and also describe how much time they are willing to invest. You may have parents who are nurses that could be responsible for keeping the medical kit stocked and helping students on field trips, while others who are in advertising could design ads for various publications. You may have a person in your booster organization who likes helping out once a week on whatever project seems to be the most pressing. Stay-at-home moms or dads seem to be some of the hardest-working folks around, and they can be an invaluable asset to you and your program. This person could take on secretarial or public relations work, including making copies, mailing correspondence, completing forms for various orchestra events, writing grants, booking trips, writing articles, or doing computer work.

As the booster club becomes more established and developed, you will want to have specific positions with job descriptions. The following model is an example you can use to establish committees that you think would enhance the quality of life for your students based on your school, community, and organization:

Steering Committee:

- President
- Vice President
- President Elect
- Secretary
- Ways and Means (fundraising)
- Treasurer
- Publicity

Subcommittees:

- Student Accounts
- Parent Helpers
- Food and Hospitality
- Uniforms
- Buses and Other Transportation
- Trip Coordination
- Chaperones
- Communications (Communications Chair, Facebook, newsletters, publicity)
- Website
- Fundraisers
- Donations and Grants

Good communication reduces confusion and keeps parents on track doing what you envision. Frequently check in with parents and guide them, if needed. Guiding a parent is usually easier than doing the job yourself. If not, then you will know to ask a different parent the next time.

Booster organizations should have by-laws that include a mission statement and various job descriptions. It is important that you, as the director, feel comfortable with the booster by-laws. Effective by-laws are the framework that governs how decisions are made and harmony is kept. Most by-laws do state that the primary role of the booster club is to support the director and to provide for the financial needs of the organization. There are examples of music booster by-laws available from NAfME.

Troubleshooting Common Booster Problems:

One of the more common problems within booster clubs is the tendency for a relatively small number of people to do the majority of the work. You can reduce this tendency by encouraging everyone to find a place within the organization. Ask parents to donate a certain amount of time to your program, whether it's five hours a year or five hours a week. Every parent has different talents and time frames, so ask them what they can contribute. After you compile the names of people who have helped in each of the fundraisers, projects, or committees, you will find that a large percentage of the organization is doing something.

The other issue you will encounter is disenfranchised parents who will say that they have never been asked to do anything within the organization. Many times, people feel awkward about volunteering or walking into a new situation. The reality is that if they would just show up, someone would tell them how to help. Veteran parents need to be trained to welcome new parents with open arms. As much as we would like to keep the veteran parents around forever, they will graduate, too. Through the use of the nominating committee and the Parent Profile Form, you can have a thriving, active booster organization. The goal is to involve everyone in the capacity that he or she feels most comfortable and to have leaders in place that you, the director, feel will do the job most effectively. When you have a great support system in place, you can devote more time to teaching students to make music and less time attending to all of the administrative jobs that a program requires.

Planning a Booster Budget

School districts can provide funding support in the form of an instrument allocation, repair account, or transportation budget. The amount your boosters will have to raise depends largely on how much of your budget is not covered by your school or district. If you receive more than 60% of your yearly budget from your school or district, consider yourself lucky! Most programs have financial needs that exceed the district funding, and it is up to the director, students, and boosters to raise funds to meet the needs of the program.

Before the start of school, write out a list of expenses in a line item format for everything not covered within the district budget (see the example in Appendix F: Operating Budget Statement for Orchestra Boosters). This line item operating budget is just a blueprint for the year. Try not to underestimate expenses, and keep in mind that things can and will change. When the entire budget is planned and discussed, divide the total amount of all budgeted expenses by the total number of students enrolled in the program. For example, if your operating budget is $9,000 and there are 100 students in the program, the fair share dollar amount per student would be $90. Each student and their family would be responsible for fundraising or paying the $90.

The Operating Budget Statement like the one in Appendix F explains how everyone will do their fair share to make up for all expenses that are not covered by the district. Some families may choose to simply write a check for the amount and not fundraise at all. Others will fundraise the entire amount. Either way, the fair share process ensures that the program is fully funded, and it provides a path for parents to get involved and support their child's program.

Before making a major decision involving finances, consult with the booster steering committee. In turn, the steering committee should also consult with you before making any major decisions. In a good booster organization, the director and parents work together to make quality decisions for young people, and music education is the driving force behind this relationship.

Field Trips

Field trips require more clear communication with students, parents, and administration than anything else you do all year. They also require extraordinary planning and extra supervision provided by chaperones. For larger trips, you may want to invite and pay for a school administrator who can take care of discipline problems and help answer tough supervision questions that can arise on the trip. Trustworthy parents can also help plan larger trips and coordinate chaperones. When delegating responsibilities, it is very important to clearly communicate how the jobs are divided so administrators, teachers, and parents are not stepping on each other's toes.

Being a chaperone is hard work, especially on overnight trips. Select the best chaperones who are up to the task of supervising students, loading buses, checking students into their rooms late at night, and getting up before students come out of their rooms. The question most chaperones ask is, "I'm here; now what do you want me to do?" Make a clear list of responsibilities and hold a well-planned chaperone meeting to help chaperones understand and do their jobs, and keep confusion to a minimum.

Chaperone Orientation Meeting:

Most programs do not have any trouble finding parents to chaperone, and every veteran director has one or two "out-of-control" chaperone stories. It is important to train chaperones just as you would train students for student leadership. Without demeaning parents, you must impress upon them their responsibility to keep students safe in a positive and professional way. There are liability issues, personal issues, and overprotective parent issues to deal with. For the chaperone, the student is the customer, and good customer relations are vital for a healthy chaperone/student environment.

Address the following topics in a chaperone orientation meeting before each significant trip:

- Policies and procedures as outlined by the director and the school/district
- The importance of being positive and prepared
- Medical and respect issues
- Medical insurance forms and liability issues
- Expectations for overnight trips and for travel by bus/plane
- Chaperone assignments and specific duties
- Encourage chaperones to ask the director if there is ever a question about anything regarding the duties or responsibilities of a chaperone or a student

Always have a detailed list of chaperone responsibilities (see the example in Appendix G: Chaperone Responsibilities). It is an exhaustive list for long, involved trips that you can alter or pair down as needed to fit your trips. Also prepare a list of students responsibilities (see the example in Appendix H: Student Responsibilities) to hand out and go over with your students. Before the trip, clearly communicate to your students the rules chaperones will be enforcing during the trip. It's not a good practice to have parents telling the students the rules; the parents' job is to keep students safe by enforcing the rules.

Chapter 17

Happiness: From Sake to Sandcastles

IN THIS CHAPTER:

- Life Is Like a Box of Sake
- Someone, Please, Just Tell Me What to Do
- Sustainability
- Sandcastles

Life Is Like a Box of Sake

Before Margaret and I got married, our favorite place to eat was a wonderful sushi restaurant in Columbia, SC. On the most special occasions, we would celebrate by ordering a "box" of sake, which meant we were ordering "the good stuff" that was served in a small wooden box instead of the standard porcelain carafe. The waitress would bring out our box and a large bottle; then she slowly poured the sake and kept pouring until it began to spill over the sides of the box.

The first time we ordered a box of sake, my initial reaction was, "Oh no, this expensive sake is spilling out of the box!"—feelings tied to that "don't spill your milk" lesson that had been ingrained in me since childhood. I quickly learned to appreciate the symbolism of this ceremonial over-pouring, and now, when I watch the sake trickle over the sides of the box, I feel the tension from recent stresses wash away while my inner voice says, "Ahhh, how wonderful; my cup runneth over."

For orchestra teachers—and all busy professionals—life is like a box of sake. Our in-boxes are frequently full, if not completely overflowing. For many of us (especially the type-A, high-strung, hard-working-so-I-can-get-better-at-this-string-instrument kind of people that we tend to be) our initial reaction to seeing our over-flowing in-box is, "Oh no! I'm not doing enough. Work faster, work harder, work longer."

Author Stephen Covey suggests that we should consider ourselves *lucky* if we still have stuff in our life's "in-box" when we pass on. My wife is a mother of two who keeps up with the children's homework, practice, and lessons; she is also a middle school orchestra teacher who teaches 160 orchestra students by herself, she is currently Orchestra President of our state music education association, and in her "free time" she plays cello and guest conducts around our state. She has a practice of retraining her inner voices that say, "I *have* to..." to now say "I *get* to...." Instead of saying, "I *have* to practice my instrument and plan a field trip for my students," she says, "I *get* to practice my instrument; I *get* to plan a field trip for my students."

How do I choose to spend the rest of my life reacting to my full in-box? First, I remind myself that this reaction is a choice, and then I choose to appreciate that I have a great job and a wonderful family; I appreciate that it's my choice to work very hard as a husband, father, and teacher; and I do feel lucky when I remember only to work as hard as I choose to work, as hard as I *want* to work.

What are we doing today? We are teaching children how to make beautiful music on stringed instruments. To do this, we must maintain our own balance as we lead them on an exciting, rewarding, and sometimes challenging journey.

Someone, Please, Just Tell Me What to Do

Jobs vary, and so do the expectations of different administrators, but the following expectations are relatively universal. If you are doing everything on this list, then you are by most accounts doing your job—and probably doing it well. Conversely, when someone is upset with you or your work, more than likely you will be able to trace the problem back to the poor execution of one or more of these expectations.

The Ten Expectations of Music Directors:

1. Supervise your students and enforce school rules to keep them safe at school and on field trips.
2. Be professional in the way you handle money, use your computer, and interact with students.
3. Be a positive, solution-oriented team player on your faculty; arrive to work on time, do your job, and don't leave early.
4. Be clear and consistent with classroom rules, expectations, and discipline.
5. Communicate frequently and positively with parents about upcoming events, student progress, and behavior.
6. Know what you expect your students to learn by the end of the year, and have a thoughtful pedagogical plan for reaching your end-of-year goals.
7. Clearly articulate what students are expected to learn each day, and how today's learning will be assessed and graded.
8. Use effective strategies to inspire students to work positively together and learn the skills and knowledge they need to reach their end-of-year goals.

9. Keep learning, and keep up with recertification requirements.
10. Enjoy your work, and maintain a healthy balance between your career and the other important people and interests in your life.

Who Do I Trust?

The best way for school orchestra directors to stay happily employed is for us to do our jobs well. But what does that mean? What are the criteria by which we measure the qualities of an orchestra teacher? Is it the number of trophies in the orchestra room? Or the ratings our groups earn at concert festival? Or is it the results of our administrator's observation? How do I know if I am doing a good job, and what could I do better? We need to know if we are doing a good job to be happy and satisfied that we are making a positive contribution to the world.

We want to be able to trust our own judgment, experience, and intuition, but we can only trust ourselves to a point—and that is especially true for young teachers. We must rely upon the people around us for different types of guidance. Our jobs require us to work with many different groups of people, including the students, their parents, administrators, and professional peers. We receive constant information, opinions, and feedback from each of these groups. Sometimes this information from the different voices in our community can be confusing, overwhelming, and even contradicting. How can we do our jobs, much less do them well, if we are not receiving clear direction from the people in our professional community? Who do we trust?

After we gain years of experience, we begin to learn when it is appropriate to listen to whom. Each group of people has some jurisdiction on information that is important to us, and when we know who to trust with information, our jobs become a little less confusing and a little more enjoyable. So, who do you ask when you have questions like the following?

- What is my job? What is expected of me?
- What am I supposed to teach?
- How do I inspire or even just communicate with students?
- Am I happy doing this job?

Your principal can answer most questions about your job and tell you what your job requires. Your principal also has the authority to tell you when you are or are not doing what is expected. Trust your administrators when they say you are doing a good job. Their praise is almost always genuine, and experienced administrators do have a sense for whether students are enjoying class and are actively and effectively learning in class. When administrators give you an evaluation, remember not to take it personally. Evaluations are part of the education business—most businesses, actually—and taking it personally is both unprofessional and painful. Listen to the feedback, learn from it, and move on.

Principals are often the first people we ask for feedback, but they do have their limits. First, they are busy, and scheduling time with your boss can be difficult. Second, unless your boss is a former string teacher, he or she will not likely be able to tell you what to teach. If you are looking for guidance about specifics related to teaching orchestra, ask other string teachers who are close to you locally, and also make inquiries in professional learning communities (like ASTA or NAfME). Your professional peers and mentors can help you determine content, instructional and assessment strategies, or even how well your students perform on a given day. Unless colleagues are able to see your work over several months and years, their assessment of your long-term progress is limited.

Most orchestra teachers take their groups to concert festival to get professional feedback from their peers. Good teachers take their students to concert festival because it can be a valuable learning process for the teacher and the students. They don't always walk away with a superior, but good teachers do walk away saying, "The students learned a lot, and even though I feel a little bruised, I know what I want to improve for next year." It's not about the ratings; it's about the learning. The silver lining is in knowing that the best teachers model courage, determination, and professionalism for their students when learning painful lessons.

Remember:
Neither you, nor anyone else, should judge your merits as a teacher solely based upon the results of a concert festival performance.

A fair evaluation, if you are looking for one, must be longer than an evaluation that takes a snapshot of your students' performance on a given day.

When do we listen to parents, and when should we ignore their opinions? It takes time to learn how to differentiate between the two, which is why young teachers are so vulnerable to bullying by bossy parents. When listening to parents, learn to separate the information about their child from the information about you and your instruction. Parents can tell teachers what works for their child and how they would like their child to be treated, but parents do not have the authority to decide what you should teach or how to teach it. Just listen to their concerns, address any misconceptions, and then move on. Beware of parents who greet you early in the year with mountains of praise, gifts, and help. Your relationship with parents is strictly professional, and the parents who try to make it personal should be handled with great caution. If you are not careful, those will be the parents who cause you the most pain.

Finally, how much weight can you give the opinions of your students? The best advice is to watch what your students do and listen to them perform on their instruments, but don't make a habit of listening to their suggestions. Teachers who do this open themselves to an avalanche of opinions, followed by a tsunami of complaints by disgruntled students who didn't get their way. It is your job—a much easier and happier job—to determine the skills students need to learn, the concert repertoire they need to study, and the destination of the spring trip. If you have questions or would like suggestions about what to do, ask mentors and colleagues that you trust; don't ask students or their parents.

There is one field of expertise in which students have valuable information to offer teachers. Students tend to give accurate and honest advice about keeping order and discipline in the classroom; despite their complaining, they do want to learn in a positive and well-controlled classroom environment, and they are experts at knowing what works and what doesn't.

Sustainability

I was twenty-six years old when I went to the doctor with stomach problems. I was in my fifth year of teaching, and I had built the orchestra programs at both of my schools into performing machines; my middle school orchestra was performing at twelve functions a year, and my high school orchestra was performing at nine. That didn't include the field trips, fundraisers, uniforms, and everything else I planned for both programs. My doctor said my stomach problems were the result of stress, and I decided I was too young to get an ulcer. It was time to make some changes.

I was doing great work, but it was not sustainable. Part of the problem with successful teachers is that we add more and more to our plates, and soon our programs and responsibilities outgrow our ability to manage them. Great teachers can easily become victims of their own success. Teachers must decide how hard they are willing to work, and then come up with a plan for covering the jobs that are less important. I am very open with my orchestra parents and my principal about how much I can work. I have identified the parts of my job that I refuse to do poorly, and the other jobs that won't get done if the parents don't do them. Parents want to help, and these types of discussions can motivate them to step up. In addition to parent help, I also look for ways to have students help do the work of running the program. Students can set up chairs, tune themselves, create programs, hang posters, distribute music, manage the library, or anything else that does not involve grades or money.

I take full responsibility for choosing to teach successful orchestra programs that require long hours, but I believe the job of teaching is also harder now than it used to be. School districts are notorious for asking teachers to do more every year, adding new educational initiatives, grading software, website requirements, and other things to our plates. And while they add new things for teachers to do, they rarely tell us what we are allowed to take off our plates to make room for all the new stuff. My last school district was led by a brilliant superintendent who was aware of this problem. Every year, teachers and administrators had a yearly conversation about "strategic abandonment" to determine what wasn't working and which initiatives should be dropped.

As orchestra directors, we should make strategic abandonment part of our end-of-year procedures. When our plates are full, and our overflowing in-boxes create levels of stress that jeopardize our health and balanced life, we need to remember to not add new initiatives until we abandon older ones. We need to have similar discussions with our boosters to periodically determine what they want to keep and what they need to discontinue. Building a program is an evolutionary process that works best when less-successful initiatives are cut to make room for better ones.

Finally, teacher burnout is real, and part of our job is to make sure we rest, see friends, enjoy family, and live life outside of school even throughout the school year. We do this so we can come to school refreshed and ready to be the best teachers we can be for our students. If you are not happy, take a hard look at your job and everything you do. Ask yourself what it would take to make your job enjoyable and sustainable, and then set up a meeting with your boss, your booster parents, or both, and make some changes. Life is too short, and you will be a better teacher for your students, a better spouse, parent, friend, and family member when you create a healthy balance between your career and the rest of your life.

Sandcastles

Every summer my family goes to the beach. My son loves to build sandcastles, and my daughter will boogie board for hours on end. For me, it is a pleasant reprieve from all the music and the relentless go-go-go life of being an orchestra director. It is a time of rest and reflection on the past year—a time to cleanse my memories of scratchy Brandenburg Concertos with the sounds of crashing waves, birds, and the wind.

We work so hard throughout the entire year to create great music with well-trained ensembles—and then it's over. Gone. Especially when I see many seniors graduating, and I look ahead at a young group the following year (what we affectionately call a "building year"), I catch myself thinking, "I just did all that work building a great ensemble, and now it's gone and I have to do it over again. What's the point? Someone, please remind me again."

I was thinking this very thing one evening as my son was watching the tide roll in, slowly erasing his sandcastle. Soon, it would be completely gone, and the following day people would walk right over that place not realizing that a beautiful creation had stood there the day before. So why do we enjoy making sandcastles, even when we know that they are temporary? For the same reason we build orchestras of students who eventually move on, and for the same reason we perform a piece of music for an audience, or possibly just for ourselves. Even though it's temporary, we have created something beautiful, and in the case of orchestra directors, we have shared that beautiful experience with children, creating meaningful and valuable memories of our work and the music we created together—memories that will last a lifetime.

Acknowledgments

To my wife, Margaret, whose patience and support have given me the time, energy, and confidence to articulate what I needed to say in the way I wanted to say it.

To Scott Rush—a mentor, colleague, and friend—for his vision, guidance, trust, and encouragement.

To Gail Barnes, Charles Laux, and Mary Wagner, for their helpful comments and suggestions in the writing process of this book.

To my music teaching colleagues from whom I learned lessons included in this book: Michael Allen, Jose Carrion, Robert Gillespie, Andrea Houde, Alison Mann, Brent Wilson, and many others.

To the teachers in my life who have directed me along my path and shaped the way I teach: Doris Fukawa, John Holzaepfel, Charles J. Hunter III, Donald Portnoy, Richard Rusack, Olene Tilton, and all of my students.

Thank you to Alec Harris for your belief and support of this project, and to all the staff at GIA who made this book possible.

To my mom, Maggie, for encouraging me to become a music teacher, and to my dad, Michael, for teaching me to listen.

Finally, to my wonderful children, Alex and Kate, for all of their hugs, sacrifice, and support.

Appendices

Appendix A: Instrument Letter to Parents

Dear Parents:

Please be very careful when getting your child's first instrument. Read this letter to avoid making a common mistake that makes learning a string instrument extremely difficult, and often pushes students to hate their instrument from the start.

The Internet has brought with it a dramatic increase in string instruments that are of *extremely* poor quality. Parents are unknowingly tricked into purchasing something that looks like a string instrument because the price is much cheaper than instruments at the local store. Here's the catch:

Cheap Internet instruments are more difficult to play and tune. They tend to break easily, and they are difficult and expensive to repair. Even when played by a professional, these instruments sound as cheap as they cost.

Students who are forced to play junk instruments tend not to enjoy their experience and quit early, simply because cheap instruments are difficult to play and tune. To avoid this, we have gone to the local stores, tested and selected models that are made with the correct materials and adequate craftsmanship to meet three minimum standards. At the very least, these instruments produce a pleasing string sound, are relatively easy to tune and play, and are manufactured well enough to hold up under reasonable playing conditions. The stores have agreed to rent and sell these instruments for affordable prices.

Be informed and consult your school or private teacher before purchasing any instrument that is not on this list.

When there is no predicting how long a child will play, we encourage parents to take advantage of the rental option. After visiting the stores, if you do not feel you can afford to rent an instrument from this list, please call the string teacher and ask for help finding a decent instrument. Stores will rent and sell cheaper instruments to compete with the Internet junk; however, to give your child the best chance of experiencing success on his or her string instrument, we ask that parents stick to the recommended list of instruments on the back of this page.

Sincerely yours,

Appendix B: The Life of an Orchestra Director

GET ORGANIZED!

Here is a sample list of responsibilities for an orchestra director. Use this list to help you reflect about the tasks your job requires, and then try writing your own list. Create a booster organization to help you delegate non-director responsibilities to parents.

SUMMER PREPARATION

1. Repair school instruments and re-hair bows.
2. Look at next year's roster, identify instrumentation needs, and reconcile school instrument inventory with student needs.
3. Prepare/update long-range plans.
4. Prepare/update end-of-semester/year tests.
5. Select Fall Concert music and sketch out music for the rest of the year.
6. Prepare/update the handbook:
    a. Plan the calendar
    b. Grading policy, including after-school rehearsal/concert attendance policy
    c. Course descriptions
    d. Student expectations
    e. Medical forms
    f. Permission slips
    g. Student/parent/teacher contract
7. Notify guidance for correct student class placement.

BOOSTERS AND FUNDRAISING

1. Prepare/update booster personnel and e-mail list.
2. Plan and write the booster by-laws with the booster steering committee.
3. Establish booster meeting calendar.
4. Establish booster yearly budget.
5. Establish fundraising calendar.
6. Fill open booster positions, and define roles and responsibilities.

ORCHESTRA CAMP AND/OR WEEKEND CLINIC

1. Create schedule.
2. Arrange facility use.
3. Hire sectional coaches and/or clinician.

4. Arrange travel and hotel for clinician.
5. Organize adult supervision.
6. Arrange student/clinician meals.
7. Follow up on attendance.
8. Prepare and send thank you notes.

FIRST DAYS OF SCHOOL

1. Meet with booster parents to update information and convey new policies.
2. Print and copy the handbook; e-mail electronic copies and link a pdf to the website.
3. Put concert music in folders and get them ready for distribution.
4. Review your first week plans for teaching policies, procedures, rules, and consequences.

COMMUNICATION

1. Update parent email addresses.
2. Maintain website (with parent help).
3. Schedule parent/teacher/student conferences.
4. Coordinate district events with other orchestra teachers.

CONCERT CHECKLIST

Fall, Winter, Pre-Festival, and Spring Concerts

1. Put date and time on the school calendar and website.
2. Book concert venue; request heating/AC, lights and sound, tables/chairs in lobby.
3. Design and print programs (get parent help).
4. Plan set-up and breakdown procedures; get help from students.
5. Publicize the concert:
   a. Create and print posters; put info on the school marquis
   b. Advertise concert at feeder schools
   c. E-mail/invite faculty, administration, and school board
6. E-mail parents and post on the website:
   a. Concert information (date, call time, start time, end time)
   b. Concert attire description
   c. Concert attendance requirements
7. Boosters: Communicate about the reception.

ALL COUNTY, ALL REGION, AND ALL-STATE ORCHESTRA AUDITIONS

1. Explain the value of trying out for honors ensembles.
2. E-mail audition information and forms, and post them on the website.
3. Distribute audition music.
4. Collect forms and fees, and register students.
5. Organize after-school clinics.
6. Hire coaches/clinicians.
7. Schedule mock auditions the week before the audition.
8. Arrange transportation or carpooling to audition site.
9. Announce the results on the orchestra and school websites, in the school announcements, newsletter, and the newspaper.

FIELD TRIP CHECKLIST

Region, All-State, Concert Festival, Spring Trip

1. Prepare tentative trip itinerary.
2. Request permission from administration.
3. Secure transportation—create bus lists.
4, Secure lodging—create room lists.
5. Plan meals—create allergy/vegetarian lists.
6. Outline chaperone duties and expectations—create student/chaperone groups.
7. E-mail forms and information to parents and post on the website:
   a. Field trip parent letter
   b. Final trip itinerary
   c. Student permission forms
   d. Field trip behavior expectations and consequences
   e. Student medical forms
   f. Room lists, bus lists, chaperon/student groups
8. Put together travel binder with student forms alphabetized.
9. Hold pre-trip parent meeting two weeks before the trip.
10. Hold a chaperone meeting one week before the trip.
11. Make plans for loading/unloading buses, checking luggage.

PRIVATE LESSON PROGRAM

1. Publicize program.
2. Contact private instructors.
3. Perform background checks.
4. Give instructor's contact information to parents.
5. Establish criteria for payment and absences.
6. Distribute a participation contract to parents.

7. Obtain facilities.
8. Assign lesson time blocks for teachers.

CHAMBER MUSIC PROGRAM AND/OR SOLO & ENSEMBLE

1. Establish chamber groups.
2. Select music and distribute parts.
3. Schedule rehearsals and arrange supervision and coaching.
4. Collect forms and fees, and register students.
5. Schedule pre-event school recital.
6. Make sure students have original scores for the judges.
7. Arrange transportation or carpooling to the event.
8. Announce the results on the orchestra and school websites, in the school announcements, newsletter, and the newspaper.

CONCERT FESTIVAL

1. Schedule pre-festival concert and arrange for facility use.
2. Complete FIELD TRIP-related forms and tasks (see above).
3. Register groups.
4. Select and distribute music.
5. Purchase extra scores for the judges.
6. Organize after-school sectionals and clinics; hire coaches/clinicians.
7. Announce the results on the orchestra and school websites, in the school announcements, newsletter, and the newspaper.

RECRUITING

1. Create recruiting posters and hang them in feeder school music rooms.
2. Prepare and print professional looking handouts about your program.
3. Contact feeder school principal or music teacher to schedule a visit.
4. Arrange transportation for demo group.
5. Visit feeder schools, perform and hand out flyers:
   a. Talk to music/strings classes, up close and personal.
   b. Show a video about the orchestra program describing class, concerts, trips etc.
   c. Have a good group perform sample warm-up exercises as well as concert pieces for the students.
6. Hold an orientation meeting for interested students/parents:
   a. Create and show recruiting video/slideshow.
   b. Meet with students and parents; answer questions.
   c. Have the top group perform for students and parents.

7. Plan an Application Night:
   a. Secure facilities for instrument testing/placement.
   b. Administer aptitude/placement test.
   c. Organize parent volunteers.
   d. Assign student assistants to testing instructors.
   e. Hire testing night staff.
8. Application Night:
   a. Design and print evaluation rubric.
   b. Evaluate student placement requests.
9. Create and send acceptance letters.
10. Place students in classes based on ability and instrumentation.
11. Hold a new orchestra parent meeting/orientation:
    a. Explain what students need for orchestra.
    b. Give overview of the calendar and schedule.
    c. Go over grading, and after-school rehearsal and concert policies.
    d. Answer questions; introduce booster board.
    e. Pair up new parents with veteran parents willing to share their phone number and answer questions about the program.
    f. Invite local music stores to parent meeting.
12. Notify guidance for correct student class placement.
13. Contact students/parents to resolve placement issues.

LAST DAYS OF SCHOOL—CLOSING PROCEDURES

1. Have upper string students clean out and wipe down instrument lockers.
2. Have lower string students clean school instruments.
3. Record repair needs and set aside instruments/bows for repair.
4. Have a couple students tighten the stands with wrenches.

TEACHER GENERAL RESPONSIBILITIES

1. Daily attendance and other records
2. Update grade book, report cards, interims
3. Grade tests
4. Attend faculty meetings
5. Serve on committees
6. Lesson plans
7. Teacher duties
8. Maintain music library
9. Listen to recordings
10. Score study and music making

Appendix C: Timeline for the Academic Year

Many orchestra teachers oversee every step of instruction from elementary through high school. This timeline includes tasks for teachers of all levels. Teachers who only teach elementary, middle, or high school can use this timeline to help coordinate with other teachers in the "pyramid" to ensure that students who start with one teacher experience quality programs and instruction through all of their school-aged years, and beyond.

JULY

- ❑ Summer organizational meeting with boosters
- ❑ Finalize orchestra calendar
- ❑ Update handbook and long-range plans
- ❑ Order method books, music, and supplies
- ❑ Print handbooks and other materials

AUGUST

- ❑ Assign school instruments to students
- ❑ Rental meeting and/or new parent orientation meeting
- ❑ Fall parent/booster meeting
- ❑ Secondary recruiting for beginning programs
- ❑ Print first grading period handouts and music
- ❑ School open house
- ❑ Emergency lesson plans due
- ❑ Long-range plans due
- ❑ Instructional calendar due

SEPTEMBER

- ❑ Beginner fast start clinics (first week)
- ❑ Fall fundraiser/letter writing campaign for fundraising

OCTOBER

- ❑ Eighth grade orchestra night at high school
- ❑ Fall concert
- ❑ Pass out holiday concert music

NOVEMBER

- ❑ All-region orchestra clinic
- ❑ Begin all-state help sessions

DECEMBER

- ❑ All-county tryouts
- ❑ Holiday concerts
- ❑ Chamber ensemble holiday performances
- ❑ Holiday performances at elementary schools
- ❑ All-state help sessions continue
- ❑ Midwest International Band and Orchestra Clinic

JANUARY

- ❑ Pass out concert festival music
- ❑ All-state auditions
- ❑ Spring fundraiser

FEBRUARY

- ❑ Sight-read literature for concert festival
- ❑ State music educators association conference
- ❑ All-state orchestra clinic

MARCH

- ❑ Pre-festival concert
- ❑ Concert festival
- ❑ Spring trip parent meeting

APRIL

- ❑ Spring trip
- ❑ Fifth grade orientation performance
- ❑ Recruiting trips to elementary schools
- ❑ Rising beginner instrument sizing, shoulder rest testing, and rental information night
- ❑ Student placement auditions for next year
- ❑ Verify with guidance about next year's student placement list

MAY

- ❏ Solo and ensemble festival
- ❏ Spring concerts: elementary, middle, and high school
- ❏ Create upcoming year's events calendar
- ❏ Orientation night for rising orchestra students new to the program
- ❏ Spring general parent meeting
- ❏ Collect all rental instruments, outstanding items, inventory, or supplies
- ❏ Settle all student accounts
- ❏ Orchestra awards ceremony/banquet or promotion ceremony
- ❏ End-of-year orchestra party

JUNE

- ❏ Clean and evaluate instruments for needed repairs
- ❏ Store instruments and arrange repairs with local shop
- ❏ Update and file music for the summer
- ❏ Order new equipment
- ❏ Facility cleaning and repair

Appendix D: Prior Commitment Form

If the student has a conflict that was planned before the required rehearsal or concert is announced, the parent must communicate this conflict in writing to the director. Established religious holidays are excused but should be communicated by the parent using this Prior Commitment Form.

Name of Student: ____

This form is due September 1st for conflicts with any event announced in August on the handbook calendar. For conflicts with events added later to the performance calendar, parents have 10 days to submit this form notifying the director of the conflict.

Today's Date: ____

Date, Time, and Name of the event the student cannot attend:

____

Please describe the reason (wedding, athletic event, etc.) for the conflict and why the student cannot attend:

____

____

____

If this event is excused, the student may be required to make up his or her grade by submitting a recording before the date of the missed event. Students must record themselves performing all of the music from the event that will be missed. For every day the recording is late, 10% will be deducted from the student's grade.

Student Signature ______________________________Date: ______________

Parent Signature: ______________________________Date: ______________

Appendix E: Parent Profile Form

The key to a successful program is the support of staff, students, and especially, the parents. If you can be of assistance in any of the following areas, please volunteer your time and talents. There is nothing more rewarding than being an active member of a fine organization, and your involvement speaks volumes about how you value the choices your child makes. Check areas of interest below, and a committee chairperson will be in touch with you!

Organize	Help Out		
________	________	**Hospitality:**	Social activities, banquets, refreshments, etc.
________	________	**Newsletter:**	Help compile the monthly newsletter
________	________	**Field Trip:**	Help plan trips, chaperone students
________	________	**Fundraising:**	Help organize fundraiser, work events

SPECIAL SKILLS AND INTERESTS

Check one or more of the areas where you can assist.

_____ Legal advisors	_____ Nurse	Miscellaneous: (use space to describe)
_____ Sound equipment	_____ CPA	
_____ Audio / visual	_____ Graphics / art	
_____ Notary public	_____ Crafts	
_____ Computers	_____ Carpentry	

(Mr.) ______________________________ Job description ____________________________

(Mrs.) ______________________________ Job description ____________________________

Please list any other skills you believe will be helpful to the orchestra:

____

____

How much time can you help?

_____ 5 hours a year _____ Several hours a month _____Several hours a week _____Daily

I can help more in the months of _________________________________.

_____ Yes, I can be on hand (on occasion) to help out during and after school.

Appendix F: Sample Budget Statement for Orchestra Boosters

Our orchestra receives $500 each year from the school district. The average yearly operating cost of this program is around $9,500 before including the costs of instrument repairs, major purchases, or field trips. The difference in funding between our operating cost and what the district provides is $9,000 which—when shared equally by our 100 students—comes to $90 per student. The fair share for this school year will be $90 per student, and this money will help pay for the General Operating Funds listed below.

General Operating Budget

- Music. $2000
- Travel Costs for Local Performances (Bus, Equipment Truck). $2000
- After-school coaching $2000
- Method Books. $700
- Concert Programs and Advertising $750
- Office Supplies $300
- Awards Banquet $900
- T-shirts $750
- Director/School Membership Fees $100

The fair share does NOT pay for needs-based scholarships, instrument repairs, or purchases, nor does it help defray large field trip costs. Grants, sponsorships, and other fundraising money will help pay for needs-based scholarships that will be made available to students on free and reduced lunch. Because every family has a different level of need, we will ask parents to pay the fees and field trip costs that they can afford, and the boosters will do their best to equitably make up the difference.

Students who wish to rent a school instrument may do so for $100 per year. This money helps pay for school instrument repairs and supplies that average approximately $2,000 each year. Students may pay the instrument rental fee up front, or add the rental fee to their fair share and work off the amount through fundraising.

Appendix G: Chaperone Responsibilities on Field Trips

Chaperones must be district staff members or parents of orchestra students. The director will select chaperones for each trip, and all chaperones must go through a background check prior to the trip. Parent chaperones may not bring other non-orchestra children, such as a student's siblings, on the trip. Being a chaperone is hard work, especially on overnight trips. Chaperones are responsible for doing the following to keep the students safe and help the trip run smoothly. If you have any questions, ***please ask the director***.

GENERAL GUIDELINES

1. Ensure that first aid kits accompany the students on any bus trip.
2. Write down the cell phone numbers of the other chaperones and the director.
3. Learn the names and needs of the students assigned to you. Give cell phone numbers to students, and have the students text back so chaperones have their numbers as well. Familiarize yourself with any allergies and special dietary needs; double-check to make sure they have food that they can eat during meals.
4. Keep students safe by controlling student environment to reduce students' risky behavior. Enforce school rules and the Code of Conduct at all times.
5. Be on time at meetings and designated checkpoints, and stay apprised of any changes or updates to the itinerary. Model appropriate behavior and use professional language with students and other chaperones. Please do not use offensive or pejorative language toward students or other adults.
6. When a student refuses to comply with a reasonable request, seek assistance from a member of the staff or the director. Do not allow students to draw you into an argument, and NEVER put your hands on a student, unless the student is a clear danger to himself/herself or others. Report any notable behavioral issues and violations of school rules to the director immediately. Disciplinary action should be left to the orchestra director who will address these issues with administration during or after the trip.
7. Do not administer any medications to students, including pain relievers (such as Tylenol). All medications must be preapproved on the student's medical form and are to be administered by a designated district staff member.

DURING BUS TRAVEL

1. Supervise the loading and unloading of all bags, instruments, and equipment on the buses. Students may load this equipment with supervision and as needed to ensure proper care of their personal instruments or school instruments.

2. Before leaving any location (food stops, bathroom breaks, competition sites, etc.), check the roll on each bus. Buses should NOT leave until every student is counted. Chaperones are expected to maintain order on the bus. They should sit in the middle rows and occasionally move around the bus to keep an eye on all students, especially those in the back.
3. When exiting the bus, one chaperone should do a final check, walking through the bus to make sure no sleeping students are left behind.

Chaperones are expected to enforce the following rules on the bus:

1. Every student must have a seat, and students should remain seated when the bus is in motion. No student is allowed to sit in the aisle or on another student's lap.
2. Students will ride the same bus for the duration of the trip and should not switch buses unless told to do so by the director.
3. Students are to be absolutely quiet during every roll call and when instructions are being given by the chaperones, director, or driver. While the bus is moving, students may speak at reasonable noise levels but not so loud that it distracts the driver.
4. Group activities on the bus should be respectful and should not involve peer pressure to coerce students into unwanted or uncomfortable situations. No lewd or disrespectful songs or other activities are allowed.
5. Bags, purses, etc., are to be stowed in the overhead compartments or under the seat, not in the bus aisles.
6. Blankets may only be used when a student has no one sitting next to him or her.

OVERNIGHT TRIPS

1. Know the rooms for which you are responsible, and know the room number and the names of all the students in each room.
2. When students are staying in a hotel, make sure long distance phone service, non-complimentary Internet, and pay-per-view TV channels are turned off at the front desk and cannot be activated by students.
3. At room checks, make sure all students are present. Students should be told when they are to report to breakfast or check out the next morning; they should also be told not to leave the room for any reason and to call the chaperone if they need help. Chaperones should give students their room phone number in case they need to contact an adult.

Appendix H: Student Responsibilities on Field Trips

1. RULE #1 – Follow directions, especially directions about boundaries—where to be and not to be. Comply with all requests made by chaperones or other adults, unless you believe the request to be unsafe or professionally inappropriate. If you completely disagree with a chaperone, find and ask the director for clarification.
2. RULE #2 – Do not bring anything on the trip that would get you in trouble at school. Prior to departure, administrators may search your bags.
3. RULE #3 – Be safe; do not engage in reckless behavior that could harm yourself or others. If you see students doing things that could cause them or another student to get hurt, please tell a chaperone or the director.
4. Follow school rules and the district Code of Conduct at all times.
5. Learn the name of your chaperone; get his/her cell number, and then text back so he/she can contact you when necessary.
6. Tell your chaperone about any allergies and special dietary needs you have. They don't know you like your parents do, so extra communication is necessary.
7. Be on time at meetings and designated checkpoints, and stay apprised of any changes or updates to the itinerary. Be respectful, and do not use offensive or pejorative language toward other students or adults.
8. Do not take any medications unless they are preapproved on the medical form; they are to be administered by an adult.

DURING BUS TRAVEL

1. It is each student's responsibility to load their bags, instruments, and equipment on the buses. Assist other students who made need extra help, especially those with larger instruments.
2. Student water bottles must be completely empty prior to boarding the bus.
3. Students are to be absolutely quiet during every roll call and when instructions are being given by the chaperones, the director, or the driver. While the bus is moving, students may speak at reasonable noise levels but not so loud that it distracts the driver.
4. If you notice a student who is missing, speak up.
5. Every student must remain seated when the bus is in motion. No student is allowed to sit in the aisle or on another student's lap.
6. Students must ride the same bus for the duration of the trip; do not switch buses unless told to do so by the director.

7. Group activities on the bus should be respectful and should not involve peer pressure to coerce students into unwanted or uncomfortable situations. No lewd or disrespectful songs or other activities are allowed.
8. Bags, purses, etc., are to be stowed in the overhead compartments or under the seat, not in the bus aisles.
9. Blankets may only be used when a student has no one sitting next to him/her.

OVERNIGHT TRIPS

1. When staying in a hotel, do not to use hotel phones for long distance calls, or use non-complimentary Internet and pay-per-view TV channels.
2. At room checks, make sure you find out when to report to breakfast or checkout the next morning. DO NOT leave the room for any reason, and call the chaperone if you need help. Chaperones should give students their room phone number in case you need to contact them. Know your chaperone's room number.

Finally, if there is ever a question about anything regarding the trip, ask a chaperone or the director.

References

Burch, Noel. "The Four Stages For Learning Any New Skill." Gordon Training International. Solana Beach, CA. 1970s.

Carnegie, Dale. *How to Win Friends and Influence People*. New York: Simon and Schuster, 1998.

Covey, Stephen. *The Seven Habits of Highly Effective People*. New York: Simon and Schuster, 1989.

Flippen, Flip. *Capturing Kids' Hearts*. College Station, TX: Flippen Group, 2015.

Jenson, Eric. *Arts with the Brain in Mind*. Alexandria, VA: Association for Supervision and Curriculum Development, 2001.

Rush, Scott. *Habits of a Successful Band Director*. Chicago: GIA Publications, 2009.

Rush, Scott, Jeff Scott, and Emily Wilkinson. *Habits of a Successful Middle School Band Director*. Chicago: GIA Publications, 2014.

Selby, Christopher, Scott Rush, and Rich Moon. *Habits of a Successful String Musician*. Chicago: GIA Publications, 2014.

Wong, Harry, and Rosemary Wong. *The First Days of School*. Mountain View, CA: Harry K. Wong Publications, 1998.

Zander, Rosamund, and Benjamin Zander. *The Art of Possibility*. New York: Penguin Group, 2000.

About the Author

Christopher Selby is an active clinician, adjudicator, and conductor, and he is co-author of *Habits of a Successful String Musician*, a string method book for upper-level orchestras (published by GIA). Dr. Selby has presented sessions at the Midwest Clinic, at four National Conferences for the American String Teacher Association (ASTA), and numerous state conferences across America. He currently directs the high school orchestras at the School of the Arts in Charleston, SC, where he led the school's Symphony Orchestra to win the 2016 ASTA National Orchestra Festival's top award of Grand Champion in the competitive public school division.

Dr. Selby earned his music education degree from The Hartt School of Music in Connecticut, and his Master and his Doctorate of Musical Arts in Orchestral Conducting from the University of South Carolina. He also earned his National Board Certification in 2002 and 2012 in the area of Early Adolescent and Young Adult Music. Before moving to Charleston, Dr. Selby taught orchestra in traditional elementary, middle, and high schools for eighteen years. He was District Orchestra Coordinator in Richland School District Two from 2001 to 2012, where he taught high school and supervised the district's orchestra curriculum and instruction, led teacher training, and facilitated district-wide orchestra assessments.

Dr. Selby has served on the Council for Orchestral Education in the National Association for Music Education (NAfME), and he was Chair of the ASTA Committee on School Orchestras and Strings. He was also President of the South Carolina Music Educators Association (SCMEA) Executive Board from 2011–2013, and President of the state's Orchestra Division from 2007–2009. He has written articles for NAfME and in ASTA's *American String Teacher*, and he was named South Carolina ASTA Orchestra Teacher of the Year in 2009.